P9-DEN-426

EUDORA WELTY

A Study of the Short Fiction

Also Available in Twayne's Studies in Short Fiction Series

Donald Barthelme: A Study of the Short Fiction by Barbara L. Roe

Samuel Beckett: A Study of the Short Fiction by Robert Cochran

Jorge Luis Borges: A Study of the Short Fiction by Naomi Lindstrom

Paul Bowles: A Study of the Short Fiction by Allen Hibbard

Raymond Carver: A Study of the Short Fiction by Ewing Campbell

Anton Chekhov: A Study of the Short Fiction by Ronald L. Johnson

Robert Coover: A Study of the Short Fiction by Thomas E. Kennedy

Julio Cortázar: A Study of the Short Fiction by Ilan Stavans

John Gardner: A Study of the Short Fiction by Jeff Henderson

Graham Greene: A Study of the Short Fiction by Richard Kelly

Shirley Jackson: A Study of the Short Fiction by Joan Wylie Hall

Franz Kafka: A Study of the Short Fiction by Allen Thiher

Gabriel García Márquez: A Study of the Short Fiction by Harley D. Oberhelman

Flannery O'Connor: A Study of the Short Fiction by Suzanne Morrow Paulson

Edgar Allan Poe: A Study of the Short Fiction by Charles E. May

Jean Rhys: A Study of the Short Fiction by Cheryl Alexander Malcolm and David Malcolm

Twayne's Studies in Short Fiction

Gordon Weaver, General Editor
Oklahoma State University

Eudora Welty. *Used by permission of Eudora Welty and the Mississippi Department of Archives and History.*

Eudora Welty

A Study of the Short Fiction

Carol Ann Johnston
Dickinson College

TWAYNE PUBLISHERS
An Imprint of Simon & Schuster Macmillan
New York

PRENTICE HALL INTERNATIONAL
London Mexico City New Delhi Singapore Sydney Toronto

Twayne's Studies in Short Fiction, No. 67

Twayne Publishers
An Imprint of Simon & Schuster Macmillan
1633 Broadway
New York, NY 10019

Library of Congress Cataloging-in-Publication Data

Johnston, Carol Ann.
Eudora Welty: a study of the short fiction / Carol Ann Johnston.
p. cm. — (Twayne's studies in short fiction ; no. 67)
Includes bibliographical references and index.
ISBN 0-8057-7936-1 (alk. paper)
1. Welty, Eudora, 1909- —Criticism and interpretation.
2. Women and literature—Southern States—History—20th century.
3. Short story. I. Title. II. Series.
PS3545.E6Z73 1997
813'.52—dc20 96-41770
CIP

The paper used in this publication meets the minimum requirements of American National Standard for Information Sciences—Permanence of Paper for Printed Library Materials. ANSI Z39.48-1984. ∞™

10 9 8 7 6

Printed in the United States of America

This book is for
Rachel and Andy Moore
and
Liz Traynor Fowler

Contents

Preface

Indeed, learning to write may be a part of learning to read. For all I know, writing comes out of a serious devotion to reading.
—Eudora Welty, "Words into Fiction"

Eudora Welty's short stories, written in the 1930s, '40s, and '50s, are almost unique in their form among American stories of that era. Today, even the skilled reader picking up an anthology of stories from this period may need some orientation to the Welty terrain, especially if he or she reads expecting something like the stories of other southern writers of the period: the broad Old Testament strokes of plot and judgment in a typical Flannery O'Connor story; the "Old Order" romanticism of Katherine Anne Porter's Miranda stories; or the plot-driven black humor of Faulkner's novels. While some of these elements do go into her stories, since the beginning of her career Eudora Welty has located her work in a tradition of British and continental writers, more so than in the continuum of American fiction. She has done so quietly but firmly, in reviews, in essays on her favorite fiction writers, and in interviews. Even in the years when many of her critics were labeling Welty as a "regional" writer of the "southern gothic school," Welty did not listen, or if she did, she did not waver from her vision of herself as a citizen of the entire world of novelists, not just the provincial teller of eccentric tales, as some critics would have her be. Her steady attention to literary tradition shows us her belief in herself as a world citizen, but more important, since Welty reads other writers with a writer's eye, the level of her attention also reveals how she is influenced by the writers she admires. Her comments on these writers can show us much about her own stories, and help us to decipher their difficult structure.

Welty's most radical departure from the American tradition of the short story has been in the shape of her story. In her reading of the nineteenth-century Russian writer Anton Chekhov, and of the British writers Jane Austen, who wrote in the late eighteenth century, and Virginia Woolf, who wrote in the early part of the twentieth century, Welty explains the way that she sees subject and point of view shaping a certain kind of story. Of Chekhov, she writes,

> The revolution brought about by the gentle Chekhov to the short story was in every sense not destructive but constructive. By removing the formal plot he did not leave the story structureless; he endowed it with another kind of structure—one which embodied the principle of growth. And it was one that had no cause to repeat itself; in each and every story, short or long, it was a structure open to human meaning and answerable to that meaning. It took form from within. (*Eye,* 74)[1]

Welty points out here how Chekhov restructures the short story. He takes away the action-based plot and replaces it with a design based on his characters' mental associations and insights. The form is shaped by "human meaning." As she says of Chekhov, stories for Welty are purely subjective; "passion is not in the sentence but in the whole. . . . [stories] run close to the nerve of our inner lives" (*Eye,* 78–79). Welty, like Chekhov, does not "tell a story" in the conventional sense of the phrase; instead, she conveys through the story a feeling for the interior life of the people she depicts. For Welty, Chekhov manages to put into concrete details and actions "expression[s] that [are] purely lyrical" (*Eye,* 78); it is the lyrical, passionate, feeling sense of everyday life that Welty depicts in her own short stories.

The story with a foundation in human emotion rather than human action will naturally have as its subject human relationships. Jane Austen's narrative style, telling the story as it wends its way through the household, holds as much sway over Welty as does Chekhov's. In her essay on Austen, Welty discusses Austen's use of community in her novels, and specifically draws a connection between community and observation:

> [W]e have nothing in our own best that corresponds to the orderliness, the composure, of that life [in Austen's day], or that meets its requirements of the small scale, the lovely proportions, the intimacy, the sense of personal security. . . . for the purpose of writing novels, most human behavior [at the present time] is looked at through the frame or the knothole, of alienation. The life Jane Austen wrote was indeed a different one from ours, but the difference was not as great as that between the frames through which it is viewed. Jane Austen's frame was that of belonging to her world. (*Eye,* 10)

Again, as she does in her discussion of Chekhov, Welty emphasizes Austen's sense of intimacy and the personal aspects of her writing; the Austen she sees is Austen in Welty's own terms. Welty emphasizes the sense of proportion and design of Austen's narrative, which the reader views through a frame that is cast very close to the personal and intimate details of everyday living. Austen's narrator is very close to the community that she represents, and this closeness shapes the reader's view of community in Austen's novels. The parlor games and neighborhood balls in Austen take on the significance of the battle of Waterloo. Because Austen's narrator holds the frame so close, these private entertainments become world-changing events, because the only world we can see through the narrator's frame is changed by these events.

Welty envies Austen's state of "belong[ing] to her world," an envy that suggests that she finds the position of her own frame of observation threatened by a contemporary sense of alienation. In this perception Welty indicates that she feels that her writing doesn't belong quite to the prevailing mode of twentieth-century fiction, a mode which she calls "the knothole . . . of alienation." This sense of longing for Austen's narrative position suggests that Welty tries to achieve a similar position in her work; she meliorates Austen's technique into her own method by bringing the things she admires about Austen into her own work, no matter if they may seem anachronistic to Welty's contemporaries. Throughout her work, Welty is carefully conscious of where the narrator of her stories stands in relation to the story she tells. Like Austen, Welty has the gift of keeping her narrators at just the right distance from the story; the narrator does not condescend to characters or situations. This is a difficult task, but Welty has wonderful instincts about where to place her frame. In a story such as "Clytie," for example, Welty's narrator allows us to see her situation almost entirely through Clytie's eyes. The abrupt ending—Clytie kills herself suddenly by sticking her head in a barrel of water—snaps our connection to Clytie. It is only at this moment that we can separate ourselves from Clytie's world and see that her family is truly suffocating. We could not begin to understand the complexity of tone in the story if it had been placed in the wrong frame.

At the time Welty wrote her essay on Austen, Austen's work was considered by many critics to be too complacent and orderly in light of the mode of alienation dominant in much mainstream fiction; the drama of domestic life seemed trivial. By identifying with Austen and acting as her apologist, Welty took the risk of empathizing with a writer outside of critical favor. Yet Austen's domestic territory is Welty's métier as well.

In validating Austen, Welty shows the confidence of her literary judgment, as well as the perceptive location of her own work in one of its appropriate contexts.

Besides associating Welty with Austen's observing narrator, Welty's language in the Austen passage above is all of a piece: "Lovely proportions," "through the frame," "frames through which it is viewed"—Welty writes about Austen's narrative stance, its "orderliness . . . composure," in visual terms, placing Austen's interest in writing about community into her own preoccupations with narrative distance and into a language congenial to her own photographic interests. What Welty says of a collection of Cartier-Bresson photographs of Russia, for instance, easily reveals her own interests and preoccupations as a writer: "One feels he has used . . . his unerring equilibrium, his recognition of the comic, and indeed his world-traveler's experience of the profundity of long despair . . . to let them show and suggest what [his subject's] real daily life is" (*WE,* 190).[2] This summarizes in a nutshell Welty's interest in Chekhov and Austen as well as her own considerable abilities. Her position as an observer is determined and balanced by her wide frame, a sense both of the comic and of the despairing.

Just as she makes note of visual and structural aspects of both Chekhov and Austen, the organization around a "structure open to human meaning" that she admires in Chekhov and "the lovely proportions" of "human behavior" in Austen, Welty also admires Virginia Woolf's use of the senses—especially the visual—in her prose. Of Woolf Welty writes:

> The extreme beauty of her writing is due greatly to one fact, that the imprisonment of life in the word was as much a matter of the senses with Virginia Woolf as it was a concern of the intellect. The scent, the gesture, the breath on the lips, the sound of the hour striking in the clock, the rippling texture of the surface in the moving air—all these things she sought with all her being to apprehend, throughout a lifetime—for they were the palpable shadows and colored reflections of the abstract world of the spirit, the matter that mirrored the reality. (*WE,* 26)

Consistent with what she venerates in Chekhov and Austen, the intimate work of art scaled to reveal the gradations of human emotion, Welty values Woolf's ability to capture an emotion in a metaphor—"scent," "gesture," "sound," "texture,"—as much as she values Woolf's powerful intellect. But a strong intelligence is the umbrella under which Welty's concerns gather. In Chekhov, Austen, and Woolf, Welty recognizes kindred minds who understand that history and fiction on a large scale often do not depict the crucial moments in life. Intimate gestures outside the mainstream of active life, like those of lyric poetry, are those that shape the individual, and in turn the individual fashions history with action. All of these writers, especially Eudora Welty, depict the determining circumstances of humanity at the root—huddled around a fire fueled by the only furniture in the house, under a quilt called "The Wide World," in a train compartment full of strangers speeding through Wales. There is in a word, in a gesture, a whole life; for Welty, as for Chekhov, Austen, and Woolf, the eye can see just as far as the heart can feel.

Welty's lyricism has over the years lulled many readers with its liquid beauty. The wonderful sound and cadence of a Welty story can carry a reader through it with dreamlike intensity. Because of this unusual form of her stories, as well as her mien as a southern woman, some readers have been unable to probe beneath the surface of the stories. Teachers often underestimate the power of professional criticism in deciding for them what they have their students read and why they have them read it. With this in mind, I begin this study of Welty with a discussion of criticism of her work. Chapter one looks at how criticism has shaped public reception of Welty's short fiction, and why much valuable criticism has come to Welty's work belatedly. In her own critical writing Welty not only emphasizes her interest in European novelists as models but also stresses the inclusiveness of her fiction: "Both reading and writing are experiences—lifelong—in the course of which we who encounter words used in certain ways are persuaded by them to be brought mind and heart within the presence, the power, of the imagination. This we find to be above all the power to reveal, with nothing barred" (*Eye,* 135). The "power" of her imagination reveals to Welty a world fraught with contradictions and paradoxes. Early criticism of her work did not perceive the contradictions there. In her own critical writing, as in the essay I quote here, Welty takes great care to guide her readers toward the complexities of her vision. I use Welty's assertions about her work as a place to begin an evaluation of her achievements as a short story writer.

Welty's most eloquent statement of her method uses a visual image; her work is a "stream" fed by "dark" and "bright" "springs" representing both the love she felt in her sheltered upbringing and the guilt she felt when she freed herself from the insularity of that upbringing. Chapter two uses her assertions about "two springs, one bright, one dark" that feed the "stream" of her fiction to survey the development of Welty's work. A life lead apart from society can leave an individual in the dark, vulnerable and unprepared to go out into the world; or such a cloistered existence can turn out a survivor, ready and eager to face the bright, open world. The two springs come together throughout Welty's stories, sometimes in mixed form, sometimes in pure form.

The paradoxical bright and dark aspects of the insular life offer an overall shape for Welty's collections of stories. Her technique in these stories is kin to the paradox, in that sometimes the incongruity between the light and the dark can be expressed only in nonsequential ways. The third chapter, then, addresses two of Welty's fundamental techniques of organizing the story. The first Welty herself identifies as "the lyric impulse." The amalgam that Welty achieves in her stories has more in common with poetry than with the orderly, cause-and-effect story. In an interview, Joanna Maclay asked Welty, "You've said that you believe that writing short stories comes out of a lyric impulse. . . . Is this different in some way from the story-telling impulse?" (*Con,* 303). Welty replied:

> It may not be. I love the told story, and I can see how certain stories and novels are descended from it. But that is, in a way, lyrical. The tale certainly appeals to the emotions that everyone feels—a sort of community of emotions—through the senses, through the ears and the voice. And I think a short story does the same thing. Often, also, the old tales dealt with a single strand of experience, just as a short story does. In the same way as lyric poetry does, it follows its own path through a certain space and time, and is a whole in itself. (*Con,* 303–4)[3]

Welty understands her method in terms of "lyric poetry," allowing her stories to organize themselves in a lyric, rather than narrative, sequence. The "strand of experience" that she traces in individual stories has its own individual path, and that path usually is circuitous, not straight; subtly marked, not indicated by flashing-neon signposts.[4]

The second narrative technique, as the imagistic nature of her criticism suggests, is visual. The Welty story, based on poetic and visual techniques, is rooted in the cultural propensity for women to be observers, the stimulus behind what I call "visual writing." Our culture finds it more comfortable for women to facilitate men's actions by observing and understanding these actions while obliquely offering subtle suggestions and correctives where they see fit. Welty's stories, however, are not the result of Welty's occupying a culturally determined role; rather, her stories show her discovery of a mode best suited to her gifts. Those gifts are primarily an ear for a good story, an eye for the relationship that objects have to one another (and I mean this in terms of both visual composition and human interaction), and an affinity for the interior moment and landscape. While these gifts are congenial with the cultural role of women, especially in the deep South, Welty's work is also a critique of that cultural role.

The final chapter considers the function of Welty's formal experimentation. Welty's technical experiments disrupt the logic of the story and make possible a radical revision of certain myths that have defined the role of women in our culture. Welty's sources for certain myths—the story of Adam and Eve, as well as the myth of "Wandering Aengus," and "Leda and the Swan"—are poems: Milton's *Paradise Lost;* Yeats's "Song of Wandering Aengus" and "Leda and the Swan."

Not only does lyric organization give a Welty story its essential signature, but it also allows her to draw her material from poetry and to associate herself with the further poetic tradition of continental literature. She enters this tradition and then uses the sanction of the lyric's organization to allow the material to "follow its own path." These myths in Welty's stories, however, follow radically different paths from those they follow in Milton and Yeats. Welty's project is an extensive "re-vision" of gender roles in our cultural myths. Though Welty has carefully located her work in a tradition of such European writers as Chekhov, Milton, and Yeats, she ultimately establishes her separate place. "Everyone to his own visioning," she writes in *The Golden Apples.* Welty's "visioning" is of a world of gender equality, where both male and female writers, for example, are judged and validated with equal vigor.

Notes

1. Eudora Welty, "Reality in Chekhov's Stories," in *The Eye of the Story* (New York: Vintage Books, 1979), 61–84; hereafter noted in the text as *Eye.*

2. Eudora Welty, "Africa and Paris and Russia," in *A Writer's Eye: Collected Book Reviews,* ed. Pearl Amelia McHaney (Jackson: University Press of Mississippi, 1994), 185–90; hereafter noted in the text as *WE.*

3. Eudora Welty, quoted in Joanna Maclay, "A Conversation with Eudora Welty," in *Conversations with Eudora Welty,* ed. Peggy Whitman Prenshaw (New York: Simon and Schuster, 1985), 203–4; hereafter noted in the text as *Con.*

4. William Jay Smith, a poet himself, points out that "Eudora Welty comes from a . . . long line [of storytellers] and her work reminds us on every page of the qualities of the ancient art of storytelling, which are often lost sight of today. The ancient storyteller was a poet, and to hold the attention of his listeners he made use of those age-old rhythmic and incantatory devices that we still find in folktales" (p. 78). See William Jay Smith, "Precision and Reticence: Eudora Welty's Poetic Vision," in *Eudora Welty: A Form of Thanks,* ed. Louis Dollarhide and Ann J. Abadie (Jackson: University Press of Mississippi, 1979), 78–94. Most of this essay is devoted to a close reading of vision as a metaphor in *The Optimist's Daughter.*

Acknowledgments

Thanks to Dickinson College for supporting my work with a Mellon Research Grant, a Dana Internship, and a Research and Development grant. These monies allowed me to employ my students Emily Wylie and Kerry Epstein as research assistants and to travel to Jackson to interview Eudora Welty. Emily's conversations about all aspects of Welty's work were invaluable to my writing process, and Kerry's efficiency and willingness to be "on call" made the final months of this project go more smoothly than I had imagined possible. Thank you both.

Natalia Chromiak in the Interlibrary Loan department of the Dickinson College Library speedily acquired even the most arcane references for me. Thanks also to Forrest W. Galey at the Mississippi Department of Archives and History for tracking down photographs in the Eudora Welty Collection.

I owe much to Raphael Gunner and Linda Rugg for conversations about theoretical issues during the formative processes of this study. I am also grateful to my colleagues in the English department at Dickinson: Sharon O'Brien, for reading parts of the manuscript at its early stages and giving thoughtful words of direction, and Wendy Moffat, for reading the final drafts and offering comments of extraordinary clarity and insight.

As always, I appreciate my family for their love and support.

Finally, thanks to Liz Traynor Fowler for insisting that I write this book, and thanks to my teachers Rachel and Andy Moore for introducing me—at age 19—to the work of their fellow Mississippian just when I needed it. My gratitude to Eudora Welty for writing her stories is implicit throughout this book.

Part 1

ANALYSIS

Eudora Welty: The Eye of Her Stories

> The story and its analyses are not mirror-opposites of each other. They are not reflections, either one. Criticism indeed is an art, as a story is, but only the story is to some degree a vision; there is no explanation outside fiction for what its writer is learning to do.
>
> —Eudora Welty, "Writing and Analyzing a Story"

Eudora Welty ends her brief autobiography, *One Writer's Beginnings,* with a three-sentence paragraph that neatly summarizes the previous 100 pages: "As you have seen, I am a writer who came of a sheltered life. A sheltered life can be a daring life as well. For all serious daring starts from within" (*OWB,* 104).[1] Welty was born in a particular time and place that has historically secured its women in a sheltered environment. The sheltered life that Welty writes about in *One Writer's Beginnings* is typical of a woman nurtured in the deep South during the early part of this century. Born in 1908, Welty is a lifelong resident of Jackson, Mississippi, daughter of an insurance executive father from Ohio and a mother from West Virginia who read avidly and passionately, who once raced back into a house smothered in flames to save a set of Dickens novels. She had two younger brothers, Edward and Walter. Welty grew up in a close-knit, extended family, she tells us, one that sheltered her and protected her from outside forces of all sorts: "Even as we grew up," Welty writes in *One Writer's Beginnings,* "my mother could not help imposing herself between her children and whatever it was they might take it in mind to reach out for in the world. . . . She stood always ready to challenge the world in our place" (*OWB,* 39). When she left her family, she did so only for a short time to attend college for three years at the University of Wisconsin in Madison, and following college, to spend a year in business school at Columbia University in New York City. After her schooling, she returned to Jackson, during the Depression, to live with her parents and to work at various jobs, such as at the new radio station atop her father's company building in Jackson and as a publicist for the Works Progress Administration. Since her young adulthood, Welty has traveled widely and held various lecturing and teaching posts, but she has always returned to her parents' house in Jackson, where she still lives and writes today. She has never married; as she says in a recent *New York Times* interview, marriage "never came up."[2] It is this Eudora Welty, southern lady of a sheltered past, that many reviewers have had in mind as they have written about her work.

This distinction Welty draws between leading a sheltered life and a daring life, between living cautiously and thinking adventurously, runs not only throughout *One Writer's Beginnings* but also throughout Welty's body of work. While she points out their marked differences, Welty simultaneously emphasizes the blurring of these two categories: out of the sheltered life comes its seeming opposite, the daring life. Welty makes it clear that her daring thinking is absolutely dependent on the nurturing care that her protected life provides. Remarkably, even when writing about her own life, Welty is unable to resist a pure writerly technique: Making one whole out of two seeming opposites, a paradoxical way of thinking and writing, is a hallmark of great writing. Throughout her work, Welty manages to hold opposites in balance, often giving the illusion that there are no opposites, that the world contains no disharmony, only harmony. This wonderful illusion of unity that Welty often achieves in her work has, ironically, handicapped her status as an artist.

Critics and readers from the beginning of Welty's career to the present have often taken Welty's ability to balance opposites—as evident in her terms "daring-sheltered" and "love-separateness"—in her work at face value, seeing the whole of Welty's work in its smooth, untroubled surface. Welty has become, for many such readers, "Miss Welty," our most amiable American writer. Such critical misreading of Welty's work as a bundle of happy, funny tales has significantly diminished her achievement as an artist. The responsibility of the critic, no matter what approach she takes or which method she subscribes to, remains that of throwing open windows to a writer's work, in order to make the writer's discoveries more clear and their delineations more accessible to readers. Critics of Welty's work who do not probe beyond its surface (though it is a very lovely surface) can have the opposite effect, that of closing the windows that could lead to deeper comprehension of Welty's vision.

Because of critical undervaluation, the literary establishment has not until very recently granted Welty the place that she deserves as one of America's great writers. And even though Welty has now been granted that status, her work in some ways remains frozen in certain kinds of critical readings that minimize or skip over the conflicts beneath the smooth surface of her work. From the beginning of her career in 1941, some of Welty's most admiring critics, in fact, have been fellow fiction writers. The Texas writer Katherine Anne Porter did well by her Mississippi counterpart and wrote an acute introduction to Welty's first published work, encouraging readers by saying that stories in *A Curtain of Green* were crafted by a well-read young writer who handled the genre of the story brilliantly. Yet in spite of Porter's careful placing of Welty in a broad literary context, most readers of Welty in the early forties and beyond insisted on stereotyping Welty as a limited, regional writer—the Eudora Welty of the sheltered life—and conceiving of her work in predictable categories. In addition to Katherine Anne Porter, novelists Robert Penn Warren, Reynolds Price, and Anne Tyler, among others, have in their essays and reviews gone against the mainstream and insisted on Welty's complex vision.[3] Robert Penn Warren wrote the first influential essay by a novelist on Welty's work, and it is often cited in current studies, a sign of its insight and influence. In the essay, "The Love and Separateness in Miss Welty," written in 1944 as a review of *The Wide Net and Other Stories,*[4] Warren uses as an epigraph a passage from "A Still Moment" (one of the central stories in *The Wide Net*) that contains the phrase "love first and then separateness." He discusses both *A Curtain of Green* and *The Wide Net* in terms of this phrase, suggesting that the two volumes of stories as a group address various aspects of the condition of the individual experiencing first the intimacy of love and then a severing of intimate ties. In analyzing the story "The Wide Net," for example, Warren suggests that "William Wallace, because he thinks his wife has drowned herself, is at the start of the story cut off from the world of natural joy in which he had lived" (p. 45); he is separated from what he loves. For Warren, then, the "love and separateness" encoded in Welty's story serves as a thematic guide from which he reads all of the stories she had written to that date. The typical Welty story, he determines, concerns a person who has loved deeply, but then is cut off—separated—from what he or she loves: "We can observe," he writes, "that the nature of the isolation may be different from case to case, but the fact of isolation, whatever its nature, provides the basic situation of Miss Welty's fiction" (p. 45). Unlike many of Welty's early critics, Warren does not stop at the surface of Welty's stories; he considers both sides of her phrase "love and separateness" as he reads her stories, and sees the complexity of this phrase unfolding in her work.

At least one important critical study has grown out of this group of novelist-critics and from Warren's study specifically. Ruth Vande Kieft's

Eudora Welty[5] follows Warren's lead, taking the Welty term "love and separateness" and developing an analysis of Welty's body of work through this term. The first book-length work to give serious consideration to Welty as a significant twentieth-century writer, this study has been one of the most important in Welty criticism, setting the themes and subjects that continue to guide critical thinking about her work. (Vande Kieft revised her book in the eighties to incorporate Welty's later work.) Nonetheless, Vande Kieft tends to view Welty's work through the persona that Welty projects, the sweet Welty of the "sheltered life," rather than the Welty who lives and writes about the adventuresome inner life. For example, while following Warren's lead and finding the life of Welty's work in "love and separateness," Vande Kieft places stress on the "love" in Welty's work. In her discussion of *The Bride of the Innisfallen,* for instance, she sees the women in the stories as lonely yet believes that they all find resolutions to their unhappiness: "Each of the heroines is abandoned by her potential or actual lover. . . . Yet each of the love-burdened heroines retains the virtues of openness to life, the capacity to love, to renew hope and joy, to achieve an inner poise, steadiness, or stillness" (p. 133). Vande Kieft's conclusion, that Welty's stories depict women who lead lives with happy endings, offers only half of Welty's duality, the "love" without the "separateness" and the unhappiness that such separation can bring. And in a 1982 essay for *Southern Quarterly,* Vande Kieft argues that Welty intentionally writes her stories with the "loving" moral that Vande Kieft herself attributes to them, asserting that Welty's "motives for writing are celebration and love."[6] Warren, by contrast, leaves open meaning in the stories to encompass both love and separation. (We need only note that early in Welty's career, Diana Trilling found Welty's vision to be not "loving" but a "vision of horror to the point of nightmare.") Vande Kieft imposes two kinds of thematic unity on Welty. Not only is it risky for a critic to declare that a writer's motives and intentions are consistent with her own ideas about a particular work, but this assumption also begs the question of how much of a writer's life we can find in her work. More important, Vande Kieft's theory sees only one facet of that life, the "loving," *sheltered* Welty, not the "separate," *daring* Welty.

Louise Westling's Welty strongly resembles Vande Kieft's. In "The Loving Observer of *One Time, One Place,*" she describes Welty as a photographer whose world is "largely sheltered from poverty and violence," and a writer whose fiction "rarely betrays any knowledge of the violent enforcement of white male authority." (Here she neglects the real violence of the gang rape at the end of "At the Landing.") Westling even finds it "tempting," as does Vande Kieft, to make the interpretive leap from her own version of Welty's work to Welty's life, imagining "the young Eudora Welty as . . . glimpsing the hidden violence beneath the gracious surface of Mississippi life but never really having the opportunity *or perhaps desire* to see it closely" (emphasis mine; Westling, 176–77).[7] Again, we have a critic composing a view of Welty's writing, "rarely betray[ing] knowledge" of violence, from the idea of Welty the person living a life in the remote South "sheltered from poverty and violence."

This view of Welty as sheltered is widely held by critics. In *Eudora Welty: A Reference Guide*, Victor H. Thompson notes that "the newspapers present Miss Welty as perhaps the most amiable and inoffensive writer that America has ever produced" (p. ix),[8] and Warren French quotes Thompson in his essay "Eudora Welty as a Civilized Writer" (French, 183).[9] In many ways French's essay epitomizes the work of critics such as Vande Kieft, Westling, and French himself, who find the essential Welty in her public self-presentation, who see her as a "sheltered" and demure southern lady. French comments on Thompson's observation: "What this statement suggests is that she is a thoroughly 'civilized' person, something that, for whatever reasons, few of our writers have been. Many of her contemporaries have proved . . . wild and flighty" (French, 183–84).[10] Even though French does position Welty's early work among other eminent works of literature, his emphasis on his perception of Welty's character and personality ultimately does her work a disservice by diminishing the importance of Welty's inner life, the Welty who practices "daring" thinking. His comments that Welty is our most civilized writer, especially in comparison with "wild and flighty" contemporary artists, begs the question of what effect, if any, one's outer demeanor has on the inner life and individual creative process.

All of these critics clearly love Eudora Welty's work and, by extension, seem to love her as well. Like Noel Polk, they "can think of nothing finer than to celebrate [Welty], in simple return, because her work is such a splendid celebration of us—of all the things that make our own lives joyful and sad, mysterious and profound" (Polk, 95).[11] And isn't this what we should do when we find a writer whose work we like? Shouldn't we celebrate that work and that writer? I think the answers are quite complex in regard to Eudora Welty. To like her personally is not to confuse her personality with her work. She herself has despaired of much of the critical estimation of her work and in her own critical essays has offered correctives to some of what has been written. Her most powerful corrective, naturally, is to ask her readers to *read* her stories.

Many readers have projected their need for a clear and ordered view of the world onto Welty's work, finding there an unambiguously happy place, or at least a narrowly circumscribed world of quaint regional shenanigans. There is a group of readers, however, who see another—equally false—version of the Welty story. For these readers, the signature of the southern writer is the so-called gothic tale, the Poe-like story that represents a series of depraved characters in unthinkable situations.[12] (We might think of this type of fiction as prose versions of B horror films—*The Texas Chainsaw Massacre* comes to mind as an apt example.) In her 1941 review of *A Curtain of Green* for *The Nation* magazine, Louise Bogan begins, "The definite Gothic quality which characterizes so much of the work of writers from the American South has puzzled critics. Is the atmosphere of the *roman noir* so skillfully transferred to America by Poe? Or is it a true and indigenous atmosphere of decaying feudalism?"[13] Except for her fellow novelists, many of Welty's early reviewers who weren't mesmerized by the beautiful language in her work read her stories primarily with their regional, southern place of origin in mind, and many, like Bogan, placed stories from *A Curtain of Green* in this category, along with her "tale" *The Robber Bridegroom* (1942), her modernization of a fairy tale that places the story of a young woman kidnapped by highwaymen in historic Mississippi on the eighteenth-century Natchez Trace. The reviewer of *A Curtain of Green* for *Time* argues that Welty "[h]as a strong taste for melodrama, and is preoccupied with the demented, the deformed, the queer, the highly spiced. Of the 17 pieces, only two report states of experience which could be called normal."[14] This stereotyping was continued by such well-known critics as Diana Trilling, who (as I mentioned earlier) wrote of *The Wide Net and Other Stories* (1943) that Welty had developed "her vision of horror to the point of nightmare."[15] Trilling also gives Welty's first novel, *Delta Wedding* (1946), the brush-off, reading it as just another southern novel about life on the plantation.[16] All in all, these critics viewed Welty's work as symptomatic of southern provinciality and of a terminal attachment to the gothic.

Trilling invokes another familiar critical category in her review of *Delta Wedding;* no longer attacking Welty's "vision of horror," she charges her of uncritically romanticizing the past of the slave-owning South.

Varying degrees of narrow readings in this vein have dogged Welty's other fictional works that follow *Delta Wedding:* the stories in *The Golden Apples* (1949); a comic novel, *The Ponder Heart* (1954); *The Bride of the Innisfallen* (1955), her last collection of stories; the two late novels, *Losing Battles* (1970) and *The Optimist's Daughter* (1972). However, with the passage of time, and as critics have considered and reconsidered them, these works have grown in critical stature. Some still question Welty's depiction of the "old South," chastising her for dwelling on the historically segregated South that kept the races apart at the cost of neglecting highly charged racial issues of the "new South." (Many of Welty's stories are set in the teens and twenties; the exceptional story "Where Is This Voice Coming From?" is told from the point of view of the assassin of the sixties civil rights leader Medgar Evers.) In general, those despairing of Welty have also found Welty's work too descriptive, too domestic, too apolitical, in short, too refined.

The good news is that since the publication of the stories of *The Golden Apples* in 1949, positive readings of Welty have been more persuasive. The critical establishment has taken note, and has accordingly awarded Welty various prizes, including the Pulitzer prize and the National Book Award. Critical praise for Welty's work became almost univocal with the publication in 1980 of her 41 collected stories, including all those in *A Curtain of Green, The Wide Net, The Golden Apples,* and *The Bride of the Innisfallen,* along with two uncollected stories, "Where Is the Voice Coming From?" and "The Demonstrators." Whitney Balliett in the *New Yorker* discusses Welty's career at length, and concludes by lauding her for her innovations: "Welty is, particularly in her short stories, an experimenter."[17] But praise and prizes do not necessarily indicate that readers have read Welty with clarity and understanding.

In his review of the *Collected Stories* in 1980, the novelist Reynolds Price gives a piercingly succinct and accurate assessment of the criticism that had addressed Welty's body of work to that point:

> [Welty's career has been a] long performance . . . and one which, though it has never lacked praise and devoted readers, has presented critics with the kind of fearless emotional intensity, the fixed attention to daily life, and the technical audacity that have mercilessly revealed the poverty of scholastic critical methods. (Price, 31)[18]

I have pointed out some of the critical methods that have failed to address Welty's work adequately. At present, several critics have begun to address the "poverty of scholastic critical methods" in regard to Welty. These critics concentrate almost exclusively on Welty's inner, "daring" aspect rather than on her "sheltered" life in the South. They do not use, as did many of their predecessors, what Price calls "the bald historical-biographical curiosity of readers and critics" (Price, 31). Members of this group apply aspects of literary theory to Welty's stories, reading them variously through the lenses of such theoretical "schools" as feminism, Marxism, and New Historicism. Among those also doing this work, Patricia S. Yaeger published an early and influential essay, " 'Because a Fire Was in My Head': Eudora Welty and the Dialogic Imagination," which first appeared in the academic journal *PMLA* in 1984. Her essay has been reprinted several times, notably in *Eudora Welty: A Life in Literature,* a collection of essays that primarily represents the use of contemporary methodology to discuss Welty's work. Yaeger applies the dialogic ideas of the Russian theorist Mikhael Bakhtin to Welty's stories from *The Golden Apples,* arguing that there are many voices, or "dialogues," in these stories. With this essay, Yaeger begins the process of recognizing and delineating the many voices and moods that Welty can capture, even in a single story.[19] Peter Schmidt's 1991 study, *The Heart of the Story: Eudora Welty's Short Fiction,* is the first book-length work to address the short stories from these newer theoretical perspectives.[20] Schmidt discusses issues of gender in his book, drawing largely on contemporary American feminist criticism. Self-conscious of his new direction in Welty criticism, Schmidt notes that his book "builds upon previous Welty criticism but questions some of the formalist and archetypal or myth-critical assumptions that have generally guided it" (Schmidt, xv). Rebecca Mark also draws on American and French feminism and its theories of intertextuality to read *The Golden Apples* in her *Dragon's Blood,* arguing that "Welty's feminist intertextuality could be called intersexuality precisely because her writing evokes an enlivening of metaphor, character, and symbol or an eroticization of the word" (p. 12).[21] These literary critics, among others, are ushering Welty's work into the most current academic criticism, which has not often examined her work.

Why has criticism been so late in coming to Welty? As Price suggests, her fiction lies outside the bounds of work that has been probed successfully by academic criticism. And its smooth and beautiful surface can act like Teflon; only the most persistent inquiries will stick or penetrate. Further, Welty herself has been remarkably successful in setting the critical agenda for her work both through what she has disclosed about her life and, more important, through her nonfiction. Given that Welty has said about feminism that "all that talk of women's lib doesn't apply at all to women writers. We've always been able to do what we've wished. I couldn't feel less deprived as a woman to be writing" (*Con,* 54), it is not surprising that feminist critics have been reluctant to address Welty's work. As with her comment on feminism, Welty has long made her opinions and beliefs available to her readers, both in interviews and in the recent *One Writer's Beginnings.* Beginning her career as a writer when much criticism entailed using the writer's private life as a lens through which to view his or her work, Welty began to insist early on that beyond the bare facts of her life, the important aspects of her being lie in her work and in her work alone. This position establishes careful boundaries around what we can and cannot know about Welty, and consequently also delimits how we may discuss her work in conjunction with her life. Welty has been remarkably influential at setting the terms for understanding her work: One despairing comment about the feminist movement delayed feminist readings of her work for 20 or 30 years.

This leverage is not, of course, unique to her as a writer. The Georgia writer Flannery O'Connor, Welty's contemporary, who died at the young age of 39, set the tone and subject matter of critical studies of her work throughout the sixties, seventies, and most of the eighties, when her critics, following her lead in her collected essays, *Mystery and Manners,* were concerned primarily with religion and its place in her fiction. Only within the past decade have readers begun to think about contexts in which to understand O'Connor's work that she did not discuss widely during her lifetime or write about in her essays: her autoimmune disease, lupus; her sexuality and her gender; her beliefs about race; her radical and anti-dogmatic religious explorations. All of these subjects, when examined through her fiction, represent a much more rich and complex version of O'Connor's work than her own critical works would suggest. Arguably, many of these fresh approaches to O'Connor's work were made possible by the publication of a volume of her personal letters, *The Habit of Being,* in 1979. To date, we have no such publication from Welty and are not likely to.[22] Critical enrichment and revaluation of Welty's work is difficult without such sources, and is, some might argue, merely speculative. Like O'Connor's early critics, Welty's critics have concentrated on her public persona as a point of entry into her work. Welty has had extraordinary control of this persona, and this control has led to a narrow reading of her work.

Welty says in the epigraph I quote at the beginning of this chapter that there is "no explanation outside fiction" for her stories; they are gifts from the writer. One way to read this caveat is as a response to critics who try to fold Welty's life back into her work. As the epigraph also intimates beautifully, Welty has written insightful and well-placed essays on technique in her stories—not that she has exhausted the subject; she has, rather, given the critic an abundance of material to work with. While one job of the critic is, as Welty suggests, to consider the stories as "visions," as absolute works of art, in order to elaborate on the technique that fosters them, another job of the critic also entails linking the writer's vision with her sociocultural place in the world. By controlling her public persona so carefully, and by firmly insisting that her work is not political, Welty has maintained for her work an anonymity among writers whom critics see as trying to change the world in which they live. Even in her autobiographical work, *One Writer's Beginnings,* Welty does not discuss social or cultural issues outside of those endemic to the immediate family. In all of her nonfictional writing, and in her interviews, Welty attempts to focus critical attention on some aspects of her technique and on circumscribed social issues of community and family, aspects of her work that she is comfortable writing and talking about.[23] Welty has tried to correct many critical misreadings of her work, primarily concerning matters of technique, but her essays are as dense as her fiction, so these correctives have been in many ways as inscrutable, and for some critics as misdirecting, as the fiction. Of course, the issues that Welty raises in her essays still need to be attended to with great critical care and industry.

Even though Welty has guided criticism of her work to some degree, one thing that the critic can do with Welty is look first at the terms she herself sets for examination of her work—such as I have begun to do with her terms "daring," "separateness," "loving"—and try to understand with some precision how she uses these terms. But to do Welty's work justice, the critic must also move with those terms beyond the demarcations that she provides for them. The critic must read her nonfiction, where Welty suggests reading techniques that will serve as a point of entry into her short fiction, where Welty is at her creative best.

The Eye of the Story (1979) and *One Writer's Beginnings* (1984), along with the essay prefacing her collected photographs, and *A Writer's Eye: Collected Book Reviews* (1994), comprise Welty's nonfiction to date. In the earlier collection of essays and reviews, *The Eye of the Story,* Welty reflects on herself as a storyteller in essays on the craft of writing as well as in pieces elucidating the work of other writers. In these meditations, as in this exemplary excerpt from her essay "Writing and Analyzing a Story," Welty begins to chisel out her unique place among writers, both contemporaries and predecessors, who have influenced her:

> It is not from criticism but from this world that stories come in the beginning; their origins are living reference plain to the writer's eye, even though to his eye alone. The writer's mind and heart, where all this exterior is continually becoming something—the moral, the passionate, the poetic, hence the shaping idea—can't be mapped and plotted. (*Eye*, 109)

The initial sentence draws a clear distinction between "criticism" and "the world," and that distinction typifies the Welty stance towards criticism: she positions her fiction in relation to the world rather than in relation to criticism of and about fiction. As she notes in the passage I quote as the epigraph to this chapter, she believes criticism and fiction to be separate but equal entities. Yet while criticism and fiction may be equal in certain ways, Welty's real emphasis is on their deep separation. "Story writing and critical analysis are indeed separate gifts, like spelling and playing the flute, and the same writer proficient in both has been doubly endowed. But even he can't rise and do both at the same time" (*Eye*, 107). Throughout her own critical writing and her interviews, she insists that stories (both her own and those of other writers) originate in the world and are transformed in the writer's mind through a process that cannot be "mapped and plotted"; that is, her stories are not linear and therefore cannot be adequately addressed in criticism, because criticism as she knows it is linear, cartographical, and plotted. In the long passage that I quote above, Welty is careful to show her critics that her stories are, despite appearances to the contrary, distinct in their nonlinearity, and thus she begins to establish her place among fiction writers as one who departs from plot-driven, conventional fiction.

In the above passage Welty discusses nonlinear writing in photographic and visual terms—"the writer's *eye,* even though to *his eye alone*" (emphasis mine). By describing nonlinear aspects of her writing in visual terms, she associates the absence of linearity with vision: the narrator functions as a photographic eye, and each story is a series of snapshots, moving in synchronic fashion rather than diachronically, or, to use Welty's own terms, moving in a "poetic" rather than a "plotted" manner. Using this assiduous but detached observer as narrator, Welty brings both the fact and the practice of an observer as overseer in snatches to her writing. I cannot emphasize enough the importance of linking visual style and visual metaphor to Welty's narrative method. The visuality that she consciously brings to her fiction defines her narrative style. One reader's response (her agent's) on reading the story "Asphodel" was that it struck him as particularly visual: "I read ASPHODEL and thought it very good and very powerful in raising pictures in the mind" (*A & A*, 72). Welty's stories are visual not only in their use of specific details and figurative language but more so in their structure, which is deliberately designed to create a feeling of dimension "in raising pictures in the mind." Hers is the narrative of the mosaic, the out-of-sequence narrative style of stories overheard, some starting at the end and working back, some repeating themselves in variants, some never reaching closure.

In "Place in Fiction," Welty connects her narrative style to the influence of place on a writer. Place allows the writer to work in a particular way, to focus, which in turn gives her vision balance, pattern, and harmony. This is quite a different understanding than that put forth by her early critics who felt place could mean only something restrictive and regional.

> It may be that place can focus the gigantic, voracious eye of genius and bring its gaze point. Focus then means awareness, discernment, order, clarity, insight—they are like the attributes of love. The act of focusing itself has beauty and meaning; it is the act that, continued in, turns into mediation, into poetry. (*Eye*, 123)

By linking place and vision, Welty gives us another angle on her narrative method, this time emphasizing that the process is one of focusing, which is a synchronic or poetic act. Synchronic writing produces fiction that is meditative—resulting in a single dilating point—rather than plotted, proceeding along a line. Inherent in the meditative, dilating process are principles of "discernment, order, clarity, insight." Even though a mode of narration is not linear and plot-driven, her implicit argument goes, it can still be clear and deliberate. Her emphasis on place, here and elsewhere, also takes us back to her differential discussion of fiction and criticism: stories, we recall again, come "from this world," "this exterior." Stories are anchored, for Welty, in a concrete place, and that place is like a single point on a map, not a plotted journey.

Putting place as a primary force in fictive inspiration immediately introduces a spatial, and thus a visual, aspect into the conception of fiction. Welty conveys her method of writing in overtly visual terms, and speaks of her visual method as resulting in a poetic text: "The act of focusing . . . turns into mediation, into poetry." For readers, this narrative style creates a fiction that is neither the episodic, carefully mapped out story of Welty's contemporary Flannery O'Connor (among writers practicing this kind of narrative writing) nor is it the collage or pastiche narrative evoked by the modernist stream-of-consciousness style of James Joyce, Virginia Woolf, or Welty's fellow Mississippian William Faulkner. Welty's stories are more like stops on the way to somewhere; when we encounter them, we walk into them as if they were places unto themselves and turn slowly, taking in all sides.

In these brief quotations from her essays, we see Welty moving her reader to these positions in relation to her fiction: that linear criticism is inadequate to address her work, that her fiction is more like a poem or photograph than the traditional story; that she understands her writing in visual terms, with the narrator as a keenly observing *eye*. With narrator as eye, rather than simply as "teller," Welty gives us a set of stories that by their nature embrace the contradictory and the paradoxical. A narrator who records rather than offering a point of view not only gives the Welty story a feeling of unplotted lack of direction but also seems to form a moral vacuum: How does the narrator feel about what she sees? More important, how should the reader feel about what she sees in the story? These are difficult questions to answer in regard to Welty's fiction. The following chapter approaches them by examining Welty's short story collections in the order in which they were published and discussing them in terms of the paradox that she sets as the guiding force for all of her work.

The Perils of the Sheltered Life

> There is no wonder that a passion for independence sprang up in me at the earliest age. It took me a long time to manage the independence, for I loved those who protected me—and I wanted inevitably to protect them back. I have never managed to handle the guilt. In the act and the course of writing stories, these are two of the springs, one bright, one dark, that feed the stream.
>
> —Eudora Welty, *One Writer's Beginnings*

The "two springs, one bright, one dark" that "feed the stream" of Eudora Welty's fiction have been considered together only in recent criticism as shaping forces in her work. As I argued in the previous chapter, many critics prefer to see Welty's work as either one or the other, exclusively bright—the loving and comic Welty, or exclusively dark—the gothic and grotesque Welty. Each of Eudora Welty's books of short fiction—*A Curtain of Green* (1941), *The Wide Net* (1943), *The Golden Apples* (1949), *The Bride of the Innisfallen* (1955)—integrates both the bright and the dark in increasingly complex, and at times confounding, ways. To unravel these complications, we can begin with Welty's assertions concerning the "stream" that runs deeply through all of her work; she suggests that the bright and dark in all of these collections represent her inquiry into the nature of the protected and isolated individual. Many characters in Welty's stories have been insulated in a community, that of either a family or a small town. For Welty, this isolation can be protective and nurturing, or it can be stifling and imprisoning. Each of her collections explores the variations—the bright and the dark—both of being secluded and of entering into a communal, social world from that position of being sequestered from the larger society.

As Welty suggests in the quotation above, the position of isolation—what she calls being "protected"—has a doubleness to it, both a bright side and a dark side. The brightness in Welty's vision at first glance may seem to result in her comic stories of women who find unexpected solutions to the claustrophobia of their lives. For instance, in "Why I Live at the P.O.," Sister spends her entire narrative explaining to us in what we come to recognize as a comic voice exactly why she does live at the post office, away from her family. It is Sister's first-person narration that provides much of the story's comedy; there is no third-person narrator here to offer the reader any mediation or meditation on her predicament. Typical of the stories in *A Curtain of Green,* "Why I Live at the P.O." leaves the reader to her own devices to determine what is funny, what is serious, and often, what has happened. As narrator, Sister dwells with such intensity on petty slights—she has to cook for two more mouths than she planned, "stretch one chicken over seven people," as she puts it—that the reader soon understands the comic nature of her self-pity. Sister never does.

"Why I Live at the P.O." is an explosion of highly comic events surrounding the return of Stella-Rondo to the family with "this child of two" after she has run off with Mr. Whitaker, the traveling photographer. Sister, a version of the older brother in the New Testament story of the prodigal son, has stayed at home cooking and cleaning for her truly wacky family: Mama, Papa-Daddy, and Uncle Rondo. Stella-Rondo returns, claiming that her child, Shirley T., is adopted (otherwise simple math would suggest that the child was conceived before her marriage to Mr. Whitaker). Sister believes that Shirley T. is not adopted, even though this is the most convenient fiction for the family, who clearly want to save face: Sister insists that Shirley T. is the "spit image of Papa-Daddy if he'd cut off his beard" and that "she looks like Mr. Whitaker's side too. . . . She looks like a cross between Mr. Whitaker and Papa-Daddy" (*CS,* 46–47).[24] In this and in most other situations, Sister refuses to go along with the family fiction. Consequently, the entire family begins to turn on her. She has placed herself in a most difficult position as an outsider within the closed system of her family.

Sister's first-person narration should put the best possible spin on her actions. Instead we get glimpses through her eyes of her jealousy of Stella-Rondo, mixed in with heavy doses of self-pity. Her jealousy seems at least partially responsible for the family's repudiation. When Stella-Rondo arrives home, for instance, the first thing Sister tells us is that Stella-Rondo stole Mr. Whitaker from her, and stole him by telling him a lie:

> Of course I went with Mr. Whitaker first, when he first appeared here in China Grove, taking "Pose Yourself" photos, and Stella-Rondo broke us up. Told him I was one-sided. Bigger on one side than the other,

> which is a deliberate, calculated falsehood: I'm the same. Stella-Rondo is exactly twelve months to the day younger than I am and for that reason she's spoiled. (*CS*, 46)

Folktales have it that every woman has one breast that is slightly larger than the other—"bigger on one side"—and Sister's reaction to this accusation is very telling. She takes it personally, denying it vehemently, when she might just as well have said, "Well, so is Stella-Rondo, and so is every woman." But, as we see over and over in this story, Sister takes every comment and accusation as an intensely personal attack. We don't know the truth about who really had dibs on Mr. Whitaker; what we learn from this monologue and others like it throughout the story is that Sister feels that she is at the bottom of the ladder in every way, and no matter what happens, Stella-Rondo will best her, because she is "spoiled." This is a case of older-younger sibling rivalry achieving its full comic potential. As with most instances of disagreement between sisters, however, this situation is not comic at all to the participants. Sister takes whatever favoritism there may actually be toward Stella-Rondo and magnifies it in her mind to such a degree that she makes the family, as well as herself, believe that she is the one who doesn't belong. She thinks that everyone conspires against her; when Uncle Rondo, drunk, leaps into a hammock with Papa-Daddy, "Papa-Daddy woke up with this horrible yell and right there without moving an inch he tried to turn Uncle Rondo against me" (*CS*, 48).

The story shows how an intensely close family can be not only suffocating but also impossible to escape. In the end, family ties are so powerful that Sister's moving to the P.O. merely intensifies her connection with and dependence on her family. They are the "main" (and almost the only) family in China Grove, and they decide to boycott the post office. At the end of the story, we learn that Sister has been in residence at the P.O. for only five days; even though she already has "everything cater-cornered, the way [she] like[s] it" (*CS*, 56), she leaves us with the sense of the insularity of her escape. She has found peace, but for how long?

> Of course, there's not much mail. My family are naturally the main people in China Grove, and if they prefer to vanish from the face of the earth, for all the mail they get or the mail they write, why, I'm not going to open my mouth. Some of the folks here in town are taking up for me and some turned against me. I know which is which. There are

> always people who will quit buying stamps just to get on the right side of Papa-Daddy. (*CS*, 56)

While Sister's escape is successful in that she leaves home, it is clear that she has not left her sheltered life. As long as she is in China Grove, she is under complete control of her family. If this comic story represents the bright side of the sheltered life, then, it also has a dark underside. Though we can see that in some ways Sister's self-righteous attitude toward Stella-Rondo brings about the deluge of familial wrath—including the entire package of firecrackers exploding in her bedroom at 6:30 A.M.—it is also clear that Sister has very little power. She exercises what little she has by taking small appliances, curios, and plants from the yard with her to the P.O. The postmistress job is an honorary, unpaid position, and even if she had a salary it isn't clear where Sister might be able to go.

The tension between Sister's limited control over her life and her over-estimation of her power creates a comic situation in "Why I Live at the P.O." But while Sister's unquestioning acceptance of her sheltered life may be comic, she does much better than Clytie, the other grown daughter living with her family in *A Curtain of Green.* Instead of moving out and interrupting her routine of cooking, cleaning, and caretaking of her screwball family, Clytie goes outside and drowns herself in a barrel of rainwater. Staring at her reflection in the barrel, Clytie sees herself and her situation for what they are: she is a young woman with no chance of escape from her tortured life of taking care of the members of her family, who are ill and insane. The similarities between Sister's and Clytie's situations point out several important aspects of *A Curtain of Green:* in this collection Welty uses the narrator's position to indicate levels of awareness in her characters. First-person narration in "Why I Live at the P.O." shows us that Sister has no detachment from her own situation. In the two other broadly comic stories in the book, "Lily Daw and the Three Ladies" and "Petrified Man," the third-person narrator gives way to long stretches of dialogue between characters, thus achieving a similar effect to first-person narration, which is comprised entirely of dialogue and monologue. In contrast, the stories with less dialogue and a more dominant third-person narrator show a more introspective side of the central character; we do not hear Clytie's voice in her story, and rely on the distanced narrator to tell us what is happening. In this volume, as with Clytie, introspection and awareness of a claustrophobic life do not usually lead to release or freedom.

Sister's tentative move toward individualism is typical of the limited autonomy of the sheltered individual in *A Curtain of Green.* Other stories in the collection—"Clytie," "Petrified Man," "Lily Daw and the Three Ladies," "A Curtain of Green"—explore the difficulties for women in a society that, while attempting to shield them from danger, may also subjugate them. Lily Daw, for example, is almost sent to a psychiatric hospital by the three women ostensibly looking out for her. She has no family, so they become her surrogates, sheltering her until she almost suffocates. She is slow mentally, and it becomes clear that her caretakers are terrified that her limited brainpower might lead to her rape. They convince her to check in to a mental hospital. She barely escapes hospital confinement (her train is pulling away from the platform) by marrying a xylophone player from the circus, who himself seems intellectually challenged at best. "Lily Daw" in many ways epitomizes the attitude toward the sheltered life in *A Curtain of Green.* Lily does not recognize her situation as inescapable—though her caretakers hope to force her into either a mental hospital or marriage—and she moves jovially through her life. The brightness in *A Curtain of Green*'s sheltered lives emanates from those characters who have little or no power of introspection. "Ignorance is bliss," or to quote Gray's line completely, "Where ignorance is bliss, 'tis folly to be wise." In *A Curtain of Green,* to understand that one is isolated is to despair.

The single exception in the entire collection to this generalization is Ruby Fisher, who attains a freedom of spirit within what has been a potentially violent marriage to Clyde, a tenant farmer and bootlegger. Ruby imagines that Clyde has killed her, and this epiphany gives her a seer's view into her potential future with Clyde. When the story ends, it seems that Ruby will remain physically in her marriage to Clyde, but psychologically, a great change has occurred: she has realized that she is being emotionally abused. We learn in the beginning of the story that Ruby's outlet from her isolation has been to hitch rides with a coffee salesman as he drives past the farm, making his rounds. This physical escape foreshadows the release that Ruby will attain psychologically with her deeper understanding of her marriage. Yet even this uncharacteristically optimistic outcome remains tentative and veiled; knowledge of a potentially violent situation does not necessarily prevent violence. Ruby remains in the sheltered situation, at risk.

As its title suggests, Welty's second book of stories, *The Wide Net,* offers a slight opening out of the sheltered life. As in *A Curtain of Green,* the stories depict women in constricted situations, but we also see women acting to loosen these bonds in ways potentially more successful than in Welty's first book. "Livvie," for example, shows the collapse of Livvie and Solomon's marriage. At the outset, it seems that this may be a liberation for Livvie, a young black girl whom Solomon has claimed in his old age as a kind of trophy or spoil for the end of his life. The narrator describes Solomon's life as a constant quest for respect:

> People's faces tell of things and places not known to the one who looks at them while they sleep, and while Solomon slept . . . his face told . . . like a mythical story that all his life he had built, little scrap by little scrap, respect. A beetle could not have been more laborious or more ingenious in the task of its destiny. When Solomon was young . . . it was the infinite thing with him, and he could see no end to the respect he would contrive and keep in a house. He had built a lonely house the way he would make a cage. . . . (*CS*, 237)

As the story commences, Solomon is sick—"a tiny old, old man"—and Livvie nurses him. This doesn't seem peculiar until a cosmetics sales agent, Baby Marie, comes to the house. In the exchange between Livvie and Baby Marie, we learn just how far from town the house is, and just how isolated Livvie has become. Not only has she never tried on cosmetics or bought anything from a sales agent but she also does not have any money of her own, and isn't quite sure if there is money in the house: "Lady, but I don't have no money, never did have" (*CS*, 234). The standard cultural arrangement between husband and wife dictates that the wife, in charge of domestic duties, is afforded the domestic purse. Solomon has kept such tight reign on Livvie that she doesn't even know about spending money for the household, much less for herself. He acquires her as the final treasure in his quest for respect. Livvie is the bird in Solomon's cage.

The image of the bird defines Livvie even at the end of the story, when Solomon dies after seeing Cash at his bedside. After the visit from the cosmetics sales agent, Livvie ventured out onto the wilderness of the Natchez Trace, her first excursion of any sort, since "Solomon had never let Livvie go any farther than the chicken house and the well" (*CS*, 232). Out on the Trace, she "saw a sight. It was a man, looking like a vision" (*CS*, 235). Cash follows her home, and they find Solomon buried deeper in his covers than before, "as if it were winter still." The quilt on Solomon's bed is "a big feather-stitched piece-quilt in the pattern 'Trip Around the World' " (*CS*, 229), as if to remind us that until

Cash comes into the bedroom with Livvie, Solomon's bed has been the extent of her world. Solomon wakes up, and after delivering a moral homily to Cash on his comparative unworthiness to be with Livvie, as well as a speech about his own unworthiness to marry one so young, Solomon dies. Livvie leaves the bedroom; Cash follows her and "[s]eize[s] her deftly as a long black cat. . . . and all at once there began outside the full song of a bird" (*CS*, 239). It is tempting to read this song as a kind of liberation for Livvie. For a moment, with Solomon's admission when he sees Cash that "Young ones can't wait," it seems that Cash will liberate Livvie from Solomon's cage. But the images of Cash seizing her like a cat are uncomfortably close to those depicting Livvie as trapped behind Solomon's bars.

The story ends with its most striking image, not of a bird but of the bottle tree: "Outside . . . the sun was in all the bottles on the imprisoned trees, and the young peach was shining in the middle of them with the bursting light of spring" (*CS*, 239). The peach tree sits among the bottle trees, on one side of the steps. The image of the blossoming peaches among the bottle trees, "with the bursting light of spring," does, after all, suggest freedom for Livvie. The flowering tree forecasts a flowering for her; she is out of the cage—her branches no longer encased in glass like the bottle trees—and at the beginning of a new, freer life with Cash.

While "Livvie" represents the "bright" stream in Welty's view of the sheltered life, it nevertheless does so in a cramped way. We still feel the claustrophobia in the relationship between Livvie and Cash; he is an acquaintance of Solomon's and is schooled in the same kind of possessive views toward women. Livvie will not go far, either physically or psychologically, from the confines of Solomon's house. As in the tales of sheltered women in *A Curtain of Green*, Livvie's story remains bright for the most part because she remains unaware of her limitations. To her, marriage to Cash is liberation, but we can see the dark spring mingling here with the bright. The final story in *A Wide Net*, however, places "Livvie" in a kind of bas-relief and gives us a fuller appreciation for the brightness of Livvie's freedom from the caged life.

Like "Clytie," "At The Landing" shows the darkest side of the isolated life for Welty's young women. Because the story follows Jenny's fate beyond her realization that she needs freedom, "At The Landing" presents a more devastating look at the dangers of insularity than does any story in *A Curtain of Green*. Jenny has remained a recluse in her grandfather's house all of her life, until he dies.

House with bottle trees/Simpson County/1941
Permission granted by the Eudora Welty Collection—Mississippi Department of Archives and History

> Up the light-scattered hill, in the house with the galleries, the old man and his granddaughter had always lived. They were the people least seen in The Landing. The grandfather was too old, and the girl was too shy of the world, and they were both too good—the old ladies said—to come out, so they stayed inside. (*CS*, 241)

The situation is similar to that in "Livvie," but in this case the old man is not merely old enough to be the young girl's grandfather, as Solomon was; he really is her grandfather. Jenny has a greater sense of her isolation than does Livvie; the all-seeing "old ladies" don't realize that Jenny has one hope, "one awareness was always trembling about her: one day she would be free to come and go." She did have the run of the house: "Jenny could go from room to room, and out at the door. But at the door her grandfather would call her back, with his little murmur" (*CS*, 242). Jenny is in effect under house arrest, and she knows it.

The story opens with the death of Jenny's grandfather. As is typical in a Welty story, however, the time line is not linear; we jump around in Jenny's experience, learning that her mother died some years before, and that sometimes "Jenny, given permission, would walk up there to visit the grave of her mother" (*CS*, 243). On one of these visits, she spots Billy Floyd, of whom "It was said by the old ladies .. [that he] slept all morning for he fished all night" (*CS*, 243). They begin an odd, protracted courtship. Jenny insists that she wants to "watch" Floyd, and she does. They rarely touch.

During the course of the developing relationship, the narration remains in Jenny's head. Her musings about Floyd and about the nature of love, while they are quite beautiful and moving, also reveal the inherent weakness of Jenny's outlook. "Jenny could see to start with that no kiss had ever brought love tenderly enough from mouth to mouth" (*CS*, 244); of Billy Floyd, the itinerate fisherman, she thinks as he rides away from her on a horse, "[S]he knew what she would find when she would come to him. She would find him equally real with herself—and could not touch him then. As she was living and inviolate, so of course was he" (*CS*, 245). These are the naive thoughts of someone who has never kissed, and has never shared a relationship with anyone outside her family. Her protected life with her "good" grandfather has left Jenny singularly unprepared to confront evil. She thinks of Floyd, and of her feelings for him, in purely idealistic terms. The high romanticism of her thoughts can only lead to her downfall.

Jenny's fall is certainly one of the darkest moments in all of Welty's work, and the most stunning condemnation of the sheltered life. The flood that Jenny's grandfather is dreaming about when he dies actually takes place. Floyd rescues Jenny from the rising water; they camp on a hilltop. Floyd takes advantage of these isolated quarters to have sex with Jenny, but certainly not the kind of intercourse that Jenny has imagined. Floyd wakes her up:

> When her eyes were open and clear upon him, he violated her and still he was without care or demand and as gay as if he were still clanging

> the bucket at the well. With the same thoughtlessness of motion, that was a kind of grace, he next speared a side of wild meat from an animal he had killed and had ready in his boat, and cooked it over a fire he had burning on the ground. (*CS*, 251)

For Floyd, "making love" to Jenny carries as much interest and weight as spearing a side of meat. In fact, he does not make love; he violates her. There is a certain foreboding tone to the narrative description of Floyd's nonchalance and "thoughtlessness" here, with its stark contrast to Jenny's romantic obsessions. When the floodwater recedes, Floyd leaves Jenny and she returns to The Landing, to her deserted house. There she cleans and pines for Floyd, and learns from "the ladies" that "just like all men [Floyd] was something of an animal" (*CS*, 255). Nevertheless, Jenny thinks that she loves Floyd, and still waxes idealistic on the subject of love: "But it was when love was of the one for the one," she thinks, "that it seemed to hold all that was multitudinous and nothing was single any more. She had one love and that was all," and that love was Floyd, "and her love was enough to pass through the whole night, never lifting the same face" (*CS*, 255–56). She is truly "lost in love," as the saying goes, and she leaves The Landing to find Floyd and, she thinks, to find her way.

Jenny's life has no more prepared her to leave The Landing than it prepared her for a relationship with Floyd. From The Landing, she comes to the river and finds a group of fishermen who tell her that Billy Floyd is out on the water: "She asked the fishermen to let her wait there with them, since it was to them that he would return. They said it did not matter to them how long she waited, or where" (*CS*, 257). When night falls, the women in the fishermen's camp cook supper, while the men entertain themselves by throwing knives at a tree. At this juncture in the story, all of the gloomy foreshadowing—Jenny's inexperience and isolation, her idealistic views of love, Floyd's crude sex, even the knives thrown at the trees—comes to fruition. The fishermen "put [Jenny] inside a grounded houseboat on the plank of which chickens were standing. . . . There were pigs in the wood." There are pigs in the camp as well (we remember "the ladies" saying that all men are animals):

> One by one the men came in to her. She actually spoke to the first one that entered between the dozing chickens. . . . About them all and closer to them than their own breath was the smell of trees that had

> bled to the knives they wore. . . . By the fire, little boys were slapped crossly by their mothers—as if they knew that the original smile now crossed Jenny's face, and hung there no matter what was done to her. (*CS*, 258)

The final scene of "At The Landing" shows Jenny being gang-raped in a chicken house by a bunch of fishermen, while their wives and children sit outside around the dying embers of a fire. The grave harm done to Jenny—Floyd's deception and the fishermen's group violence—can be attributed in large part to her upbringing. By keeping her apart from society, Jenny's grandfather kept her from learning how to interact, how to understand the varieties of love and lust, how to protect herself from violation. Though Jenny survives her recognition that she is isolated, she is not able to survive beyond that realization because she hasn't learned to recognize evil. And even if she had, it is not clear that her recognition of it would have been enough to protect her. Jenny's story represents the darkest side of the sheltered life; it leaves the protected individual entirely vulnerable outside of its protection. The irony is full-blown: the more strictly a person is guarded, the greater the danger she faces when she goes out into the world.

As the final story in *The Wide Net,* "At the Landing" carries particular weight. Throughout the stories of this collection, as well as those in *A Curtain of Green,* Welty has examined the guarded life; "At The Landing" recapitulates her findings. *A Curtain of Green* indicates that the sheltered life provides an adequate—and even happy—life for those unaware of other possibilities and unfazed by their isolation. Welty brings this supposition into *The Wide Net* but complicates the situations and shades the emotional entanglements, showing us her characters' actions and development over longer time spans than those encompassing any of the stories in her first volume. The stories in *A Wide Net* seem to function as Welty's laboratory, where she is able to develop situations that she put forward in *A Curtain of Green.* She asks in "At The Landing," what if the sheltered life brought harm instead of protection to those too naive to recognize their vulnerability? Welty deepens her inquiry into the drama of the isolated life, and "At The Landing" summarizes her findings, murky and somber discoveries about the nature of the sheltered life, up to this point in her work.

As works depicting the sheltered individual in a closed community, both *A Curtain of Green* and *A Wide Net* augur the subject matter of the interlocking stories of Welty's third book of short stories, *The Golden Apples.*

Set in the community of Morgana, the stories, by focusing on Morgana's different members, offer a prismatic view of Welty's experimentation with the relation of self to family and community. Just as the longer stories of *A Wide Net* represent a deepening of Welty's concerns with the drama of the isolated life, the interconnected stories of *The Golden Apples* show Welty broadening these concerns. No longer are we in a singular situation, seeing only one brief span of a life from a single point of view; these stories allow us, and the characters, breathing space. We begin to see how different individuals cope with isolation both over a period of time and within a slightly larger community.

As in the stories of her previous two collections, some individuals in Morgana fare better under the protective umbrella of a close family or community than do others. Welty lists the "main families" of Morgana as a preface to the book, inviting us to consider individuals within families, and families within communities. We first read about the MacLains and the Raineys, in "A Shower of Gold"; "June Recital" also features the Raineys, as well as the Morrisons and Miss Eckhart and her mother. When we look back at the list after reading these two stories to situate ourselves more securely in Morgana, we see that Miss Eckhart and her mother are not on the list. Miss Eckhart is not from Morgana, nor would she and her mother be considered a proper family by native Morganans, much less one of the main families. In other words, even before we read a word of *The Golden Apples,* we can discern from this list the clannish nature of the town and the provincial way that it views family and community. We may also discern from this list and its omissions an indication of narrative distance in *The Golden Apples.* By omitting Miss Eckhart, arguably the central character in the work, from the list of Morgana's main families, the third-person narrator indicates a slightly ironic stance that will last throughout the book. The narrator may represent something that is true within the framework of Morgana, but then she may also step back and show us another truth, one that lies outside the town's framework. Miss Eckhart is not "main" from the point of view of the characters enclosed within Morgana's narrow world, though she is certainly a central figure if we look at Morgana from the position that the narrator gives us.

Merely by her singular existence, Miss Eckhart challenges the prevailing ways that Morganans live. But whether or not Miss Eckhart's way of living is an alternative to the claustrophobia of family and community is a question Welty leaves open. On one hand, Miss Eckhart's life seems ideal. She is free to follow her own passion and art, and as the town's piano teacher she shepherds most of the children through their beginning and intermediate keyboard repertoires. Thus as a music teacher, she has the pleasure of her music and the added pleasure of being with children. On the other hand, Miss Eckhart does not seem happy or at peace with her life. When one of her pupils, Cassie Morrison, reflects in "June Recital" on Miss Eckhart and her legacy, she reports various rumors about Miss Eckhart's failures in love. It is rumored that "She had been sweet on Mr. Hal Sissum, who clerked in the shoe department of Spights' store" (*CS*, 296). As far as Cassie knows, the two never even dated. When Mr. Sissum drowns, Miss Eckhart "would have gone headlong into the red clay hole" (*CS*, 299) of his grave if the minister hadn't grabbed her. This silent but powerful outpouring of grief suggests that Miss Eckhart harbors an equally powerful feeling for Mr. Sissum; she may, after all, wish to have a family, to "fit into" Morgana. Mr. Sissum's death slams the door on this possibility.

Miss Eckhart lives alone with her mother. After the funeral, we begin to realize what an unhappy life Miss Eckhart leads, from the devastating sadness of the narrator's comment that Miss Eckhart is "a poor unwanted teacher and unmarried. . . . Of course her only associates from first to last were children; not counting Miss Snowdie" (her landlord; *CS*, 306–7). Cassie reports seeing her slap her mother viciously, and "[t]hen stories began to be told of what Miss Eckhart had really done to her old mother. . . . Some people said Miss Eckhart killed her mother with opium" (*CS*, 307). Whether or not these rumors are true, they offer a glimpse into the kind of atmosphere in which Miss Eckhart exists in Morgana. The community is not kind to her, and Cassie concludes that "Her love never did anybody any good" (*CS*, 307). What seems on the surface to be a potentially enriching life of following one's artistic passion and passing that passion on to the young becomes, in the fishbowl of Morgana, just as devastating an experience for Miss Eckhart as for any other Welty character caught within a closely guarded family. Miss Eckhart dies alone in a mental institution in Jackson, which reminds us of Lily Daw en route to a mental institution until her suspect husband-to-be arrives at the train station and plucks her off the train. If we look to Miss Eckhart, Lily Daw, and characters like them, the choices for a life in a sheltering community seem rather bleak: either marriage or confinement in a mental ward.

Other individuals in *The Golden Apples* seem to survive the rigors of the intensely sheltered, myopic community better than Miss Eckhart, and give us a different view of community. Yet these are all members of the youngest generation of Morganans, and we are not shown in *The Golden Apples* how their lives will play out. Both Loch and Cassie Morrison early on thrive on their Morgana upbringing. In "June Recital" and in "Moon Lake," each exudes in youth a levelheadedness and balance of spirit that is rare in a Welty character. As a young adult, Loch leaves Morgana for New York, presumably for a contented life: "He likes it there," Cassie says. Cassie, however, stays in Morgana, teaching piano and obsessing over her mother's suicide (she plants hyacinth bulbs in a pattern that spells out her mother's name), and is not as happy as her brother.

Unlike Loch and Cassie, Cassie's friend Virgie Rainey has struggled under the scrutiny of Morgana. Her family is so poor that her mother dyes shoestrings with pokeberry juice to fashion for her a laced-up collar like the one on the sailor blouse in the town store. All the girls in Morgana make fun of her poverty. Virgie also struggles in her family; her independent spirit lets her musical ability shine—she is Miss Eckhart's star pupil—yet the refinement of music and the arts are totally beyond her family's grasp. The goats are allowed into the parlor in the Rainey house, where they snack on Virgie's old practice piano.

The final story in *The Golden Apples* finds Virgie confronting her mother's death, and with this death Virgie breaks all ties to family and community. At her mother's funerary viewing, Morgana tries to reach out to Virgie, but "[t]hey were all people who had never touched her before who tried now to struggle with her, their faces hurt. She was hurting them all, shocking them" (*CS*, 435). She packs up her mother's house, sells the cattle, and readies to leave Morgana. Cassie connects Virgie with Loch: " 'You'll go away like Loch. . . . A life of your own, away—I'm so glad for people like you and Loch, I am really' " (*CS*, 457). For Cassie, the focus of Loch's and Virgie's future is on their ability to control or "own" their life, and to lead that life "away." These are things, it seems, that Cassie cannot now do in Morgana. With Virgie, Welty suggests for the first time in her stories that something unmitigatingly bright can come of isolation for one who understands the narrowness of small-town life and who suffers its shackles. Welty leaves open the possibility for Virgie and for Loch that the sheltered, isolated life they have known in Morgana, with its magnified attention to the individual, has prepared them to go out into the world. Perhaps there can be, after all, some redemption from the insular life; the scrutiny that the small town places on the individual can, it seems, give one an impression of importance and the confidence that accompanies such importance.

With Virgie, Welty shows us that it is possible that the kind of life Morgana offers can also foster a rich and perceptive inner life. The pressures that townspeople and family have placed on Virgie Rainey seem in the end to act on her as pressure and heat act on coal: they form a diamond. The images in the final sections of "The Wanderers" suggest that with the death of her mother, Virgie is able to release some of the anger and resentment that have built up in her: "like suggestions and withdrawals of some bondage that might have been dear, now dismembering and losing itself. . . . the vanishing opacity of her will. . . . in the next moment she might turn into something without feeling it shock her. . . . As though for a long time she had been extremely angry" (*CS*, 440–41). Living in a sheltered environment, as Welty indicates, can be lovely with its protective shell, but that shell can also press and retain heat. For some—Miss Eckhart, Cassie and her mother—this pressure causes a breakdown. Virgie, though, seems to emerge from the intensity of her environment poised with self-knowledge. In the end, she asks herself, "Could she ever be, would she be, where she was going?" (*CS*, 459). All signals suggest that she will come into herself, for in the final sentences of the story, Virgie sits alone in the town square with an old beggar woman and nothing to her name—these very facts would be anathema to Morgana wags—yet she hears "the world beating" in her ears. Not only does Virgie show her self-confidence by sitting in the wrong place with the wrong person and with the wrong trappings of social status but she simultaneously shows that she is full of knowledge and creativity. The world that she hears "beating" is a world of myth and imagination: "The horse and bear, the stroke of the leopard, the dragon's crusty slither, and the glimmer and the trumpet of the swan" (*CS*, 461). These images have nothing to do with Morgana or with the Mississippi countryside; they are purely the stuff of myth, awaiting Virgie's fashioning. We leave Virgie in full possession of her self, negating all that the shelter of Morgana has offered, perhaps, but also flourishing out of the strength that she has built up in defiance of Morgana's probing and pressure. We suspect that Virgie will find her way through the kinds of situations that damaged Jenny in "At The Landing"; we have seen already her resolve and defiance in the face of the Morganans' tauntings; we have seen her intense understanding of music, with its passions and disappointments.

With the stories of *The Golden Apples,* Welty is able not only to suggest a bright light at the end of Virgie Rainey's insular life but also to intensify her scrutiny of the sheltered individual, if for no other reason than that the interlocking stories allow a revisitation of characters at various stages in their lives. In all three books, protection of the individual can result in harm, or at least in a static condition in which certain individuals—Livvie, Cassie Morrison, Lily Daw, for instance—can move only from one circumstance of protection to another. Jenny is certainly Welty's most memorable character of this type, though *The Golden Apples* presents several characters who try to leave Morgana, or try to exist outside of the social system, but cannot. The MacLain twins, Ran and Eugene, each flee Morgana—Ran leaves his wife and tries to live alone; Eugene moves to San Francisco, where he, too, is in a troubled marriage—but in the end, both return to home base, in states of defeat. Ran goes back to his wife, even though she does not love him; Eugene leaves San Francisco and his wife to return to his family in Morgana, where he dies. The sustained quality of *The Golden Apples* allows Welty to show the effects of a sheltered life over the course of a lifetime; significantly, she again chooses to explore the dark side of that life. Nevertheless, Virgie Rainey, the most convincing example of the bright side, the one who seems to profit from her experience, is left at the end of *The Golden Apples* on the brink of her life. Welty's emphasis here is on Virgie's victory over her experience rather than on Virgie's experience in Morgana.

A Curtain of Green focuses on shelter as entrapment; characters live a secluded existence, alternatives to which they cannot even imagine. Escapes—such as they are—are provisional, closed, unsatisfactory: Clytie and the wife of Powerhouse commit suicide; Sister moves to the post office; Ruby Fisher hitchhikes to get away from her farmhouse. The next collection, *The Wide Net,* presents characters who live in similar circumstances yet in some cases are able to contemplate escape. Their view of the world is wide, like Solomon's quilt and William Wallace's net. The tension in these stories arises from the characters' partial understanding of their options; they may see more of the world within their grasp, but like the characters in *A Curtain of Green,* they still cannot claim it for their own. Characters in *The Golden Apples* act out the tension between the dark and light streams with even more intensity than in either of the previous volumes. They share similar situations with characters in previous works, but some—Virgie, Cassie, Miss Eckhart, perhaps—seem to understand their predicament with more subtlety. They know that community shelter is at once safe and light, yet can also be smothering and dark. By the end of *The Golden Apples,* Virgie Rainey has made a true escape from this dualism by gaining self-consciousness. The interlocking stories of *The Golden Apples* also allow Welty to broaden her inquiries into the sheltered life; in Morgana we can visit and revisit individuals as they confront the pleasures and limitations of living under the microscope of their fellow citizens. *The Bride of the Innisfallen* both "falls" in line with its predecessors as a discussion of the sheltered life and shows a "falling off" in the intensity and closeness of the narrator to the diverse situations represented in the volume. Yet in their variation on the theme of shelter and in their presentation of a more distant narrator, the stories confirm both Welty's consistency and experimentation within the genre.

Welty's short story collections are autonomous and beautiful works, yet each volume also suggests connections to the others. Each collection is an individual project, questioning and reflecting its own emotional place, and each collection also points toward its successor. With her final collection, *The Bride of the Innisfallen,* Welty follows the pattern that she establishes in *A Curtain of Green* and *The Wide Net* and codifies in *The Golden Apples.* A writer often begins her career with a set of questions about a subject, and in the course of examining these questions, deepens them. We can look at the connections among these books in terms of Welty's developing sophistication as she weighs the benefits against the perils of shelter. Or to recall the terms with which she ends *One Writer's Beginnings,* Welty asks with increasing intensity, "[C]an the sheltered life also be a daring life?"

The Bride of the Innisfallen shares explorations into the sheltered life with Welty's other collections. Following the tour de force of *The Golden Apples,* however, this book represents a leveling of Welty's concerns. The more muted questioning in this volume allows Welty to extend her interest, both geographically and historically. The stories range from an account of a woman who decides after taking the ferry from England to Ireland to leave her husband, to the narrative of two sisters fleeing their plantation in the wake of Union troops' pillaging of the estate. Welty allows more of the brightness into her stories here than she has previously. Many characters have gained the same kind of self-consciousness as Virgie in *The Golden Apples,* but we see them moving farther from shelter than Virgie does. Many characters in *The Bride of the Innisfallen* are either in the midst of or at the end of a purposeful journey.

At its outset, "The Burning" seems to represent business as usual. Two central characters hang themselves after they are forced out of their home; we see again the devastation that people withdrawn from the world at large may experience. But in some ways, with these two deaths the story is only beginning. "The Burning" is a unique story in Welty's canon; it is Welty's rare, straightforward look at the Civil War. Here we see Welty extending far beyond the reach of previous work, moving back into the South's most troubled historical moment.

"The Burning" opens on a Southern plantation in the path of General Sherman and the Union army's burning march through Mississippi. A Union soldier rides his white horse into the parlor, to "inspect beforehand." He and his companion are met by the two sisters, Miss Myra and Miss Theo, and their slave, Delilah. Besides a group of house slaves, these are the only living inhabitants of the plantation; as Miss Theo tells the soldiers, " 'Then inspect. . . . No one in the house to prevent it. Brother—no word. Father—dead. Mercifully so—' " (*CS*, 484). The Union soldier gets Delilah to do his bidding—"Hold my horse, Nigger"—while he rapes Miss Myra on the parlor floor. Miss Theo comforts her sister, stroking her hair: "My poor little sister. . . . Don't mind this old world" (*CS*, 484). It seems this statement has been the sisters' mantra during the war; they have remained sequestered in the dreamworld of their mansion with their servants as the war raged around them. As they leave the house with Delilah, Miss Theo confesses, " 'Word *was* sent to us to get out when it was sent to the rest on Vicksburg road. Two days' warning. I believe it was a message from General Pemberton' " (*CS*, 487). The sisters epitomize the protected women of the nineteenth-century South, bound to their home: " 'Oh no, of course we couldn't leave,' said Miss Myra" (*CS*, 487). The story's ending literalizes this statement; they cannot survive without the protective walls of the plantation and the insular Southern culture they represent. Both Myra and Theo, with Delilah's assistance, hang themselves.

The jolt of the two sisters' gruesome death almost overshadows the story's ending. What at first seems like a long denouement after the central action of the story on reflection becomes the central action of the story. Delilah, the sisters' slave, does not hang herself with them, and she returns to the plantation. There she confronts the burned shell of the house, and finds among the burned-out ruins a carved mirror that had hung in the parlor:

> Though the mirror did not know Delilah, Delilah would have known that mirror anywhere, because it was set between black men. Their arms were raised to hold up the mirror's roof, which now the swollen mirror brimmed, among gold leaves and gold heads—black men

> dressed in gold, looking almost into the glass themselves, as if to look back through a door, men now half-split away, flattened with fire, bearded, noseless as the moss that hung from swamp trees. . . . In this noon quiet, here where all had passed by . . . she waited on her knees. (*CS,* 492–93)

The frame of this mirror is carved to depict Moors holding the glass; as Delilah holds up the mirror, it reflects her face, along with Jackson in the background. The symbolism here is rich. At this moment in history, the institution of slavery—the "black men"—does hold up a mirror to the South, reflecting the image of desolation and destruction that the city of Jackson represents. The nature of the antebellum South, and indeed of the entire country, was reflected in the way it treated slaves. The institution of slavery is one of the deepest stains on the fabric of the country; through its very existence we can discern the character of the nation at that time in history. The mirror also reflects the future of the South in the face of Delilah, a freed slave. In the reflection, then, we see the darkest moment in the nation's history—the destruction of the Civil War, and the brightest—the face of a free slave.

"The Burning" is Welty's most balanced consideration of the insular life, and epitomizes the balance of *The Bride of the Innisfallen* as a whole. The two aristocratic sisters cannot survive their cloistering, whereas Delilah, suffering the ultimate restriction of slavery, survives. The story is one of Welty's most highly allegorical stories as well; the nature of the sheltered life takes on broad historical significance in "The Burning," the sisters representing the victims of an entirely corrupt way of life and Delilah representing the great light that springs out of the dereliction of the slave-owning South. After she studies the potent images in the mirror, Delilah rises up to walk to Jackson, "stilted in Miss Myra's shoes," symbolically walking in the shoes—taking the place of—her white mistress. When she comes to the Big Black river, she lowers herself confidently into its waters, much as Virgie Rainey does in "The Wanderers": "She has forgotten how or when she knew, and she did not know what day this was, but she knew—it would not rain, the river would not rise, until Saturday" (*CS,* 494). As it does with Virgie, Delilah's immersion in the river suggests her first immersion into life, because she is free. And she seems to have an uncanny knowledge that she will be safe, that she can swim in the river of life.

We can only imagine the depth of Delilah's "passion for independence" as she realizes her freedom. It is this passion that Welty notes in the quotation beginning this chapter as the impetus behind writing all of her stories. In this quotation Welty also uses the potent image of the stream as she writes about coming into her own independence, one fed by those bright and dark springs rooted in the sheltered life. Welty thinks in images; the stream not only serves as one of the central images around which she organizes her short story collections but also is one she calls on specifically to represent the positive awareness of an insular life, and the embracing of the "wide world" beyond that insularity.

Clicking the Shutter, Arresting the Gesture: Eudora Welty's Passionate Looking

> I have a visual mind. That's the way I see things, so that's the way I write. I try to concentrate what I say in stories into visual images—landscapes, portraits, seasons, all the aspects plain to the eye. I work hard on these things.
>
> —Eudora Welty, interview, 1965

Eudora Welty tells us that the core of her imagination is visual, that she sees her stories in the form of scenes and snapshots. Welty surmises that her visual sense and her love of photography came from her father, Christian Welty, and his fascination with the camera he brought out to record all special occasions. Photography has a profound influence on Welty's mode of writing, teaching her that "Life doesn't hold still," as she explains in *One Writer's Beginnings.* "Photography taught me that to be able to capture transience, by being ready to click the shutter at the crucial moment, was the greatest need I had" (*OWB,* 84). Welty's formal career as a photographer never really materialized, though two exhibitions of her photographs were mounted in New York, and five selections from her photographs have been published to date. As she explains her choice of vocation, she tells us that she "felt the need to hold transient life in *words*—there's so much more of life that only words can convey. . . . The direction my mind took was a writer's direction from the start" (*OWB,* 85). Yet while Welty obviously did feel her primary medium to be language, she did not hold photography in abeyance but continued to use a camera until 1950, when she left her Roliflex on a bench in the Paris metro and, out of anger at her carelessness, did not replace it.[25]

A serious interest in using the camera, such as Welty's, requires more than mere mastery of the relationship between film speed, shutter speed, and the size of the lens aperture, the technical aspects of photography. To be a photographer is to internalize a special way of seeing, and Welty's photographic visual sense shapes her prose in many ways. Welty herself has written about the relationship of vision and writing in her work, and as she suggests, the relationship is a very complicated one. "The camera was the hand-held auxiliary of wanting-to-know" (*OWB*, 84), and for Welty, "wanting-to-know" may extend from being curious about a thing and the way it looks to trying to ascertain the many layers of a complex personality and contemplating the nature of human relationships. Welty's photographs themselves cover this range; she has taken many stills of objects and of landscapes, capturing the beauty of things, but her most evocative photographs are her portraits of individual faces that she encountered during her travels around her home state in the Depression years, and those pictures of individuals interacting, that "[stop] a moment from running away" and show "that every feeling waits upon its gesture" (*OWB*, 84–85).

The two photographs reproduced here illustrate the way Welty catches individuals in moments of revelation. In the posture and face of the young girl, Welty captures a complex set of feelings. Her stance is casual and relaxed—she leans back on her left foot—but the way she holds the umbrella, tipped on its side over her shoulder, gives her posture a deliberate swagger. Her face, somewhat overpowered by the bow in her hair, looks painfully at the camera. Her eyes are puffed almost shut and her lips are slightly parted. Has she been crying? Is she about to speak? The various and contradictory elements of this portrait come together to suggest vulnerability, but also tenacity; the girl wishes to pose for the camera in her Sunday best, even through some sort of personal sadness. She relies on her clothes to prop her up emotionally.

The photograph entitled "Brothers" is not as emotionally complex as the portrait of the girl. The brothers grin at one another as if they are sharing some joke or secret. The straightforwardness of the grins suggests their closeness and geniality, neither quality necessarily a given in sibling relationships. The photograph also shows family resemblance in looks, as well as in mannerisms. Their grins are the same, and both boys wear caps. In each portrait, Welty uses her camera to probe into the inner lives of her subjects. She waits until just the right moment, when her subjects open up to the camera a "gesture" that reveals "feeling," to use Welty's words; they have shown her camera something that it wanted to know. From the gestures captured in these pictures, we can see beginnings of stories, but these stories are presented to us in synchronic (nonsequential) fashion. We receive all information in one glance, and we can put it in sequence for ourselves—as I

Sunday school child/Jackson/1930s
Permission granted by the Eudora Welty Collection—Mississippi Department of Archives and History

do in describing the photographs here—in any order we choose. As Welty says, "I'm a visual-minded person" (*Con,* 348).

For Welty the medium of the story most closely resembles the medium of the narrative painting, where the painter makes his view of a story-telling incident clear by using these techniques: perspective, to show, for instance, which characters are important, which belong

Brothers/Jackson/1930s
Permission granted by the Eudora Welty Collection—Mississippi Department of Archives and History

together, which are hostile to one another; line of vision, to expose exactly what the most important point of the painting is, and where the viewer should stand in order to focus on it; framing, to control the story, to capture the part of the story and the scene that the painter wants to engage and, as important, to leave out that part of the story that the painter wants to omit.

Welty practices a version of narrative painting in several of her photographs. The perspective of "The Tomato-Packers' Recess" is carefully shaped. The man playing the guitar is the focal point of the photograph not just because he sits at the center of the grouping (and not just because he wears a cowboy hat with a beautiful three-fingered crease) but more because many of the subjects seated around him look at him and are seated at angles deferential to his position. The young boy standing below the porch even has his back to the camera so that he can look up at the guitarist. The relationship between the individuals in the photograph shows us the point of emphasis.

Line of vision here is established by the base of the porch slanting across the bottom quadrant. The neck of the guitar parallels this slant, but because it is tilted at a slightly higher angle, the line it makes with

Tomato-packers' recess/Copiah County/1936
Permission granted by the Eudora Welty Collection—Mississippi Department of Archives and History

the porch boards forms a V. The base of this V, or arrow, is in the lap of the guitar player. Other lines of vision also form in the photograph, most of them drawn by the eyes of the crowd. If we simply follow with our eyes the eyes of the packer at the tuning pegs of the guitar, for instance, we are taken to a different part of the photograph than we see if we follow the main sight lines established by the porch and the neck of the guitar. The same is true for other pairs of eyes in the photograph. Notice how few men look into the camera.

These effects are all dependent on the framing or the cropping of the photograph. Either at the moment the camera's shutter clicked or later, during printing in the darkroom, Welty positioned the players within the frame of the photograph to emphasize the centrality of the guitar player. There could be, for example, something larger or more disruptive going on within a 360-degree range of Welty's gaze, but as a photographer framing this scene she has the power to shut out, as well as to emphasize, what she chooses. The inferences we draw from this photograph are entirely dependent on the choices Welty makes in perspective, line of vision, and framing. The narrative photograph or painting tells a story, but like Welty's stories, it tells its story synchronically. The series of images are presented simultaneously, and the viewer relies on the photographer's techniques of perspective, line of vision, and framing to guide his or her eyes toward the important details.

When we think of how visual techniques find their way into prose fiction, we are inclined to think primarily of description and metaphor. Welty uses these devices brilliantly in her work, but Welty has also thought deeply about seeing in a broader sense. Welty's visual sense, informed by her sustained use of the camera, is the genesis of her writing, shaping her imagination and her technique in story telling, in her relationship to the story, and in her selection of the parts of the story she chooses to tell. The techniques Welty masters as a photographer shape her stories as well as her photographs.

Welty's Visual Prose: A Primer

Given Welty's visual mind, we should not be surprised to find that she uses a visual technique as the fundamental organizing principle in her stories. Individual stories often seem like a collection of scenes or snapshots rather than the sequential, causal telling of a plot. Early in her career, Welty often combined this synchronic narrative strategy with a journey motif; the linear structures of the journey anchored her use of her visually grounded technique, giving a shape to the emotional revelation that an action-filled plot would otherwise provide a more traditional story. For example, in "A Worn Path," Phoenix Jackson walks from her house in the country into town to get medicine for her grandson. The inherent structure of the journey frees Welty to combine memory and dream as she captures the wanderings of the old woman's mind.

While Phoenix travels along the path to town, her mind meanders throughout the events of her past. Welty achieves a similar effect in another story in *A Curtain of Green,* "Death of a Traveling Salesman." In this story Welty traces the journey of Bowman, a shoe salesman, on "his first day back on the road after a long siege of influenza" (*CS,* 119). Because Bowman is "feverish, and . . . not quite sure of the way" (*CS,* 119), he has a car accident. He leaves his car and walks to a nearby farmhouse, where he first misjudges, then discovers something very surprising to him about the relationship between the man and woman living there. The conceit of Bowman's illness, which gives him a foggy mind, like the device of Phoenix Jackson's advanced age, allows Welty to weave various disconnected scenes across the straight lines of his physical journey.

While Phoenix Jackson's mind flashes memories and stories from her past across the canvas of her journey, the canvas of Bowman's story is more dreamlike than it is filled with memory. Throughout, the salesman struggles with a dual perception. Bowman tries to discern what is happening inside his body—"His chest was rudely shaken by the violence of his heart" (*CS,* 126)—as well as to understand the relationship he has discovered between the farmer and his wife. As we read through the story, we wrestle both with the nonsequential, synchronic nature of the narrative as well as with understanding the connection between Bowman's thoughts and the objects of his focus, between his insight and his sight. The emphasis on the disruption of linear narrative by a visual, narrative sequence, and the focus on Bowman's scrutiny of the marriage together suggest a disruption of Bowman's identity as a salesman. The career of a salesman depends primarily on two things: the linear journey from one place to the next, without rest, a sense of destination, or time for introspection; and the use of speech and language to establish superficial relationships in order to make the sale. The life of the salesman, when considered as a series of stops and starts, resembles the structure of the typical Welty story. As I described them in chapter one, Welty's stories are like stops on the way to somewhere, though in Bowman's life, the stops don't imply progress, since he has no destination.

Throughout "Death of a Traveling Salesman," Bowman's struggle with the connection between the couple's relationship and his own inner life allows Welty to concentrate her visual technique on composition and viewpoint rather than on metaphor and description to drive a straightforward plot. For instance, Bowman's recollections of the places he has stayed, as well as his image of himself in those places, are represented visually, in terms of distance and framing. The story opens with the salesman reviewing his "fourteen years on the road." In his delirium he can only "remember little rooms within little rooms, like a nest of Chinese paper boxes. . . . And he himself . . . in the wavy hotel mirrors had looked something like a bullfighter, as he paused for that inevitable instant on the landing" (*CS*, 119–120). In this vivid opening, Welty tells us several things about Bowman's character and about the way she will structure the story. Bowman's self-perception is warped, or "wavy": when he looks in the mirror, he sees a bullfighter rather than his true self; his career in sales has left him without opportunity for self-knowledge. The simile of the Chinese paper boxes shows us the nature of his memory: it functions synchronically, or vertically, like one box stacked inside the other, rather than moving in a linear and time-bound fashion, like one box stacked beside the other. In spite of the nature of his job, one that demands that he live a life of linear travel, Bowman can no longer think of himself in such terms at this point in his life. The narration broadcasts that the telling of "Death of a Traveling Salesman" will be alinear, reflecting Bowman's psychological upheaval in spite of his professional travels, which are presumably in a straight line, from one destination to the next.

The telling of this story, instead of constructing some action-packed plot, is essentially a narration of Bowman's perception. This kind of telling reinforces the essentially visual technique that drives the story. Because we see the other two characters in the story from Bowman's point of view as he questions his vision of himself, we notice what he notices about them: their individual capacity to see and, symbolically, to perceive and communicate. Of Sonny, the narrator notes through Bowman's eyes, "There was effort even in the way he was looking, as if he could throw his sight out like a rope" (*CS*, 124). Bowman notices the power and direction of Sonny's perception; he controls it as he would a lasso. Bowman observes as he converses with the wife that "she was not really talking to him, but following the thing that came about with words that were unconscious and part of her looking" (*CS*, 125). The young wife somehow is able to communicate more directly in images without the mediation of language. In her world, communication is a process in which idea is translated directly into gesture or "thing." Sonny and his wife confront Bowman with two ways of perceiving and communicating that he has not understood before. Sonny's perceptions are driven from within and active, not externally driven and passive, as are Bowman's. His identity as a salesman has led him from short-term goal to short-term goal, with no other coherence or direction: he has "travelled *for* a shoe company," allowing the company rather than himself control of his perception. Bowman recognizes that this mode of communication represents the ideal relationship between two people: the desire for that rare and impossible union, the union of understanding (seeing) and communication (language). In other words, the ideal for the lover is to communicate great passion without speaking. For the lover, as with Sonny's wife, the first step toward this kind of communication is to communicate with gesture. Both through visual techniques and the language of vision, Welty shows us Bowman's essential drama: because he has not been in control of his life's journey, he has not experienced the essential element in life: an intimate relationship with another person. The hotel rooms he remembers as boxes within boxes are all empty.

Welty carries out her plan of organizing the story visually by presenting Bowman's "looking" in snapshot form. With each new snapshot, Bowman gains a greater understanding of the relationship he observes and of his own comparative emptiness. When the salesman comes to the farmhouse, Welty frames his vision of the house: "It was a shotgun house, two rooms and an open passage between, perched on the hill. The whole cabin slanted a little under the heavy heaped-up vine that covered the roof, light and green, as though forgotten from summer. A woman stood in the passage" (*CS*, 121). Welty intersperses views of the house from Bowman's point of view throughout the story; with each repetition of these views, we get a sense of how the salesman's point of view is shifting. As the visual sense of the house shifts in the narration, we feel him moving closer and closer to the emotional center of the house, the relationship between the man and the woman, and closer and closer to the ideal of seeing and speaking as one gesture. Emphasizing the scenic nature of Bowman's perception, Welty here shows him drawing an analogy between what he sees and a painting he recalls being among his family possessions:

> The room was enclosed in the gloom of yellow pine boards. He could see the other room, with the foot of an iron bed showing, across the passage. The bed had been made up with a red-and-yellow pieced quilt that looked like a map or a picture, a little like his grandmother's girlhood painting of Rome burning. (*CS*, 122–23)

At this juncture in the story, Bowman's vision has moved through the house to the bedroom, but he sees only the foot of the bed, not the entire bed. He must continue to look before he perceives what is at the center of this room, what the bed represents: "A marriage, a fruitful marriage." At the moment of his discovery, Welty repeats a detail from the distinctly pictorial description of the bedroom. As the woman sits down, "The pattern on the quilt mov[es]." At this moment, Bowman sees the whole quilt (and by extension, the whole bed); symbolically he sees simultaneously the "pattern" of their relationship, and its vitality, or "movement." Bowman then describes the relationship between the husband and wife to himself, emphasizing the purity of communication without the clutter of language, communication through the gesturing head or the raised eyebrow:

> There was nothing remote or mysterious here—only something private. The only secret was the ancient communication between two people. But the memory of the woman's waiting silently by the cold hearth, of the man's stubborn journey a mile away to get fire, and how they finally brought out their food and drink and filled the room proudly with all they had to show, was suddenly too clear and too enormous within him for response. . . . (*CS*, 129)

His moment of recognition is powerful enough that Bowman—perhaps for the first time in his life—feels something "too enormous within him," and he is without language to describe it. The narration simply trails off in an ellipsis. Bowman recognizes the flaws in his ways of perceiving and communicating, and thus recognizes the inherent poverty of his life. He decides to stay the night with the couple because of the promise of heightened self-awareness. When Sonny frees his car, Bowman realizes, "Now that he could go, he longed to stay. Of what was he being deprived?" (*CS*, 126). When he sees the full scene of the bedroom, he perceives the nature of their relationship, and the nature of his deprivation, even though "he had not known yet how slowly he understood" (*CS*, 129). For Bowman, vision and understanding are inextricably linked; when he begins to see clearly, he also begins to understand. Welty shows us these things through her scenic organization of the story. The seemingly disjunctive ordering of scenes allows us to mimic Bowman's growing self-knowledge. We begin to see as he begins to see.

Metaphor and Description in *A Curtain of Green*

In Welty's fiction vision can be in the form of a metaphor, an object representing something bigger and deeper than itself. Loch's telescope in

"June Recital" and Clytie's last glimpse of her face in the reflective pool in "Clytie," for example, are each uses of visual metaphor that point to larger issues: the telescope suggests Loch's developing perspective on the world outside as he matures into adolescence, and Clytie's reflection indicates the belated discovery that her face is the face—and the identity—she has unknowingly searched for throughout her life.

Along with metaphor, Welty also uses the visual technique of pure description to extraordinary effect in all of her stories. The quick color, like Uncle Rondo's pink kimono, for instance, can situate a permanent image in the reader's mind. Welty's depiction of Uncle Rondo in this contraption is one of the great comic moments in "Why I Live at the P.O.": "It wasn't five minutes before Uncle Rondo suddenly appeared in the hall in one of Stella-Rondo's flesh-colored kimonos, all cut on the bias, like something Mr. Whitaker probably thought was gorgeous" (*CS,* 48). To intensify the visual image, and thus the comic effect, later in the story Uncle Rondo accidentally squirts catsup down the front of the kimono.

Description can work most profoundly in Welty's work to carry and evoke emotion. In "A Piece of News," Welty represents a storm's passing with a descriptive metaphor of a wagon crossing a bridge. The story opens with Ruby Fisher running in out of the rain, but the metaphor of the rainstorm takes on a deeper meaning by the end. Ruby has seen a newspaper story about another Ruby Fisher, whose husband has shot her in the leg, and she realizes that such a thing could very easily happen to her: "It was as though Clyde might really have killed Ruby, and as though Ruby might really have been dead at his hand" (*CS,* 16). After reading this news story, Ruby will never accept Clyde's brutality in the same fashion again; the story ends with this telling description: "It was dark and *vague* outside. The storm had rolled away to *faintness* like a wagon crossing a bridge" (*CS,* 16; emphasis mine). Nature's storm by the end of the story has metamorphosed into the emotional storm stirring between Ruby and Clyde, brought to a head by the newspaper from another county that tells of violence done to another Ruby Fisher.

At first glance, the language of this storm passage may seem straightforward rather than evocative of deeper emotional content, but a closer look shows that the depth of the language lies in a couple of unusual word choices: "vague" and "faintness." "Vague" connotes something ambiguous and unintelligible. These are not attributes we usually associate with the weather or the time of day, but rather we link them to inner perceptions and emotional weather. "Faintness" represents the imperceptible, dull, indistinct, while also evoking weakness, as in "faint of heart" or "faintness of breath." Stress on these two words opens out the emotional content embedded in the two sentences that at first seem only to describe the weather. What lies ahead, or on the "outside," of the marriage is "vague," but for the moment the tension between Ruby and Clyde has "rolled away," "become faint," it seems, because Clyde perceives Ruby's recognition of his potential for violence. Clyde's random outbursts of violence have been his method of intimidating, and hence of controlling, Ruby because she has never known what to expect from him. He has kept her always on guard. Now that she is onto his game, the workings of the relationship are more "vague." Ruby has crossed an emotional bridge, as this quick visual description tells us, because she has been forced to confront her husband's violence.[26] As this brief ending of "A Piece of News" displays in Welty's hands, descriptive passages can assume a complicated function, working on several levels at once to suggest both an external, visual occurrence and to represent an internal, emotional change or revelation. Welty uses the metaphor here as she used framing in "Death of a Traveling Salesman" to draw the relationship between vision and emotional revelation. Welty's unusually dexterous use of these fundamental visual methods—metaphor and description—as well as her complex use of photographic framing and organization suggest how carefully she directs her attention to visual techniques.

"A Memory" and the Visual Style

The stories I have discussed thus far as "visual stories" all come from Welty's first collection, *A Curtain of Green* (1941). One of the more enigmatic and visually interesting stories in the collection, "A Memory," releases Welty's visual techniques from the linear underpinning of the journey that she uses in "A Worn Path" and "Death of a Traveling Salesman." "A Memory" serves not only as a touchstone in the collection, crystallizing Welty's fictional method for all of its stories, but also presents some of the philosophical difficulties in Welty's framing technique, especially when framing implies control of one individual over another. "A Memory" begins with the narrator's reminiscence of her coming of age. The narrator recalls sitting on the beach as a young girl, awash in memories of the school year and her first crush, on a boy whom she has never met but whose wrist she has most certainly brushed against. While she sits on the beach recalling this narrative, she frames the action around her (the frolicking of a family of "common" people) within a rectangle of her fingers, as she is learning to do in her painting class. Thus Welty opens this story with one of her primary visual techniques, the frame of vision. This act of framing gives us a quick view of the scene and indicates that the narrative method will be visually directed, as it is in other stories we have examined from *A Curtain of Green,* rather than progressing in a straight line. We know to expect, then, a method of organization more scenic and poetic than linear and plotted. Here is the narrator's reflection on the conflation of her memory of her love and her observation of the events going on around her:

> As I lay on the beach that sunny morning, I was thinking of my friend and remembering in a retarded, dilated, timeless fashion the incident of my hand brushing his wrist. It made a very long story. But like a needle going in and out among my thoughts were the children running on the sand, the upthrust oak trees growing over the clean pointed roof of the white pavilion, and the slowly changing attitudes of the grown-up people who had avoided the city and were lying prone and laughing on the water's edge. I still would not care to say which was more real—the dream I could make blossom at will, or the sight of the bathers. I am presenting them, you see, only as simultaneous. (*CS,* 77)

The narrator presents two distinct, though somehow related, "stories" here "only as simultaneous." The nature of these two juxtaposed stories offers further clarity of method. What starts off as a "very long story" in this passage ends up as "the dream I could make blossom at will." This shift from long story to instantaneous dream is significant. The story of her tryst with her beloved is not long, not even a story at all in the conventional sense, but an encounter lasting a split second, a brush-by on the staircase. We learn here, if we have not learned already from reading previous stories in *A Curtain of Green,* such as "Death of a Traveling Salesman," that the narrator has a special definition of story, and it may be more like a blink of an eye that becomes "dilated, timeless" than like an extended and connected series of events. The event story that the narrator juxtaposes with her remembered dream story is not conventional either. Rather, this "sight of the bathers" is "like a needle going in and out among [her] thoughts." The narrator tells us that "through some intensity" she "had come almost into a dual life, as observer and dreamer" (*CS,* 76), and this is an accurate and telling description of what this longer passage describes; she dreams and observes at once, and the result is an interlocking series of observations with the lyrical, visual logic of a dream.

While "A Memory" at first seems to be about the coming of age of love, a reading through the story with this expectation may be strangely unfulfilling. The narrator as a young girl doesn't have any contact with the object of her love besides the light touch on the stair. And the voice of the adult relating this childhood memory does not tell the story we might expect—that when she gets older, she does have a lover, but never the same intensity of feeling that she had for her first love. Since the narrator does not fulfill the reader's desire for information or closure in this matter of love, we must reconsider the story to find out what subject the narrator does address. When we review the passage quoted previously, the story's subject becomes the coming of age of Welty's particular artistic vision and method. Unlike any of the other visually directed stories in *A Curtain of Green,* "A Memory" does not use the visual method to show development of insight in a central character; in fact, the narrator of the story is striking in her lack of movement or insight, just as she is remarkably unwilling to relate more information about her lover. The truly static nature of this story suggests that we need to look to other issues to find its subject matter, and these other issues concern the visual techniques Welty uses throughout *A Curtain of Green.*

Welty's Representational Method: Visual Technique in a Verbal Medium

Some 40 years after publishing "A Memory," Welty delivered a series of lectures that became her autobiographical work, *One Writer's Beginnings.* In the course of these lectures, she remarks on her visual method, and details the principle behind the narrator's framing in "A Memory" as well as in other stories of *A Curtain of Green.* As she wrote "Death of a Traveling Salesman," Welty discovered that

> My temperament and my instinct had told me alike that the author, who writes at his own emergency, remains and needs to remain at his private remove. I wished to be, not effaced, but invisible—actually a powerful position. Perspective, the line of vision, the frame of vision—these set a distance. (*OWB,* 87)

This passage describes Welty's method in terms explicitly drawn from the visual arts. When we take these terms back to "A Memory," we see that the narrator of this story resembles Welty's account of her methods. Welty is a private person, she tells us, who wishes to remain "invisible" in her stories; the young girl remains invisible as well. She never meets her love, nor does she interact with the family on the beach. Further, as we know, Welty writes and represents herself consistently in paradoxical constructions: invisibility is not weakness, or erasure, as we might expect, but rather its opposite, power. (The most powerful gods in religion and mythology, for example, are depicted as being invisible.) By the end of "A Memory," we can see the young girl becoming aware of this power of invisibility; she delivers a long incantation on the depravity of the "common" family on the beach in which she clearly considers herself socially superior to the family, even without seeing them except from a distance.

After professing her desire to be hidden, Welty goes on to develop the visual metaphor suggested by her word "invisible": "Perspective, the line of vision, the frame of vision—these set a distance." This language is comprised of technical terms from the world of the visual arts, primarily photography and painting, and establishes the relationship between the artist and her work. Welty tells us in visual language, as she has told us all along in her essays, that she understands herself as a writer in the position of an observer. The opening of "A Memory," which shows the young girl framing the scene as she does in painting class, coupled with the complex method of telling the story that the older narrator develops, parallel Welty's own description of herself as storyteller. "A Memory" serves in one sense as Welty's earliest *Ars Poetica;* Welty uses the story to set out her method of writing for herself and for her readers.

Writing within the specific visual boundaries of an observer, she takes interest in perspective, a term that the visual arts uses to delineate the spatial relationship between objects. In Welty's stories, perspective reveals relationships between individuals and between individuals and their surroundings; it "set[s] a distance," and that distance can be immense, as it is between the girl and the family on the beach. Welty also points out that she must be acutely aware of line of vision, the position from which her readers will read her work. And she explains that she is an observer who must understand how to "frame," or circumscribe, the portrayals and action in a story. As Welty uses perspective, line of vision, framing, she summarizes, she must set herself up as an observer/narrator at just the right distance, so that the panorama of the story will be as she wishes: not too close to the reader, or certain things will be left out of the visual frame, and not too far from the reader, or the emphasis will fall away from the subjects she wishes to explore and emphasize.

Narrator and Distance in "A Memory"

While the narrator does not seem to grow or change during "A Memory," the story does give us a complex view of Welty's narrator. "A Memory" seems to be one of Welty's most personal works of fiction. Because the first-person narration represents the coming of age of an artist, the distance between writer and narrator seems very slight. Welty herself has said that this story represents her memory of daydreaming on train trips she took as a girl with her father: "The [young girl's finger] frame only raises the question of the vision. It has something of my own dreaming at the train window" (*OWB,* 89). Yet the story's first-person narration and subject matter create a misleading sense of intimacy; it is very difficult to locate and attribute certain feelings in the story. Though we know that the story is the older narrator's remembrance of herself as a child, for example, when we finish reading "A Memory," we are not sure how the older narrator feels toward herself as a child; the language relating the child's crush on her schoolmate is oddly noncommittal and emotionally flat. On one of the rare occasions when the older narrator does express an opinion about the obsessive love she is remembering, she casts it in a strangely distant, negative syntax: "I remember how he used to swing his foot as he sat at his desk—softly, barely not touching the floor. Even now it does not seem trivial" (*CS,* 77). Note how the narrator is unable to put her feelings about this memory into active or positive language but casts her emotion negatively, "it does not seem trivial." How shall we read this sentence? It does not *seem* trivial, but is it? If it does not seem trivial, what does it seem to be? What is the significance of this memory to the narrator; why is she recalling it with such detail? If the memory is so important, why is she unable to be straightforward about it?

One answer, I believe, lies in the narrator's emphasis on vision and in Welty's understanding of the relationship between vision and feeling. Both "Death of a Traveling Salesman" and "A Piece of News" indicate that sight and insight are connected in Welty's stories. Welty discusses the link between observation and sensitivity in her essay "Place in Fiction" (from *The Eye of the Story*), which she composed after *A Curtain of Green.* The link she makes in this essay between looking and feeling offers a gloss on "A Memory." Welty defines observation in terms of focus: "Focus then means awareness, discernment, order, clarity, insight—they are like the attributes of love. The act of focusing itself has beauty and meaning; it is the act that, continued in, turns into mediation, into poetry" (*Eye,* 123).

Welty defines "focus" as a metaphor for the mental process of concentration, a metaphor that is just one indication of the centrality of the visual to Welty's writing and to her thinking about writing. Second, by comparing the act of focusing and the sensation of love, Welty gives a particular slant to each term. For example, she equates the attributes of focus—"awareness, discernment, order, clarity, insight"—with those of love. While these may well be some characteristics that we associate with mental focus—the act of thinking about a narrow subject—Welty imbues the physical, mechanical act of visual focus with these qualities as well. In other words, feelings, for Welty, govern how vision is trained and focused; interior feelings affect not only what the exterior gaze is trained on but the intensity, duration, and discerning power of that mechanical gaze as well. Her character the naturalist painter Audubon muses in a later story, "[I]n man the enlargement of the eye to see started a motion in the hands to make or do, and . . . the narrowing of the eye stopped the hand and contracted the heart" (*CS,* 195). For Welty, the extension or contraction of one's vision connects directly to the extension or contraction of the heart: the larger the "eye," or field of focus, the larger the "heart," or capacity of feelings; likewise, the narrower the field of focus, the more contracted the capacity of feelings.

Not only does the feeling generated by love determine the direction, duration, and intensity of the physical act of focusing, but focus also affects—more strikingly—Welty's understanding of the nature of love. Welty defines "the attributes of love" matter-of-factly, as "awareness, discernment, order, clarity, insight." Because this definition of "love" is in the service of a definition of "focus," we naturally "focus" on focus in this passage; yet if we look squarely at the qualities that Welty claims for love as she concentrates on her definition of "focus," we see that these qualities she gives to love are quite unusual. In this passage, Welty gives us a love emphasizing objectivity and distance, qualities that we don't automatically associate with love. The love Welty uses to determine her subject matter and intensity, and which undergirds her work, in other words, is more dispassionate than passionate. We recall

Welty telling us that as a writer she "wished to be, not effaced, but invisible—actually a powerful position." Part of that power, it seems, lies in the ability to control the irrationality of love by keeping it at a distance.

In her story "A Still Moment" (in her second collection, *The Wide Net*), Welty details the artist/visionary's particular attitude toward subjects as one of "love and separateness." As I discussed in chapter one, Robert Penn Warren's insightful essay early in Welty's career turns on the significance of love and separateness to her work. This phrase sums up Welty's understanding of how passion and observation come together in her work. At the conclusion of "A Still Moment," which depicts a momentary meeting on the Natchez Trace between the nineteenth-century highwayman James Murrell, the minister Lorenzo Dow, and the naturalist painter John Audubon, Dow has a moment of realization after witnessing with pure horror Audubon's shooting a white heron in order to preserve it as a model for his studio:

> In the woods that echoed yet in his ears, Lorenzo riding slowly looked back. The hair rose on his head and his hands began to shake with cold, and suddenly it seemed to him that God Himself, just now, thought of the Idea of Separateness. For surely He had never thought of it before, when the little white heron was flying down to feed. He could understand God's giving Separateness first and then giving Love to follow and heal in its wonder; but God had reversed this, and given Love first and then Separateness, as though it did not matter to Him which came first. (*CS,* 198)

While this is a complex passage in a difficult story, it stands as a revelatory moment for each of the seemingly different men. Earlier in the story, the narrator has connected the men in this way: "What each of them had wanted was simply *all.* To save all souls, to destroy all men, to see and to record all life that filled this world—all, all" (*CS,* 196). The heron is symbolic of each of their desires. When Audubon shoots the bird, all realize, in the words of Dow, that this devouring love that offers complete physical possession of the object of love is merely destructive, and not possible. Dow realizes that the things in life that human beings desire most, that we love the most, are those same things that we must be most careful to keep ourselves from. If we follow our emotions and try to close the gap of separation, we will consume and destroy the object of our feelings. This is Welty's narrative stance in a nutshell: what she loves, she writes about, but what she loves, she keeps at a distance.

Welty writes of first discovering this method and process with one of her first stories, "Death of a Traveling Salesman." When she began to write the story, she says,

> As usual, I began writing from a distance, but "Death of a Traveling Salesman" led me closer. It drew me toward what was at the center of it. . . . In writing the story I approached [the cabin] and went inside with my traveling salesman, and had him . . . figure out what was there: . . . 'A marriage, a fruitful marriage. That simple thing.' Writing "Death of a Traveling Salesman" opened my eyes. And I had received the shock of having touched, for the first time, on my real subject: human relationships. (*OWB*, 87)

Welty's understanding that her subject is human relationships parallels Bowman's realization that his life is void of human relationships. Welty shows her awareness of her position as the observing narrator, first at a great distance, then drawing closer and closer. She links this narrative position with her "real subject: human relationships." She is intrigued by the idea of love and how it works in a relationship. At the same time, she must not experience this love but only observe it, creeping toward its center but not actually touching it or entering into it, only "touch[ing] . . . on" it. Always, for Welty, love is intertwined with spatial distance: "love and separateness," love with the attributes of focus: "awareness, discernment, order, clarity, insight." With this understanding of Welty's narrative stance embodying the paradoxical relationship of distance controlling desire, we can return to "A Memory." One explanation for the narrator's withholding both irony and scorn toward her younger self is that she recognizes in her actions as a child the seeds of her older artistic vision. Her detached vision as a child leads her to a role in adulthood similar to Welty's, the objective, distant observer and artist.

"The Secure Sense of the Hidden Observer": Welty's Concealing Vision

Thus far, as I have discussed how vision operates in Welty's fiction, I have remained primarily within the terms that Welty sets for her readers. There is a dark side of Welty's connection of vision and feelings, however, one that Welty does not allude to directly in her essays but that lies at the heart of "A Memory." As I have suggested earlier Welty's detached visual sense as a narrator affects both the technical and the emotional aspects of her stories. For Welty, visual distance implies emotional distance, and though she tells us that her method is to venture closer and closer to her subject, the way she details this method in "A Memory" shows that the emotional proximity she is able to attain with her subjects is often not very close. This emotional distance suggests two points of origin in the narrator as artist: shyness and the need for control. Both of these points dictate the tone and action of "A Memory."

Shyness may seem an unreasonable explanation for the narrative detachment in "A Memory." Welty herself, however, remarks on her own shyness as a girl and as an adult in *One Writer's Beginnings:* "I have always been shy physically. This in part tended to keep me from rushing into things, including relationships, headlong" (*OWB,* 21). In "A Memory" we see similar shyness and the reluctance to enter "headlong" into a relationship: the younger narrator claims to love the boy passionately, but she has not allowed herself to get close enough to him to know anything about him. She is too shy to get to know him, and their only physical contact has been their momentary touch on the stairwell, so she obsesses on an overwrought story throughout "A Memory": "It is strange that sometimes, even now, I remember unadulteratedly a certain morning when I touched my friend's wrist (as if by accident, and he pretended not to notice) as we passed on the stairs at school." Such a physical moment would loom large to the physically shy, as it most certainly does in the psyche of the narrator: "sometimes, even now" she remembers it, and remembers it with the wonderful use of the word "unadulteratedly." The older narrator's assurance that she did not even figuratively commit adultery as she thought of touching the boy is certainly hyperbolically funny, but she contradicts her assertion with the figurative carpe diem image of loss of virginity, the blooming of the rose: she thought "endlessly on this minute and brief encounter which we endured on the stairs, until it would swell with a sudden and overwhelming beauty, like a rose forced into premature bloom for a great occasion" (*CS,* 76). Certainly this obsessive fantasy over the slightest contact with the boy (which the narrator tells us that he only "pretended not to notice"—but surely it was so slight that he did not notice at all) is a familiar gesture for the very shy, intense preadolescent observer. The surprise here is that the adult narrator is as focused on this incident as her young self was; hers is the language of adultery and virginity; she valorizes this incident by infusing it in the retelling with the language of adult sexuality—muted, distant, and symbolic sexuality, but sexuality nonetheless.

Shyness, and thus narrative distance, also characterizes the other physical moment that the narrator recalls in "A Memory," the boy's bloody nose in Latin class; a vivid, uncontrollable, attention-getting malady of just the sort that would mortify a shy child. In her adult retelling of this scene, the narrator naturally focuses on the blood, but also infuses the telling with a dramatic flair that suggests something larger:

> I remember with exact clarity the day in Latin class when the boy I loved (whom I watched constantly) bent suddenly over and brought his handkerchief to his face. I saw red—vermilion—blood flow over the handkerchief and his square-shaped hand; his nose had begun to bleed. . . . I remember the very moment. . . . this small happening which had closed in upon my friend was a tremendous shock to me; it was unforeseen, but at the same time dreaded; I recognized it, and suddenly I leaned heavily on my arm and fainted. Does this explain why, ever since that day, I have been unable to bear the sight of blood? (*CS*, 76)

As a girl, she imagines his life and desires him because she could never bring herself to speak with him, much less to touch him. As an adult, she has returned to these physical memories so often that they seem to represent to her in some complicated way her continuing sexual shyness, symbolically alluded to first by image of loss of virginity, "a rose forced into premature bloom for a great occasion" (*CS*, 76), and then by her being "unable to bear the sight of blood," a symbol of a woman's sexual maturity in terms of both her menstrual cycle and her loss of virginity.

Even though this first layer of the story concerns one of the most important aspects of being human, the narrator's attitude toward her sexuality, this layer also exposes the adult narrator's deliberately passive and neutral language toward her younger self: her remark that "Even now [these events do] not seem trivial" is an understatement. Though we know that these moments from her childhood are of great importance, such language makes us feel as if the older narrator has broken away from the story. It seems that her failure to have a relationship with this boy, because of her own shyness, prefigures her adult failure to succeed in love.

There is a second layer and tone to the story, however, one that is emotionally aggressive and in its way just as perplexing as the first layer of emotional distance and sexual shyness. When the adult narrator relates a memory of her younger self first seeing the family of swimmers who join her on the beach, the muted description that characterizes her memory of her first love erupts into abstract, yet disdainful, criticisms directed toward this family on an outing. Her condescension toward them stands out in bold contrast against the otherwise cool emotional language in the story:

> I did not notice how the bathers got there, so close to me. Perhaps I actually fell asleep, and they came out then. Sprawled close to where I was lying, at any rate, appeared a group of loud, squirming, ill-assorted people who seemed thrown together only by the most confused accident, and who seemed driven by foolish intent to insult each other, all of which they enjoyed with a hilarity which astonished my heart. There were a man, two women, two young boys. They were brown and roughened, but not foreigners; when I was a child such people were called "common." (*CS*, 77)

Her judgment of the family here is scornful and harsh; they are "loud, squirming, ill-assorted . . . foolish . . . such people were called 'common.' " Even as we observe this in the story, however, we must pull back and ask ourselves, "Which narrator feels this way; is it the young girl sitting on the beach, or the adult who is telling us of the memory of sitting on the beach?" Because it is a conundrum, an adult remembering herself obsessing over a memory as a child, a memory of a memory, as it were, Welty's story makes it particularly difficult to locate the source of the loathing toward the bathers. Whether or not we can conclusively identify the source, contempt for the family is distancing in itself, no matter which narrator feels it: we see through narrative eyes no attempt to understand the swimmers, no effort to imagine living as they live. The mind, as well as the physical person, of both narrators stays quite far from these characters; they are "distant observers." Just as the story is a memory within a memory, the disdain for the group of swimmers serves as a kind of distance within distance: the dislike intensifies because of its uncertain location.

What are we to make, then, of the adult narrator's cool tone toward her younger, impassioned self, and the harsh judgment that both narrators seem to place on those not part of their emotional fabric, such as the swimmers? Usually such contrasts in tonal color suggest an irony of some sort. But to conclude that the adult narrator possesses an ironic sense of herself as a girl would be a misreading. Rather, both the detachment that the adult narrator shows in relation to her younger self and the detachment that each narrator shows toward the swimmers and for the world outside of herself, may spring from the extreme shyness, physical and psychological, that Welty's narrators feel toward the world, a shyness that is acute in early adolescence but also remains a definitive part of the adult narrator's being.

The narrator both as a girl and as a woman obviously finds the family physically repellent, but her observation of them nevertheless seems disproportionate. As the man piles sand around the woman's legs,

> [The woman] stared fixedly at his slow, undeliberate movements, and held her body perfectly still. She was unnaturally white and fatly aware, in a bathing suit which had no relation to the shape of her body. Fat hung upon her upper arms like an arrested earthslide on a hill. With the first motion she might make, I was afraid that she would slide down upon herself in a terrifying heap. Her breasts hung heavy and widening like pears into her bathing suit. Her legs lay prone one on the other like shadowed bulwarks, uneven and deserted, upon which, from the man's hand, the sand piled higher like the teasing threat of oblivion. A slow, repetitious sound I had been hearing for a long time unconsciously, I identified as a continuous laugh which came through the motionless open pouched mouth of the woman. . . . The woman continued to laugh, almost as she would hum an annoying song. I saw that they were all resigned to each other's daring and ugliness. (*CS*, 78)

The narrator tells us that she was "afraid" that the woman would collapse in upon herself, in a "terrifying" mound. As we wonder what the object of fear is here for the narrator, she offers us several clues: she tells us that the family's boisterousness and uninhibited physicality "astonished her heart" (*CS*, 77); out of this "hilarity," the man piles sand upon the woman's legs "like the teasing threat of oblivion" (*CS*, 78); and at the end of the passage I have quoted, she sees them "resigned to each other's daring and ugliness" (*CS*, 78). All of these speech acts suggest the speaker's fear of bodily excess, as if the family's collective physical abandon were leading them to a singular loss of control, hurling them into "oblivion." The strongest statement of the narrator's fears occurs at the most physically revealing moment in the story:

> Once when I looked up, the fat woman was standing opposite the smiling man. She bent over and in a condescending way pulled down the front of her bathing suit, turning it outward, so that the lumps of mashed and folded sand came emptying out. I felt a peak of horror, as though they were of no importance at all and she did not care. (*CS*, 79)

Though the narrator has uttered the word "breasts" earlier in the story—"her breasts hung heavy and widening like pears in her bathing suit," and the sand goes "down inside her bathing suit between her bulbous descending breasts" (p. 78)—here she avoids naming the woman's breasts. This signifies the nadir of her revulsion to the family's missing sense of physical decorum, her "peak of horror," as she calls it, at the woman's lack of attention and lack of modesty about her most defining feature. To the budding adolescent girl, the younger narrator, a woman's breasts are the objects of her total attention and shyness about her soon-to-be developing body. That the swimmer has no sense of presence about her body is the most unimaginable set of circumstances for the young girl, and triggers her severe reaction.

Shyness and sensitivity, however, are not the only emotions at issue here. True, the young narrator is hypersensitive about her own body, but she is also an acute observer of the way others view and use their physicality. The sharpest and most repulsed reaction she has to the family is when the tables are turned, when they actually observe her body: "The man smiled, the way panting dogs seem to be smiling, and gazed about carelessly at them all and out over the water. He even looked at me, and included me. Looking back, stunned, I wished that they all were dead" (*CS*, 78). This startling overreaction does not initially make sense in the context of an adult's emotional world. Yet for a young girl, conscious as she is of her body, this reaction has the validity of a visceral response. The narrator's young self understands that looking can be a means of garnering control and possession, as her imprisonment of her subjects in the frame of her fingers at the beginning of the story indicates. So when the object of her gaze, the man, turns his gaze on her, she feels all the power of control, containment, and possession directed at her. She cannot stand being contained by these "common" people; their lack of care about the body invades her shyness, and just as important, she loses control when the tables are turned on her, when she does not command the gaze.

The adult narrator does not color this response—or any of the young girl's responses—with the leavening of her adult judgment. She seems to believe that this particular observation—wishing the death of the "common" swimmers—like the rest of her narrative, stands on its own, with minimal commentary. On reflection, the intensity of the gaze that characterizes the young narrator's experience may serve as an explanation of the older narrator's behavior. This shy woman must remain detached from experience because she is afraid of scrutiny and of losing her privacy. The narrator links vision and body quite closely here. The more intense the narrator's gaze, the more detached the body of the narrator becomes from the experience. The gaze seems to intensify both the desire for the invisible body and the viewer's sensation of an invisible body, in other words, the desire for what Welty calls her wish as an artist to be "invisible." When the gaze is turned on the narrator, she loses her invisibility, and thus her power and control.

When she loses control of the gaze, she loses control of the subject that she has held within her frame. At this moment, she resorts to what Welty admits is the stronger tool: words. The child puts her companions on the beach back into their frame of reference and back into her control by labeling them "common," located much below her place in the socially stratified South, she thinks, and that must be the most damning fate that the child can imagine, for her just as tragic as death.

Even though the swimmers' invasion of her body by way of their intrusive gaze explains the narrator's violent language and reaction, some readers will argue that instances like this throughout Welty's work suggest that she has a blind spot that results in her condescending to her characters. Welty herself has this to say in the preface to her *Collected Stories* about her relationship to her characters:

> I have been told, both in approval and in accusation, that I seem to love all my characters. What I do in writing of any character is to try to enter into the mind, heart, and skin of a human being who is not myself. Whether this happens to be a man or a woman, old or young, with skin black or white, the primary challenge lies in making the jump itself. It is the act of a writer's imagination that I set most high. (*CS*, xi)

The obvious contradiction to Welty's assertions here of "loving" her characters is this matter of the narrator's memory including a vision of "common" people on the beach. As in so much of Welty, however, we must consider both sides of the issue, the separateness with the love.

Still, "A Memory" remains troubling. It is consistent with Welty's method of synchronic representation in *A Curtain of Green* that the contrast between the older and younger narrator represents growth. Had Welty shown the narrator's growth as a linear process of evolution, she would have negated the visual method that she is trying to perfect in *A Curtain of Green.* However, "A Memory" also demonstrates the shortcomings of this particular visual method. As I have noted, this story is strangely static. Moreover, it seems to lack narrative guidance: we are forced to make connections ourselves, both between the events of the narration and between the narrator's two states of mind at different points in her life. The cues that Welty places in the story—such as the narrator as "dreamer-observer"—show us the way to make these connections, if we wish. Yet even after we make the connections and "draw our own conclusions" (to quote Sister in "Why I Live at the P.O."), the violent description and labeling of the family on the beach are disturbing.

It seems to me that the most satisfying way to read "A Memory" is as a story that reveals the limitations of the single-frame device that the young narrator uses (and that Welty herself uses in many of the stories in *A Curtain of Green*). By freezing an individual or group in a single frame, the artist can capture the moment. But on these terms, framing is merely an act of appropriation, one that can be used both by and against the observer. The choice seems false, either a limited representation or no representation at all. If this is the case, then the single frame in the artist's hands is quite limited. The single snapshot, ironically, does not begin to impart the whole picture. To do that, Welty needs to turn to the structures of myth.

Welty's "Re-vision": The Myth of Confluent Genders

> [F]reedom ahead is what each story promises—beginning anew. And all the while, as further hindsight has told me, certain patterns in my work repeat themselves without my realizing. There would be no way to know this, for during the writing of any single story, there is no other existing. Each writer must find out for himself, I imagine, on what strange basis he lives with his own stories.
>
> —Eudora Welty, *One Writer's Beginnings*

The extensive depth and breadth of Eudora Welty's reading, as Katherine Anne Porter points out in her preface to *A Curtain of Green*, includes classical Greek myths, Celtic myths, and Mississippi folktales: Welty read "the ancient Greek and Roman poetry, history and fable," Porter writes. "From the beginning until now, she loved folk tales, fairy tales, old legends, and she likes to listen to the songs and stories of people who live in old communities whose culture is recollected and bequeathed orally" (Porter, 285–86).[27] Our cultural myths were a part of Welty's consciousness from the beginning of her reading life, so much so that Welty herself says that myth flows out of her as she writes as one might use salt and pepper during a meal. If we follow this metaphor, Welty uses myth to enhance the flavor of her stories. In other words, Welty does not import myth into her work in order to preserve the myth; rather, she uses myth in the service of her own stories.

Readers of Eudora Welty's short fiction have long remarked on her use of myth, some from classical sources and others filtered through the lens of W. B. Yeats's poetry. Only a few years after *The Golden Apples* (1949) was published, Harry C. Morris pointed out this extensive presence of Greek myth in Welty's stories, "from the births of the early heroes to the return of Odysseus to Ithaca" (Morris, 34).[28] In doing so, he set out to draw a one-to-one correspondence between specific mythological characters and characters from Welty's stories. Most criticism following Morris has approached Welty's use of myth in *The Golden Apples* (indeed, throughout her stories) as he does, looking for correspondences and seeing Welty's use of myth as a way of "reestablishing . . . myths in modern terms" (Morris, 34). Such an approach is valuable and informative but stops short of defining the essential function of myth in Welty's work.

The term "confluence" describes one of the "chief patterns" of Welty's work with myth. As she closes *One Writer's Beginnings,* Welty writes, "I'm prepared now to use the wonderful word *confluence,* which of itself exists as a reality and a symbol in one. It is the only kind of symbol that for me as a writer has any weight, testifying to the pattern, one of the chief patterns, of human experience" (*OWB,* 102). She sprinkles the salt and pepper of various myths throughout her stories, and in doing so she disrupts the original plot of each myth and recombines various elements from various myths. With this recombination, Welty achieves a "confluence," or coming together, of various myths into new wholes.[29]

The pleasure in reading contemporary writers is not just the pleasure of seeing a reflection of one's own society in the writer's work but the more significant sensation of seeing there a vision of the future. That vision can be either hopeful or despairing, depending on the writer's temperament. Throughout her body of stories, Welty not only experiments with visual narrative techniques, as I discuss in the previous chapter, but she also is swept up in the task of the visionary, to imagine or reimagine fictive terms for our existence that shift the ground of the present in radical ways. Welty's use of myth is central to this visionary project. She has said, "My natural temperament is one of positive feelings" (*Con,* 96). This "positive" temperament allows Welty to present her readers with a vision of hope centered on "re-vision" of the myths that have defined Western society.

Although Welty does not associate herself with writers who think of themselves primarily in terms of gender, her project in rethinking how myth shapes culture does place her in such a group. The American feminist poets Adrienne Rich and Alicia Ostriker have written eloquent and thoughtful essays on women writers and the revision of myth. Rich coined the term "re-vision" in her 1971 essay "When We Dead Awaken: Writing as Re-vision,"[30] and uses it polemically; she believes that women writers must "re-vision—in the sense both of reimagining and revising"—the myths at the core of the Western tradition of literature. Unless women first reinvent these myths, Rich argues, they will not be able to have a literature of their own but merely will be borrowing from male traditions and male language and unable to express fully female culture. Alicia Ostriker supplements and adapts Rich's ideas with her phrase "stealing the language."[31] Unlike Rich, Ostriker doesn't ask the question, Do women have or need a separate language from men; is the female experience so radically different from the male that it implies a uniquely female way of seeing and thinking, and thus representing that experience in myth and work? Instead, Ostriker demonstrates how American women poets have set about not to invent a new language but to revise the stories and myths at the center of our culture.

> Whenever a poet employs a figure or story previously accepted and defined by a culture, the poet is using myth, and the potential is always present that the use will be revisionist: that is, the figure or tale will be appropriated for altered ends, the old vessel filled with new wine, initially satisfying the thirst of the individual poet but ultimately making cultural change possible. (pp. 212–13)

Anytime a writer, male or female, uses a cultural story, he or she is trafficking in myth. But almost without exception, these myths central to our culture have predominantly been told in male voices, from male perspectives. Only relatively recently in the history of the written word have women been literate; the power of the word has historically belonged to men. One of our defining myths, for example, is the account in the Book of Genesis of Adam naming all the animals in Eden, while Eve, his wife, does not have this power. The message to women is that they are in a subordinate position to language, without power to name and by extension even to write. When a woman writer retells the story of Adam and Eve, as many—including Eudora Welty—have done, she will invariably tell the story of Eve from a female perspective, allowing both men and women to see and grasp Eve's position with a different kind of knowledge. The importance of the female voice as a recorder of our history and culture, Ostriker argues, is that "revisionist myth-making in women's poetry is a means of redefining both woman and culture" (p. 211).

One result of Welty's revising myth is her blending of categorical boundaries, especially those separating male and female. Thus, any attempt to place Welty in a category must be qualified, especially in such a politically charged category as feminism. She has spoken often about politics in her art, as she does here in an interview with folklorist Bill Ferris:

> I think there are places for political outspokenness, but in my mind, it should be done editorially, and in essays and things that are exactly what they seem. But I think a work of art, a poem or a story, is properly something that reflects what life is exactly at that time. That is, to try to reveal it. Not to be a mirror image, but to be something that goes beneath the surface of the outside and tries to reveal the way it really is, good and bad. Which in itself is moral. I think a work of art must be moral. The artist must have a moral consciousness about his vision of life and what he tries to write. (Welty in Ferris, 17)

Even as she argues here for the apolitical nature of her work, she also emphasizes that she does have a position and a point of view from which she writes—as do all writers—and that point of view is what she calls "a moral consciousness about [a] vision of life." Let us say, then, that Welty's "moral . . . vision of life" may not be a political or feminist vision in a narrow sense of these terms but is rather her view of "life . . . exactly at that time," as she sees it.[32] But as Doris Lessing says, famously, "The personal is political." The most profound politics are those inseparable from being itself. We shall set out to explore here Welty's point of view, mingled with desire, as she considers the myths that have shaped and continue to shape our culture, re-visioning them to express her "moral" point of view, including her critique of the way our culture categorizes women and men. Welty's idea of the moral entails a radical reshaping of cultural myth.

Re-Visioning Eve in *A Curtain of Green*

Critical attention to Welty's use of myth in her stories has focused primarily on the stories in *The Golden Apples*, as well as on several stories outside this collection with Greek myth at their core, such as "Circe" and "Petrified Man." Here, I will consider Welty's use of myth as a coherent re-visioning project, discussing first her earliest stories in order to establish a context in which to place the extensive revisions in *The Golden Apples*.

The central myth winding its way through *A Curtain of Green*—that of Eve in the garden of Eden—is one of the dominant myths in Western culture. The source of Welty's myth, John Milton's epic poem *Paradise*

Lost, has gone unnoticed in criticism of Welty's work, though there is plenty of evidence outside the stories to suggest Milton's importance to Welty. In her introduction to *A Curtain of Green,* Katherine Anne Porter notes that Welty read Milton, as well as other influential poets, in her youth, since "[s]he had at arm's reach the typical collection of books which existed as a matter of course in a certain kind of Southern family, so that she had read . . . Shakespeare, Milton, Dante, the eighteenth-century English and the nineteenth-century French novelists . . . before she realized what she was reading" (Porter, 285–86). However, as Welty tells us, her reading of Milton was a bit more than an unconscious "matter of course." *Paradise Lost* is a work that Welty's mother loved: "[My mother's] mind was filled with *Paradise Lost,* she told me . . . showing me the notebook she still kept with its diagrams" (*OWB,* 52).[33] The mythic story of Adam and Eve in Paradise as John Milton tells it has a personal and powerful resonance for Welty.

As with most important cultural myths, the values set by the archetypal events in *Paradise Lost* have remained unquestioned as cultural definitions and truths. Readers of *Paradise Lost* have begun to point out the aspects of the poem that define Eve as powerless or evil. When she first assumes consciousness after God has created her from Adam's rib, Eve turns over her power to Adam; as Christine Froula points out, she "utters the words which consign her authority to Adam, and through him to Milton's God, and thence to Milton's poem, and through the poem to the ancient patriarchal tradition" (Froula, 327). Eve addresses the absent Adam when she retells the story of her birth: "O thou for whom / And from whom I was form'd flesh of thy flesh, / without whom am to no end, my Guide and Head" (4.440–43).[34] She has learned very well that she is subordinate to Adam in every way: she is physically made from his flesh, and she has no "end"—no destination in life's journey—without Adam to tell her where to go and what to do. As Eve's role in Milton's poem develops, the reader continues to see the myth of the dutiful wife tending the garden, while Adam's primary task is to speak to God. As Adam explains when Eve asks if she can work apart from him, "nothing lovelier can be found / In Woman, than to study household good, / And good works in her Husband to promote" (*PL,* 9.232–34). According to Milton, Eve's role is to support her husband and to clean up after him. Eve cannot speak to God, and she acquires God's knowledge only as it is mediated through Adam. She knows nothing about her life in the garden through direct communication with the being who put her there.

Eve's famous failure occurs when she disobeys the only rule in the garden: she eats the forbidden fruit from the Tree of Knowledge. Traditional reception of the story of Adam and Eve in the garden places the blame for everything that goes wrong squarely on Eve's shoulders. Her disobedience ultimately results in both Adam' and Eve's expulsion from Paradise. Consequently, according to tradition, all men and all women continue to suffer punishment for Eve's sin: men must work in order to eat—before the fall, food was provided by God in Paradise—and women must suffer the pain of labor in childbirth. As one of the defining stories about women in our culture, the story of Eve's failure continues to resonate in debates about the ability of women to perform certain tasks—to fly planes in combat, to run multinational corporations, to write novels. "Our first mother," as Milton calls Eve in his poem, sets a precedent for all women, one that has bolstered a cultural directive: a woman's duty is to keep house and support the endeavors of men. If she ventures outside of these duties, and if she tries to enter men's domains—the realms of knowledge and power—then failure, even disaster, will follow.

The cultural definition of a woman's role drawn from Milton's version of the Adam and Eve story offers a particularly difficult obstacle for the woman writer. Like all professionals, writers look to models from the past as they develop their craft. A male writer reading Milton might see there a sanction for his work; after all, Adam's first task is to name the things around him, and to communicate with God. Naming and communication are at the heart of the writer's vocation. But the woman reading Milton can see explicit directives against her, not only against her taking on any vocation at all that does not at its heart support her husband but also specifically against the writerly vocation, since she cannot name and cannot speak directly to anyone but her husband—and, of course, Satan.

Revisions of Milton's Eve: The Polar Opposites in *A Curtain of Green*

It is fitting and inevitable that Eudora Welty's first publication addresses the problematic cultural directive that comes from John Milton's myth of Adam and Eve in Paradise. Not only is this myth problematic from a cultural standpoint for Welty, an obstacle that any female writer must surmount, but it also has the added power of having been her mother's favorite work of literature. In Welty's first collection of stories, *A Curtain of Green*, she contemplates her mother's world in the form of an extended meditation on Eve's aborted search for self-knowledge.

Two stories form the poles of the work: "A Piece of News," in which a young woman's blossoming self-love expresses itself in independence, and the title story, "A Curtain of Green," which explores a woman's guilty silence after the accidental death of her husband. In each story, Welty addresses the Miltonic issues of naming, silence, and knowledge, beginning a process of revision that gives these powers to women. She completes this revisionary process that she begins in *A Curtain of Green* in her later volume *The Golden Apples.*

Of all the stories in *A Curtain of Green,* "A Piece of News" most clearly shows the young writer revising and stealing from Milton. The central figure in the story, Ruby Fisher, lives in an isolated farmhouse with her violent husband, Clyde. We first see her as she comes in from the pouring rain and places her rain-soaked body over a section of newspaper that contains a story about another Ruby Fisher "who had the misfortune to be shot in the leg by her husband this week" (*CS,* 13). These words seem to come off onto Ruby's skin, like tattoos, and as the story progresses the text on her body mingles with—rather than imposes upon—her very being, allowing Ruby knowledge of herself and of her relationship to Clyde.

Initially, Ruby makes a failed attempt to see herself separately from the story in the newspaper and from her husband, Clyde. Her failure is described in mirror images, images that would seem odd without the underlying context that Eve's birth scene provides for the story. Eve stares at her reflection in a pool, like Narcissus, and falls in love with her own image (*PL,* 4.440–91).[35] Ruby looks instead into another of the four elements, a fire that "might have been a mirror . . . trying to see herself." In the scene, reminiscent of Adam calling Eve away from her mirror image, Ruby cannot imagine seeing her own image without Clyde in the picture with her:

> At last she flung herself onto the floor, back across the newspaper, and looked at length into the fire. It might have been a mirror in the cabin, into which she could look deeper and deeper as she pulled her fingers through her hair, trying to see herself and Clyde coming up behind her. (*CS,* 13)

Ruby cannot see herself apart from Clyde, just as Eve is unable to remain staring at herself in the pool. Adam lays an extraordinary guilt trip on Eve—you are made out of my flesh and bone, how can you run away from me—in order to pry her away from her reflection. Eve describes herself as finally "yielding" to Adam, and yield she does, finding her own sense of beauty and of knowledge outdone by Adam, "excell'd by manly grace / And wisdom, which alone is truly fair." Eve gives up her entire sense of self and cedes everything to Adam and to his way of knowing. Welty understands that Adam's interruption of Eve's self-admiration, symbolic of her attempt to gain self-knowledge, leads ultimately to her fall. At the moment of her temptation, Eve is not secure enough in her own way of knowing to refuse the offer of a fruit that, Satan promises, will give her the kind of external confidence, in the form of knowledge, that she lacks. Milton describes Satan's effect on Eve: "His words replete with guile / Into her heart too easy entrance won . . . in her ears the sound / Yet rung of his persuasive words, impregn'd / With Reason, to her seeming, and with Truth" (*PL*, 9.734–35; 737–38). How might Satan's words have affected Eve had she been allowed to cultivate her own reasoning abilities instead of relying on Adam to think for her?

Unlike Eve, Ruby Fisher has a second chance at self-discovery, and this one is uninterrupted, allowing for the beginnings of self-assertion and self-love that alter her life. When Ruby pulls the newspaper from beneath her and looks at it, the narrator describes the action as one of simultaneous discovery of self and of language, in a manner more like Adam, who immediately looks up to God after he is created:

> Then she squatted there, touching the printed page as if it were fragile. She did not merely look at it—she watched it, as if it were unpredictable. . . . she frowned now and then at the blotched drawing of something and big letters that spelled a word underneath. Her lips trembled, as if looking and spelling so slowly had stirred her heart.
>
> All at once she laughed.
>
> She looked up.
>
> "Ruby Fisher!" she whispered. (*CS*, 12–13)

" 'Ruby Fisher!' " Like Eve, whose first perception (seeing her reflection in a pool and mistaking the reflection for her self) tests the boundaries of fact and illusion, Ruby Fisher finds her name in a literal way—in the newspaper—which causes similar, though ironic, confusion. Symbolically, by reading her name Ruby discovers language and names herself in the same instance. Clyde does not interrupt Ruby's second meditation, as Adam interrupted Eve's by calling her away to him from her mirror image. Instead, Welty allows Ruby to create a fantasy that, however cruelly, allows her to attain self-knowledge. Ruby's death fantasy is somewhat melodramatic:

> At once [Ruby] was imagining herself dying. . . . Underneath a brand-new nightgown her heart would be hurting with every beat, many times more than her toughened skin when Clyde slapped at her. Ruby began to cry softly, the way she would be crying from the extremity of pain; tears would run down in a little stream over the quilt. Clyde would be standing there above her, as he once looked. . . . He would say, "Ruby, I done this to you." She would say—only a whisper—"That is the truth, Clyde—you done this to me." (p. 14)

Ruby's imagined story tells Ruby about her relationship to Clyde: he slaps her, and it hurts. He controls her with his violence: "That is the truth, Clyde," she realizes, "you done this to me." We recall that Clyde's first act in Welty's narrative is to "poke at Ruby with the butt of his gun, as if she were asleep" (p. 15). But as he is soon to learn, Ruby is no longer asleep to the implications of his actions; she realizes that Clyde is responsible for her lack of self-knowledge. The image ending the story, a description of the storm clearing from the evening sky, carries the emotional weight of the narrative, as description does so often in Welty: "The storm had rolled away to faintness like a wagon crossing a bridge" (p. 16). Ruby is able to calm herself after her outbreak with Clyde, and the narrator leaves us with the sense that Ruby has crossed a bridge of self-realization and has burned it behind her.[36] This is the real "Piece of News."

Welty's revision of Eve's self-knowledge in "A Piece of News" extends Eve's aborted acquisition of it and, by implication, of independence. Ruby Fisher may be an impoverished farmer's wife, but even she can be a woman of substance. The imagery of the story connects it with the two aspects of *Paradise Lost* responsible for Eve's temptation by Satan: her lack of the power of naming and her lack of self-knowledge, both of which Satan promises Eve she can have by eating the forbidden fruit. Ruby Fisher symbolically acquires language when she lies down on the newsprint and it comes off on her wet body; the words literally become a part of her. And when she reads there about Ruby Fisher, shot by her husband, she sees herself and her life clearly, as if she had studied them in a mirror. This kind of self-knowledge may free Ruby from the isolation that any individual faces when her experience is mediated through another's, as Ruby's often has been through Clyde's. Ruby attains the kind of self-knowledge unavailable to Eve in *Paradise Lost.* Welty's version of woman's acquisition of self-knowledge, significantly, shows a woman seeing her own name in a written text. Welty supplies what she has been missing as she reads *Paradise Lost;* she could not see a recognizable version of herself there, only a woman instructed to live a vicarious life. In "A Piece of News" she begins to rectify the situation.

Like "A Piece of News," the title story of *A Curtain of Green* also demonstrates how Welty uses *Paradise Lost* as a framework for her fiction. In "A Curtain of Green," however, the epic serves as a frame for the exploration of individual guilt rather than individual insight. In the story, Welty dramatizes the paralyzing effect that guilt has over the central character, Mrs. Larkin. Mrs. Larkin, inexplicably in terms of her story, feels guilty for the act of God that kills her husband; the origin of her guilt lies in the framing narrative of *Paradise Lost,* connecting her to Eve and her experience in Eden.

Several wry jokes in the narrative allude to archetypal elements of Milton's work. Mrs. Larkin's husband is killed, for instance, when a tree falls on his car, an act which combines death, falling, and a tree. As in Milton's Eden, where the Tree of the Knowledge of Good and Evil stands at the center of Paradise, in "A Curtain of Green" a fruit tree watches over the garden: "[Mrs. Larkin] would move to the shelter of the pear tree, which in mid-April hung heavily almost to the ground in brilliant full leaf, in the center of the garden" (*CS,* 108). Welty remembers vividly a nursery rhyme from her childhood and recounts, it in *One Writer's Beginnings:* "Pear Tree by the garden gate / How much longer must I wait?" (*OWB,* 22). Indeed, this might be a fitting epigraph for "A Curtain of Green," Mrs. Larkin's silent prayer: just as Mrs. Larkin constantly relives the memory of seeing the tree crush her husband's car, she also suspends her life and simply waits to die. After one such memory we see the garden from Mrs. Larkin's point of view: "Everything had stopped once again, the stillness had mesmerized the stems of the plants, and all the leaves went suddenly into thickness. The shadow of the pear tree in the center of the garden lay callous on the ground" (*CS,* 109). Again, as in "A Piece of News," the description bears the emotion of the moment; the pear tree echoes both the fallen state of humankind and the tree that fell on Mr. Larkin. Mrs. Larkin's guilt has left her powerless to escape the bonds of either event. Her life is an endless replay of her guilt about her husband's death, an endless repetition of "Everything . . . stop[ping] once again."

Mrs. Larkin's constant, but pointless, responsibility, like Eve's main task in *Paradise Lost,* is to tend a very wild garden. Welty shows us the garden from the neighbors' point of view: "To the neighbors gazing down from their upstairs windows it had the appearance of a sort of jungle, in which the slight, heedless form of its owner daily lost itself" (*CS,* 109). Eve's obsession with gardening, Milton makes clear, is part of the reason she succumbs to temptation. Rather than working with Adam, Eve wants the freedom of tending the garden more artistically alone, and alone she is prey to temptation. Similarly, Mrs. Larkin is obsessed with her wild garden:

> It might seem that the extreme fertility of her garden formed at once a preoccupation and a challenge to Mrs. Larkin. Only by ceaseless activity could she cope with the rich blackness of this soil. Only by cutting, separating, thinning and tying back in the clumps of flowers and bushes and vines could she have kept them from overreaching their boundaries and multiplying out of all reason. The daily summer rains could only increase her vigilance and her already excessive energy. And yet, Mrs. Larkin rarely cut, separated, tied back. . . . To a certain extent, she seemed not to seek for order, but to allow an over-flowering, as if she consciously ventured forever a little farther, a little deeper, into her life in the garden. (*CS,* 108)

Yet, unlike Eve before she eats the forbidden fruit, Mrs. Larkin has no interest in establishing an artful, ordered garden. Her utter despair causes her to do the opposite of creating any sort of self-image, or of attaining self-love. She instead tries to lose herself in the "over-flowering" of the garden. And unlike Ruby Fisher, who is allowed the moment of self-discovery that Eve is denied, Mrs. Larkin does not attain self-knowledge or self-expression through language: "People said she never spoke" (*CS,* 109). Even if she does emit some sound, the garden absorbs it, further emphasizing her loneliness, despair, and loss of identity:

> But her voice hardly carried in the dense garden. She felt all at once terrified, as though her loneliness had been pointed out by some outside force whose finger parted the hedge. She drew her hand for an instant to her breast. An obscure fluttering there frightened her, as though the force babbled to her, The bird that flies within your heart could not divide this cloudy air. . . . She stared without expression at the garden. (*CS,* 110)

Here, too, the perverse echoes of *Paradise Lost* continue. The "outside force"—the voice of God—that keeps Adam and Eve company in Milton's Paradise merely threatens Mrs. Larkin; even the Holy Spirit that Michael promises Adam as a comfort after the Fall seems to strike Mrs. Larkin not as the dove of peace but only as an "obscure fluttering."

The final scene in "A Curtain of Green," showing Mrs. Larkin's death, points to its literary antecedent *Paradise Lost* as well as to "A Piece of News," its polar opposite. Just as Ruby Fisher enters her house and initiates her self-discovery because of rain, Mrs. Larkin leaves all sensual awareness when she is prone, "a shapeless, passive figure on the ground" with "her open eyes closing at once when the rain touched them" (*CS*, 112). Mrs. Larkin shows the destruction of the individual life when it is lived through another; she has been so consumed into her husband's identity that at his death, most of her dies with him. She is left very little of her self—literally she is without a voice—and left with the irrational guilt that is a woman's heritage from Milton's poem; women are responsible for all the evil that happens to mankind.

Other women in *A Curtain of Green* also come to tragic ends as they struggle to forge their identities. Gypsy, the wife of Powerhouse, the jazz pianist, apparently cannot survive without the reflective presence of her husband; during his performance, he announces that he has just received a telegram about her suicide. Even though she is a character purely of his narration, and quite probably is his fiction, the story told by a man of a woman's absolute dependence on his presence for her survival echoes the theme of *Paradise Lost* that Welty is revising in *A Curtain of Green.* In her story, Clytie discovers herself as she looks "into the slightly moving water . . . in her nearsighted way," seeing there her reflection. This is the most straightforward echo of Eve's experience in Welty's book.[37] Clytie has been forced to care for her sickly (mentally as well as physically) family as if she were their servant. She has no real life of her own; when she goes into town, we see her searching intently for something in the faces of passersby.[38] In the final paragraph of "Clytie," we learn that it is self-knowledge she has sought. When she finally sees her own reflection, "It was the face she had been looking for, and from which she had been separated." When she manages to turn her face away from others and look into her self, she sees her reflection in the water. But unlike Ruby Fisher, Clytie cannot bear what she finds within herself. She dives into the barrel of rainwater and is found there, dead, "with her poor ladylike black-stockinged legs up-ended and hung apart like a pair of tongs" (*CS*, 90). For Gypsy and for Clytie, death is a deliberate action, their way out from under the endless wheel of mediated experience grinding them away.

The Golden Apples and Multiple Myth

The Golden Apples is Eudora Welty's most complex work. Neither purely a collection of short stories nor a novel, Welty's book is a grouping of interconnected stories about the residents of the fictional town of Morgana, Mississippi, a name itself derived from myth. In Welty's words, Morgana is "a made-up Delta town. I was drawn to the name because I always loved the conception of *Fata Morgana*—the illusory shape, the mirage that comes over the sea. . . . My population might not have known there was such a thing as *Fata Morgana*, but illusions weren't unknown to them, all the same—coming in over the cottonfields" (*Con*, 98). Morgana's illusionary nature provides a perfect setting and environment for Welty's mythic revisions. Myths, stories, even manners and codes of behavior take on dreamlike qualities in Morgana, and as such become much more mutable and pliable. Welty uses this combination of dreaminess and myth to great effect.

King MacLain and Images of Zeus

King MacLain, though physically absent from Morgana during much of Welty's narrative, in many ways epitomizes her juxtaposition of the dreamlike setting of Morgana with the cultural truths of myth in order to shift the nature of myth. We are introduced to King, figuratively the king of Morgana, in the first story in the work, "Shower of Gold." Katie Rainey narrates the story of Snowdie MacLain, King's wife, who is an albino. Shortly after the marriage, King disappears for the first of many times, leaving behind only his black hat on the shore of the river. Some think he has drowned; Katie Rainey offers this opinion:

> Time goes like a dream no matter how hard you run, and all the time we heard things from out in the world that we listened to but that still didn't mean we believed them. You know the kind of things. Somebody's cousin saw King MacLain. Mr. Comus Stark, the one the cotton and timber belongs to, he goes a little, and he claimed three or four times he saw his back, and once saw him getting a haircut in Texas. (*CS*, 267)[39]

Not only does "time [go] like a dream" in Morgana, but King also moves in and out of the world in illusory fashion. In Morgana, King has taken on mythic status: he is a chimera. Initially even the question of his existence is mythic. His actions, too, suggest a world of myth. We first see him through Katie Rainey's eyes. Snowdie comes to announce, "I'm going to have a baby too, Miss Katie. Congratulate me" (*CS*, 266). Katie then describes Snowdie in this way: "She looked like more than only the news had come over her. It was like a shower of something had struck her, like she'd been caught out in something bright" (*CS*, 266). The reference here to the title, "A Shower of Gold," and to the myth it invokes is unmistakable. For readers familiar with Greek myth, this story conjures up the myth of Danae and her rape by the god Zeus. Danae's father, having heard the prophecy that he would be destroyed by his daughter's offspring, locks her in a cell so she cannot have children. Zeus comes into the cell in a "shower of gold" and rapes her. Danae's offspring by Zeus, Perseus, eventually carries out the prophecy and kills Danae's father, though accidentally. At this point in "A Shower of Gold," we don't yet have an intimation of King's offspring doing him in, but anything seems possible in the dreamy, mythic world of Morgana.

Welty does more with King that simply equate him with the Zeus of "A Shower of Gold." When King appears again in *The Golden Apples* he does so years after his marriage to Snowdie. Mattie Will Sojourner sees him—or thinks she does—in the woods. He is a "white glimmer," a hallucination perhaps, passing from tree to tree, asking about birds: "You boys been sighting any birds this way?" he asks Junior Nesbitt and Wilber Morrison (*CS*, 334). Then he flits away. The genius of this story, "Sir Rabbit," is its dreamlike quality. It seems that King is in the woods. It seems that King rapes Mattie Will in the woods. It also seems that Mattie Will has had a sexual encounter with King's twin sons, Ran and Eugene (echoes of Zeus's mythic twins Castor and Pollux) in her adolescence. The narration blurs the actions together so successfully that it is hard to tell one from the other. And hard to tell if either is anything more than Mattie Will's daydream. This illusionary, phantasmic quality is an element of most of the stories in *The Golden Apples*, but it dominates "Sir Rabbit" and each of the stories involving King or his sons, suggesting *Fata Morgana.*

In "Sir Rabbit" King is associated with the mythic form of Zeus as a swan. The narrator of the story describes the feathery aftermath of Mattie Will and King's intercourse:

> Mattie Will subsided forward onto her arms. Her rear stayed up in the sky, which seemed to brush it with little feathers. . . . presently Mr. MacLain leaped to his feet, bolt awake, with a flourish of legs. . . . Mr. MacLain beat his snowy arms up and down. (*CS*, 340)

With King's "snowy arms," Welty connects him to another mythical rape, that of Zeus appearing to Leda in the form of a swan and leaving her pregnant with two eggs containing the twins Castor and Pollux, and Helen and Clytemnestra. As she does with Danae's rape, Welty presents yet another classical myth in which women don't fare well. Castor and Pollux are good sons who go on to perform heroic deeds. But myth places the daughters in untenable situations, where their actions lead to the deaths of many men. Helen deserts her husband, King Menelaus, an event which precipitates the Trojan War. Clytemnestra kills her husband, King Agamemnon, after his return from Troy. This myth of evil women, however, does not surface in "Sir Rabbit." In "Sir Rabbit," Welty does not give any sense of King MacLain's female offspring; only the twins make a cameo appearance in this story. Welty's technique in *The Golden Apples* is to evoke myth or cultural truth distinctly, but not completely. By connecting King so clearly to the mythic adventures of Zeus, Welty leads us to expect the connections to continue; we expect to meet King's female offspring later in the work, and expect them to cause monumental catastrophe. But in a Welty story, myths are often introduced in order to be revised.

Welty draws her version of the mythic Zeus in "Sir Rabbit" from one of William Butler Yeats's mythic poems, "Leda and the Swan." This sonnet describes the rape of Leda, beginning with her unsuspecting and violent capture by the swan-god—"A sudden blow; the great wings beating still / Above the staggering girl"—and ending with a compelling question about the effect the rape has on Leda: "Did she put on his knowledge with his power, / Before the indifferent beak could let her drop?" The description of Mattie's rape by King unmistakably echoes these Yeatsian lines:

> When she laid eyes on Mr. MacLain close, she *staggered*, he had such grandeur, and then she was caught by the hair and brought down as suddenly to earth as if whacked by an unseen shillelagh. Presently she lifted her eyes in a lazy dread and saw those eyes above hers, as keenly bright and unwavering and apart from her life as the flowers on a tree.

> But he put her on, with the affront of his body, the affront of his sense too. No pleasure in that! *She had to put on what he knew with what he did*—maybe because he was so grand it was a thorn to him. Like submitting to another way to talk, she could answer to his burden now, his whole blithe, smiling, superior, frantic existence. And no matter what happened to her, she had to remember, disappointments are not to be borne by Mr. MacLain, or he'll go away again. (emphasis mine; *CS*, 338)

Welty echoes Yeats's "staggering" at the beginning of her description, and her "whacked" matches up nicely with Yeats's "sudden blow." And since Yeats is an Irish poet, Welty can't resist adding an Irish "shillelagh" to her references. Most notable here is Welty's addition to Yeats's poem, or completion of it. Mattie Will does "put on his knowledge with his power": "She had to put on what he knew with what he did." By transferring King's knowledge to Mattie Will through his sexual assault, Welty attempts a revision of Yeats's poem, and by extension a revision of the interaction between the raping god Zeus and his powerless, passive female victims. Instead of being merely a victim of King's sexual whim, Mattie Will also takes something in exchange: his knowledge. The knowledge here seems primarily of a sexual nature; Mattie Will can meet King on his turf, can respond in kind to his sexual prowess. The normally passive rape victim's active response to the rapist may seem like a Pyrrhic or slight victory, but symbolically this empowerment is significant. Language, as the story of Adam and Eve in the garden tells us, is the prerogative of men. Mattie Will takes this language from King: "Like submitting to another way to talk, she could answer to his burden now, his whole blithe, smiling, superior, frantic existence." Mattie Will has an answer for King, and she speaks to him in his own language. Of course this revision is not entirely satisfying. Mattie Will, no matter what other power she acquires, still must "submit," since she is still sexually violated by King.

The cultural currency that Welty exchanges by engaging the myth of Zeus as an all-powerful sexual predator, in the person of King MacLain, is the currency of male power and privilege. She establishes this myth with Katie Rainey's description of King and of Snowdie's pregnancy in "A Shower of Gold," and she begins to dismantle it (through an omniscient third-person narrator) with Mattie Will's subtle exchange of power with King during her rape. Though the rape of Leda produces two female offspring whose lives serve as linchpins for male violence, Welty focuses her revision of myth on different kinds of female victims, the passive female victims of rape. With this revision, Welty concentrates on empowering the victim of an individual act of violence rather than on the immense violence spiraling around Helen and Clytemnestra. For Welty, justice must begin with the individual.

Multiple Revisions of "Wandering Aengus"

In addition to Greek myth, Welty engages the myth of "Wandering Aengus" in each of these two stories.[40] Welty entitles her entire collection after the final lines in W. B. Yeats's poem "Song of Wandering Aengus," a poem portraying the protagonist's longing quest after an illusionary woman.[41] Like the Greek myths she uses in these stories, Welty uses the story of "Wandering Aengus" as the mythic identity for several quite disparate characters. The cultural "truth" of Yeats's poem dictates that men have license to "wander," to chase after visionary women and sexual fantasy, while women, on the other hand, are merely the objects of the vision and fantasy, not allowed to be aggressors or pursuers in the affair. The poem is so important, I quote it in its entirety. It sets these terms:

I went out to the hazel wood,
Because a fire was in my head,
And cut and peeled a hazel wand,
And hooked a berry to a thread;
And when white moths were on the wing,
And moth-like stars were flickering out,
I dropped the berry in a stream
And caught a little silver trout.

When I had laid it on the floor
I went to blow the fire aflame,
But something rustled on the floor,
And some one called me by my name:
It had become a glimmering girl
With apple blossom in her hair
Who called me by my name and ran
And faded through the brightening air.

Though I am old with wandering
Through hollow lands and hilly lands,
I will find out where she has gone,

And kiss her lips and take her hands;
And walk among long dappled grass,
And pluck till time and times are done
The silver apples of the moon,
The golden apples of the sun.

The essence of Yeats's poem is Aengus's desire for something "glimmering" and ethereal that draws him from place to place but remains forever just out of his reach. This mythic structure may be read in explicit sexual terms: a man's sexual "wandering" after his ideal fantasy woman. It may also be read as a myth of artistic inspiration; the true artist is obsessed with a vision and will follow it, in her art, wherever it leads. Welty makes use of both levels of the poem. In each instance, she revises the essential significance of the Aengus myth, the myth of male sexual wanderer and of male artistic wanderer.

The role of Aengus is another of King's roles begun in "A Shower of Gold" and continuing throughout *The Golden Apples.* King, in one way or another, embodies most of the elements of the poem. He begins his wandering shortly after his marriage to Snowdie and, like the figure of Aengus, wanders obsessively in and out of reality, after an unnamed, unpictured ideal. Like those of Aengus, many of King's reappearances in the stories occur in the woods—he sends Snowdie "Word ahead: 'Meet me in the woods,' " (*CS,* 264), and the first time he disappears after his marriage he leads everyone to think that he has drowned in the river. Welty reasserts King's role as the wanderer in the woods in "Sir Rabbit"; he walks into the woods after a lifetime of mysterious wandering. But Welty also makes Mattie Will another figure of "Wandering Aengus." Just as Welty empowered Mattie Will sexually, she also empowers her by giving her this male role. Mattie Will's full name is Mattie Will Sojourner, "sojourner" meaning "wanderer." Further, the narrator tells us that after King leaves Mattie Will in the woods, "she moved. She was the mover in the family" (*CS,* 339). Mattie's moving in the final paragraphs of the story, after King has raped her, is more interior and metaphoric than is King's wandering. The principal characteristic she takes on from the Aengus myth is an ability to pursue rather than be the object of pursuit, to take pleasure rather than be the object of pleasure. After King leaves her, she wanders through the woods—"Morgan's woods, it used to be called"—(*CS,* 340) until she finds him, and this time it is he who is vulnerable, sleeping under a tree.

> She stamped her foot, nothing happened, then she approached softly, and down on hands and knees contemplated him. Her hair fell over her eyes and she steadily blew a part in it; her head went back and forth appearing to say "No." Of course she was not denying a thing in this world, but now had time to look at anything she pleased and study it. (*CS*, 339)

Mattie Will's power is expressed in terms of contemplation and gaze, that is, in terms of knowledge and power: she can now "look at anything she pleas[es] and study it." To put this in terms of "Wandering Aengus," Mattie Will has the newfound power that myth tells us is granted to men. She can chase her visions if she wants to. Mattie Will reflects on her encounter with the MacLain twins in the final paragraph of the story, and this reflection seals her newly acquired knowledge and power. She is able to feel sexual pleasure: "As she ran down through the woods and vines, this side and that . . . it stole back into her mind about those two gawky boys, the MacLain twins. They were soft and jumpy! . . . For the first time Mattie Will thought they were mysterious and sweet—gamboling now she knew not where" (*CS*, 340–41). By giving Mattie Will the role of Aengus, Welty revises the myth to encompass woman as actor. Mattie shifts from being the passive object of the chase to being the active wanderer. Welty reverses Yeats's use of the myth, allowing woman to pursue sexual power and sexual pleasure.

The particular beauty of myth is its layered quality. Nowhere is the transformation more subtle than in Welty's revisions of King's two sons, the twins Ran and Eugene. Each son is allotted a story of his own, and in each instance the son is in a troubled marriage, though he does not cope with marriage in the wandering way of his father. Neither Ran nor Eugene is able to step into his father's role of Zeus or Aengus.

Ran MacLain has married Jinny Love Stark, and Welty begins the story of this marriage after it has broken up. Ran rents a room in his boyhood home, now owned by a stranger. His wife has returned to her parents. The story, "The Whole World Knows," unravels almost to its completion before the narrator discloses the problem with the marriage. Jinny Love, it seems, has had an affair, quite publicly, with Woodrow Spights, a member of one of Morgana's "main families." The double edge of this story has been honed on this fact: Ran has not taken over King's legacy as the sexual wanderer but has, instead, married a sexual wanderer in Jinny Love. The title of the story is drawn from Ran's consolation. What "the whole world knows" is that public opinion and scorn is much greater for the woman who has affairs than for the man. Snowdie MacLain tells her son, "The whole world knows what she did to you. It's different from when it's the man" (*CS*, 390). Snowdie obviously is torn between her two interests; on one hand, she is a woman. On the other, her husband has spent their marriage wandering after his sexual fantasies, and her son's wife has had a very public affair. She sides with social mores and condemns the sexually active woman with a greater penalty than she does the sexually active man. In doing so, she also chooses to side with both her husband, the sexually active man, and her son, the cuckolded husband.

Snowdie also tells Ran, "Son, you're walking around in a dream" (*CS*, 380). This dreamlike nature of the story again invokes the idea of *Fata Morgana.* Ran's dreamlike story, as he tells it, is an encyclopedia of depressed self-abuse. The living thing he has most empathy for is the dog, Bella, dying in the yard from stomach cancer. As he listlessly takes Maideen Sumrall to a hotel in Vicksburg, instead of having sex with her, he pulls out a gun and tries to kill himself. The gun misfires. Ran's suicidal depression could be a result of his crumbling marriage. The story opens, however, with Ran's plea to his absent father: "Father, I wish I could talk to you, wherever you are right now." Throughout the story, we hear him talking to his father as a regular part of his imaginary life, adding to the dreamy cast of the story. Though most of these comments are offhanded or have to do with small details of Morgana (the weather, the houses), Ran does implore his father for a diagnosis: "[W]hat ails me I don't know, Father, unless maybe you know" (*CS*, 385). The final lines of the story go out to both King and Eugene: "Father! Eugene! Where you went and found, was it better than this?" Ran adds, "And where's Jinny?" (*CS*, 392). Ran believes that his father can help with his state of mind, but his depression has more to do, it seems, with his generation and changing gender roles. Unlike his father, he is unable to wander through the world in quest of a visionary love. Instead, his whole world is Morgana, and he has found a woman who wanders on him; it is Jinny who should be asking "Where's Ran" if the "Wandering Aengus" myth is to follow along male gender lines. Significantly, when Ran halfheartedly takes up with Maideen Sumrall after he leaves Jinny, Maideen informs him that her mother's maiden name is Sojourner, wanderer. Ran describes, "And now I was told her mother's maiden name. God help me, the name Sojourner was laid on my head like the top teetering crown of a pile of things to remember. Not to forget, never to forget the name of Sojourner" (*CS*, 386). "Sojourner" is Ran's crown, both the heritage that does not come from his father and the consequence that he suffers from

Jinny. In the dreamlike world of Ran's Morgana, Welty emphasizes anew her revision of the Aengus myth. It is not King's son who takes on the mantle of the sexual wanderer but, instead, both his son's wife and his mistress. Like Mattie Will, Maideen Sumrall is also a Sojourner.

Eugene, unlike Ran, has strayed from Morgana, and Ran seems to think that he is a wanderer, like their father. "Music from Spain" follows "The Whole World Knows" in *The Golden Apples* and adjusts Ran's erroneous assumption about Eugene. The story follows Eugene on a day when he slaps his wife at breakfast, then wanders through the streets of San Francisco instead of going to his job as a watch repairman. During most of the day he is accompanied by a famous Spanish guitar player (modeled on Andrés Segovia) whom he has heard the night before at Aeolian Hall. Eugene's story calls up all sorts of myths and other cultural stories; some readers have, for example, connected Eugene's journey through San Francisco with Dante's through hell. Both see various strata of their locations, and both see in a new light people whom they recognize, each guided by an artist—Virgil guides Dante, just as the guitarist leads Eugene. But because Eugene is the son of the archetypal wanderer in *The Golden Apples*, King MacLain, the story is, like "The Whole World Knows," at its heart an exploration of Eugene as an extension of the myth of the wanderer. As it turns out, Eugene is no more the successor to his father's legacy than is his twin, Ran.

In one sense, the dramatic action in this story, as in "The Whole World Knows," has taken place as an antecedent to the story. The daughter of Eugene and his wife, Emma, has been dead for a year. In another way, though, the story opens with a dramatic action: Eugene slaps his wife over the breakfast table.

> One morning at breakfast Eugene MacLain was opening his paper and without the least idea of why he did it, when his wife said some innocent thing to him—"Crumb on your chin" or the like—he leaned across the table and slapped her face. They were in their forties, married twelve years—she was the older: she was looking it now. (*CS*, 393)

When we learn in the third paragraph that Fan, their daughter, has died, certain things about this incident and the narrator's description of it begin to fall into place. The pressure in the household has built to such a degree that Eugene finally cracks, slapping his wife. We learn as we read through the story that "The slap had been like kissing the cheek of the dead" (*CS,* 396). Emma has mourned Fan so deeply that she has withdrawn from everything else in her life, especially from Eugene: "Mourning over the same thing she mourned, he was not to be let in. For letting in was something else. How cold to the living hour grief could make you! Her eye was quite marblelike" (*CS,* 399). We learn, too, that possibilities of another child are slim; the wife is nearing the end of her childbearing years, and has refused Eugene's sexual overtures since Fan's death.

Eugene walks out of the house after he slaps his wife. As he walks toward the jewelry shop where he repairs watches, he impulsively decides to skip work. He begins to wander the streets of San Francisco. He sees the Spanish guitar player, whose recital he attended the previous evening, just as he is about to step out in front of an oncoming car. Eugene grabs his coat, saving him from the impact, and they strike out together. Because the Spaniard doesn't speak English, Eugene carries on a silent monologue during their travels through the city. In his monologue, Eugene is naturally consumed with the state of his marriage and with the meaning of his violent outburst against his wife. In addition to the morning's outburst, though, Eugene meditates quite elaborately on the role of the artist. While this subject is initiated by the presence of the guitarist, the intricacies of Eugene's thoughts on the role of the artist suggest that this is a subject that he has thought about often. How Eugene's relationship with his wife connects to the artist's place in the world seems obscure without the underlying mythic text of Yeats's "Song of Wandering Aengus."

Eugene's place in his marriage is colored by his relationship to his father. By combining the subject of marriage with that of the artist's place in society, Welty takes us back to Yeats's text and deepens considerably its correlation to *The Golden Apples.* In the poem, Aengus wanders in search of a vision; a fish has metamorphosed into a beautiful woman. In a larger, symbolic sense, one of the meanings that this poem can support concerns not just the sexual passion of a man for his ideal fantasy woman but also the passion with which individuals pursue any vision. The "fire in his head" becomes the fire inside any artist that demands creativity. Welty's introduction of the Spanish guitarist in "Music from Spain" points to this deeper meaning in Yeats. The Spaniard becomes for Eugene a kind of representative artist, and as such he has the cultural power to show him the way to cope with his own, unarticulated passions. Welty again redirects the Aengus myth of the sexual wanderer, but in this version she elevates the myth to a higher level rather than reversing gender roles, as she has done with Mattie Will, Jinny Love, and Maideen Sumrall.

Eugene and his guitar player "[w]alked city squares in the sun until some meditative mood between them bound them like consenting speech" (*CS*, 412). With this bond between them, they wend their way to the sea, or, as Eugene describes it, "Land's End!" Eugene continues to struggle with his life, assessing and reassessing the journey that has gotten him there. "How could he put a watch back together?" he wonders, thinking about his life in terms of a metaphor of his work. He then moves to the image of the wanderer: "[H]e thought how the making and doing of daily life mazed a man about, eyes, legs, ladders, feet, fingers, like a vine. It twined a man in, the very doing and dying and daring of the world, the citified world" (*CS*, 413). Eugene, unlike his father, King, and, we learn, unlike the Spaniard, is stuck in his journey. He has no destination, and instead is moving through life in a confusion of paths. Reaching "Land's End" symbolizes for Eugene a break in this pattern. If there is no land, there can be no maze.

Coming to the sea in itself is not enough of a catalyst for Eugene's release; the Spaniard's presence as guide is also necessary. As they walk along the cliffs above the beach, Eugene thinks, "The Spaniard went as sedately as ever along the edge . . . had he been here before too?" (*CS*, 420). The answer to this is yes; the Spaniard has, as an artist, been to this metaphorical edge. At this point, he begins to show Eugene how to escape his mental torture. Eugene speaks aloud to himself, " 'You assaulted your wife. . . . But in your heart,' Eugene said, and then he was lost. It was a lifelong trouble, he had never been able to express himself at all when it came to the very moment. And now, on a cliff, in a wind, to . . ." (*CS*, 420). He trails off, losing the ability to articulate his feelings. The articulation of our deepest and most perplexing emotions is exactly what we depend on artists for. The artist must not only experience life out on the edge but also be equipped to come back from the edge and communicate the experience to us. Eugene seems to intuit this; as his speech drops off, he grabs the Spaniard around the waist: "Eugene clung to the Spaniard . . . almost as if he had waited for him a long time with longing, almost as if he loved him, and had found a lasting refuge." The Spaniard, the artist, does not, in the end, disappoint Eugene, though his response is unexpected: "The Spaniard closed his eyes. Then a bullish roar opened out of him. . . . What seemed to be utterances of the wildest order came from the wide mouth. . . . It was a terrible recital" (*CS*, 421).

In the next instant, both Eugene's and the Spaniard's hats blow away. Eugene runs after them, but in the end they are gone: "[Eugene] felt himself lifted up in the strong arms of the Spaniard, up above the bare head of the other man. Now the second hat blew away from him too. He was without a burden in the world" (*CS*, 422–23). This combination of seemingly irrational acts—the Spaniard's roaring and his lifting Eugene high above his head—explains the significance of the hats. An artist's activity is mostly irrational and purely emotional, having very little to do with the "head." So when the artist shouts, he shows Eugene that feelings don't need to be articulated in a rational way to be expressed; sometimes it is best to feel rather than to think. Eugene is able to follow the Spaniard's lead—he is literally lifted up by the artist—and he allows his hat, symbolic of his thinking, to blow away. Only at this moment is he "without a burden in the world." And only at this moment is he able to leave the mental maze that he has been wandering through since Fan's death. He breaks through to a personal vision that stops the cycle. The vision first appears in its previous, unresolved form, his mind "circling":

> Pillowed on great strength, he was turned in the air. It was the greatest comfort. It was too bad that circling in his mind the daylong foreboding had to return, that he had yet to open the door and climb the stairs to Emma. There she waited in the front room, shedding her tears standing up, like a bride, with the white curtains of the bay window hanging heavy all around her. (*CS*, 423)

Eugene's "foreboding" fear is of business-as-usual with his wife when he returns home at the end of the day. But by the Spaniard's second spin, Eugene sees another, clearer vision:

> When his body was wheeled another turn, the foreboding like a spinning ball was caught again. This time the vision—some niche of clarity, some future—was Emma MacLain turning around and coming part way to meet him on the stairs. . . . She lifted both arms in the wide, aroused sleeves and brought them together around him. He had to sink upon the frail hall chair intended for the coats and hats. And she was sinking upon him and on his mouth putting kisses like blows, returning him awesome favors in full vigor, with not the ghost of the salt of tears.
>
> If he could have spoken! It was out of this relentlessness, not out of the gush of tears, that there would be a child again. . . . He was

> upborne, open-armed. He was only thinking, My dear love comes. (*CS*, 423)

This second vision breaks Eugene out of his emotional desolation. And like all great visions, it also seems to communicate to those around him. When he returns home, Emma greets him cordially, lovingly, as if a new era has dawned in the household. We are left to assume that Eugene's vision becomes reality.

Neither Ran nor Eugene follows their father's path as a wanderer after sexual passion. Both have been true to their marriages, though both have deeply troubled relationships with their wives. Unlike Ran, however, whose story ends in despair, Eugene finds a new—improved—model for wandering. The Spaniard, "alluring . . . the perfect being to catch up with. . . . a stranger and yet not a stranger," takes on immediately the role of the ethereal King MacLain: charismatic, otherworldly, there and not there. Yet the Spaniard is more of a journeyer than a wanderer; Eugene muses that the Spaniard perhaps "could produce a beautiful mistress he had somewhere" but instead decides that "It was more probable that the artist remained alone at night" (*CS*, 407). The guitarist also takes on the artist's role of teacher and leader for Eugene. King was never at home to teach or to lead, but the Spaniard, while "the formidable artist [is] free" (*CS*, 406), also "everywhere seem[s] too much at home" (*CS*, 405). It is the paradox of being both mentally free and somehow stable, tied to one's surroundings, that King MacLain, in his role as Wandering Aengus, lacks. This paradox is lacking in the Yeatsian telling of Aengus's story as well. Ran begins himself to collapse the roles of the wanderer, the artist, and his father:

> Eugene saw himself for a moment as the kneeling Man in the Wilderness in the engraving in his father's remnant geography book, who hacked once at the Traveler's Tree, opened his mouth, and the water came pouring in. What did Eugene MacLain really care about the life of an artist, or a foreigner, or a wanderer, all the same thing—to have it all brought upon him now? That engraving itself, he had once believed, represented his father, King MacLain, in the flesh, the one who had never seen him or wanted to see him. (*CS*, 409)

With the Spaniard and his relationship to Eugene, Welty reshapes altogether the nature of the Aengus model: a person can follow his vision, his "fire," but does not necessarily have to do so as an itinerate or an unreliable wanderer, supplying neither emotional nor physical stability for others. The Spanish guitar player provides Eugene with several things he needs: he is at once a model, a guide, and an emotional anchor—all of the aspects that King MacLain, as Wandering Aengus, could not give his sons. We have seen Welty perform two kinds of revision of Yeats's "Wandering Aengus." On one hand, she changes the gender of the sexual traveler, and on the other, she privileges the artistic interpretation of the myth over the sexual, showing that the Spanish artist's gifts to Eugene are superior and more valuable than anything that King in his role as Aengus has to offer.

Art, Gender, Transcendance, Myth

Though the revisions we have seen thus far are significant, Welty most radically revises the Aengus story in *The Golden Apples* in "June Recital," the story of Cassie and Loch Morrison, Virgie Rainey, and their piano teacher, Miss Eckhart. In the story, Welty collapses her two revisions and presents us with a female version of the artist-Aengus model. In "Sir Rabbit" and "The Whole World Knows," Welty suggests that the sexual-Aengus role can be filled by women; both Mattie Will Sojourner and Jinny Love Stark take on the sexual impetus in their relationships. But Welty offers a much more complex portrait of Miss Eckhart, Morgana's resident piano teacher and musical artist, than she does of either Mattie Will or Jinny Love. Cassie and Loch Morrison's house is next door to the MacLain house, where Miss Eckhart has her studio. "June Recital" is a story told on two levels; one, Loch's looking through the windows of the now-deserted house, and seeing an old woman (Miss Eckhart) come into it, string the parlor with "ribbons of newspaper . . . starting with the piano, where she weighted down their ends with a statue" (*CS*, 282), and try to set fire to the house. Upstairs, Virgie Rainey carries on her regular afternoon sexual tryst with a sailor. Loch watches both scenes with rapt eyes, though as a young boy, he doesn't always interpret accurately what he sees.

The second level of the story is Cassie's. She is in her room, preparing to go off to college, and she hears the opening bars of Beethoven's "Für Elise" from next door: Miss Eckhart plays the phrase intermittently as she prepares to burn down the house. This familiar strain of music touches off Cassie's memories of years of lessons with Miss Eckhart, Virgie Rainey's lesson following her own every week. "Für Elise" had been Virgie's piece before she moved on to more complex repertoire, and the piece touches off memories of lessons and recitals past. Cassie, even though she doesn't know that the music comes from Miss

Eckhart's fingers, or that Virgie Rainey is upstairs next door, begins to put together in her mind the difficult emotional relationships between herself, Virgie, and Miss Eckhart.

Laced in among Cassie's rich memory horde, lines from Yeats's "Song of Wandering Aengus" appear in small groups, until the end of the story, when Cassie lays down to sleep. Then she remembers the poem in its entirety.

> Into her head flowed the whole of the poem she had found in that book. It ran perfectly through her head, vanishing as it went, one line yielding to the next, like a torch race. All of it passed through her head, through her body. She slept, but sat up in bed once and said aloud, " '*Because a fire was in my head.*' " Then she fell back unresisting. She did not see except in dreams that a face looked in; that it was the grave, unappeased, and radiant face, once more and always, the face that was in the poem. (*CS*, 330)

Cassie's reminiscences of her "June recital" days, her piano lessons with Miss Eckhart and Virgie Rainey, have led her to a subconscious revelation. That revelation, one she struggles to have throughout the course of her recollections, is quite clearly tied to the vision in "Song of Wandering Aengus"; awake, she can experience only pieces of this truth, in single lines of the poem. Asleep, she grasps the whole.

In "June Recital," the artistic community in Morgana is predominantly female, foreshadowing the revision of the female artist as Wandering Aengus. Welty makes it clear that Miss Eckhart, while merely Morgana's piano teacher, is in her way also an artist. Miss Eckhart is an outsider—as is the Spaniard, as is the prototypical artist in a Welty story—though it is never clear where she is from: "[I]t was because she was from so far away, at any rate, people said to excuse her, that she couldn't comprehend. . . . Miss Eckhart's *differences* were why shame alone had not killed her and killed her mother, too" (*CS*, 302). Miss Eckhart's foreignness becomes most clear to Morgana when her reaction to a fierce attack by a black man is to go on with her life rather than to move out of town in shame. Miss Eckhart, like the Spaniard, is a world citizen, at once at home and out of place everywhere; moving to another place, for her, would change nothing. Miss Eckhart envisions her status as a world citizen for Virgie Rainey as well: "Virgie would be heard from in the world," Miss Eckhart insists. Morgana does not understand what this means. To all who hear her, Miss Eckhart simply reveals "her lack of knowledge of the world. How could Virgie be heard from, in the world? And 'the world'! Where did Miss Eckhart think she was now?" (*CS*, 303).

Like the Spaniard, Miss Eckhart is also a guide. In her way she offers guidance to Virgie and Cassie, though without the direct results that the Spaniard achieves with Eugene. Once during a daytime thunderstorm, Miss Eckhart does the unaccustomed and plays the piano for Virgie, Cassie, and Jinny Love. Cassie, "[u]neasy, almost alarmed," divines that "What Miss Eckhart might have told them a long time ago was that there was more than the ear could bear to hear or the eye to see, even in her" (*CS*, 301). Like all good teachers and guides, Miss Eckhart teaches her lessons so that they unfold in her students gradually, when they are ready to face them. In Cassie's reconstruction of Miss Eckhart's life and teachings, we see vividly how lessons are borne to fruit successfully in memory. Miss Eckhart, as the prototype of the artist, teaches Cassie to see herself more clearly. As Cassie hears "Für Elise" through her window a third time, she begins the process of seeing her inner self with some clarity and understanding:

> her uncritical self of the crucial present, this Wednesday afternoon, slowly came forward—as if called on. Cassie saw herself without even facing the mirror, for her small, solemn, unprotected figure was emerging staring-clear inside her mind. There she was now, standing scared at the window again in her petticoat. . . . She had seemed to be favored and happy and she stood there pathetic—homeless-looking—horrible. Like a wave, the gathering past came right up to her. Next time it would be too high. The poetry was all around her, pellucid and lifting from side to side,
>
> "*Though I am old with wandering*
> *Through hollow lands and hilly lands,*
> *I will find out where she has gone. . . .*"
>
> Then the wave moved up, towered, and came drowning down over her stuck-up head. (*CS*, 287)

As with the final paragraph of the story, where Cassie is able to dream the full text of Yeats's poem, in this intense moment of self-realization Cassie's developing self is tied closely both to Miss Eckhart and to something essential in "Song of Wandering Aengus."

Miss Eckhart is linked directly to "Song of Wandering Aengus" through more than Cassie's recitation of the poem as she remembers her. Miss

Eckhart is at once as powerful as King MacLain, the first Wandering Aengus in these stories, and she is also his opposite: "[King and Miss Eckhart] always passed without touching, like two stars, perhaps they had some kind of eclipse-effect on each other" (*CS*, 296). Like two polar stars, each with its own true gravity and course, Miss Eckhart and King MacLain respect their individual likeness and power. This likeness originates with the myth each character represents, the Wandering Aengus in search of something to quench the fire in the head. Miss Eckhart is distinct from King MacLain in this role, however; it is Miss Eckhart alone, of all the various characters in *The Golden Apples* who fit the role of Wandering Aengus, who experiences literally the "fire" in her head. Through Loch's eyes the narrator of the story first suggests the resemblance. As Miss Eckhart is stringing the parlor with newspaper, the narrator tells us, "Soon everything seemed fanciful and beautiful enough to Loch; he thought she could stop. But the old woman kept on. This was only a part of something in her head" (*CS*, 283). Miss Eckhart's passion at this moment is to set fire to the source of her art—the piano, and the place where she practiced that art—her studio at the MacLain house. The passion to burn her artistic past is the "something in her head." As she struggles to set the fire—in Loch's eyes, "Everything she did was wrong, after a certain point"—she perseveres with the same intensity: "She kept putting her hand to her head" (*CS*, 284). When she manages to set her fire, it is snuffed out by two passing men, Old Man Moody and Fatty Bowles. When she tries to set it again, Miss Eckhart sets her hair on fire:

> while they talked, [she] tried it again. She was down on her knees cradling the lump of candle and the next moment had it lighted. She rose up, agitated now, and went running about the room, holding the candle above her, evading the men each time they tried to head her off.
>
> This time, the fire caught her own hair. The little short white frill turned to flame. (*CS*, 322)

The "frill" of her hair in flames literalizes and materializes what is otherwise a metaphor in Welty's text: Miss Eckhart does actually have a fire in her head. The literalization of the metaphor signifies that Miss Eckhart is the essential representation of the Wandering Aengus figure in *The Golden Apples.*

As I have pointed out, Welty sets up a dreamlike atmosphere in Morgana, an atmosphere in which all stories and actions become pliable, elastic, and ultimately changeable. As the most literal example of the various characters who represent Wandering Aengus, Miss Eckhart represents a complete shift in the signification of the myth. King MacLain, Welty's original Aengus, comes to represent a layer of this particular myth that will ultimately die out in Morgana. Neither of his sons, Ran and Eugene, takes up King's mantle; neither is the kind of wanderer with sexual passion as his driving force. Eugene's guide, the Spanish guitarist, indicates a more sophisticated kind of Aengus figure, one who strives after the passions of artistic, rather than sexual, endeavor. The replacement of King with the Spanish artist suggests ultimately the kind of shift that occurs in the mythology of the human driven to seek a passionate vision at all costs. In Western culture, the freedom to seek one's passion, whether sexual or artistic, has belonged solely to men. Welty does allow both Mattie Will and Jinny Love to take on the role of the sexual wanderer, but she does not place this role at the center of her mythic revision. Both characters play minor parts in the world of Morgana. With the Spanish artist, and most significantly with Miss Eckhart, Welty shifts the myth of Aengus onto two characters whom she describes as being, at their moments of highest passion, both entirely absorbed in artistic endeavors and having dual gender identity. When Eugene envisions the Spaniard in a moment of artistic contemplation, he both feminizes the artist and connects the Spaniard to Miss Eckhart's studio through the sibyl framed on her studio wall:

> Eugene felt untoward visions churning. . . . The Spaniard with his finger on the page of a book, looking over his shoulder, as did the framed Sibyl on the wall in his father's study—no! then, it was old Miss Eckhart's "studio"—where he was muscular, but in a storylike way womanly. (*CS*, 408)

At once both muscular and womanly in Eugene's vision, the Spaniard takes Eugene back first to his father's—King's—study, but then, most tellingly, to Miss Eckhart's studio. Here Eugene figuratively replaces his father with Miss Eckhart. Eugene remembers a picture of the sibyl hanging over the piano.[42] The mythic sibyl is a woman, most often depicted predicting the future and offering prophecies to those who seek her out. Hence Eugene's vision of the Spaniard's finger on the page of a book represents the sibyl's book of blank pages that she fills with her prophecies. The sibyl, as Virgil represents her, also guides Aeneas through the underworld. As I have discussed, the Spaniard as an artist becomes both Eugene's prophet and his guide, so the sibylline association to him is exactly symbolic of what takes place in "Music from Spain," prophecy and guidance. The further implications of this vision of the Spaniard as sybil concern the redirection of gender—the Spaniard as sybil is not entirely feminized; he remains muscular, indicating an attempt to neutralize the artist's gender identity.

Miss Eckhart, associated with the sibyl in Eugene's vision, like the Spaniard loses her gender identity at the moment of highest artistic vision. She plays for Cassie, Virgie, and Jinny during the storm:

> The piece was so hard that she made mistakes and repeated to correct them, so long and stirring that it soon seemed longer than the day itself had been, and in playing it Miss Eckhart assumed an entirely different face. Her skin flattened and drew across her cheeks, her lips changed. The face could have belonged to someone else—not even to a woman, necessarily. It was the face a mountain could have, or what might be seen behind the veil of a waterfall. There in the rainy light it was a sightless face, one for music only—though the fingers kept slipping and making mistakes they had to correct. And if the sonata had an origin in a place on earth, it was the place where Virgie, even, had never been and was not likely ever to go. (*CS*, 300–301)

Like the Spaniard, Miss Eckhart's identity and the crucial moment of artistic passion is dual—or, more exactly, ambiguous. She has an entirely different face, one that is "not even . . . a woman['s], necessarily."

New Myths: Compromise and Escape

"Moon Lake" and Confluent Genders

A Curtain of Green begins Welty's revision of that part of the Adam and Eve myth that is the most destructive aspect of the cultural imperative defining how a woman may exist. In this work, Welty offers overwhelmingly negative perspectives, showing how living without the expressive power of language, and therefore without identity—their self-expression instead mediated through the language and experience of men—destroys women. Not content to leave this situation in the negative, however, Welty touches on the myth again in "Moon Lake," one of the stories from *The Golden Apples.* Moon Lake is at the center of a girl's camp, where well-bred girls from the town of Morgana have been sent for the summer, along with orphans from a local home. In the scene most explicitly linking "Moon Lake" to *Paradise Lost,* Welty focuses, as she does in "A Piece of News," on naming and language as the currency of power.

Easter, the "leader" of the orphans ("Easter was dominant among the orphans" [*CS*, 346]), takes two of the girls from town—Jinny Love Stark and Nina Charmichael—to a secret place she has found on the opposite shore of Moon Lake. They settle there on a sandbar, and Nina begins to write her name in the sand, while Easter lies in a boat tied to the shore: "[Nina's] own hand was writing in the sand. Nina, Nina, Nina. Writing, she could dream that her self might get away from here—that here in this faraway place she could tell her self, by name, to go or to stay" (*CS*, 355). As she finishes her writing, Nina wades out and pushes Easter's boat until it becomes unmoored, and Nina is able to control it: "For a moment, with her powerful hands, Nina held the boat back." Writing her name in the sand seems to give Nina an unaccustomed strength. As she realizes this, the idea of a pear pops inextricably into her mind:

> Again she thought of a pear—not the everyday gritty kind that hung on the tree in the backyard, but the fine kind sold on trains and at high prices, each pear with a paper cone wrapping it alone—beautiful, symmetrical, clean pears with thin skins, with snow-white flesh so juicy and tender that to eat one baptized the whole face, and so delicate that while you urgently ate the first half, the second half was already beginning to turn brown. To all fruits, and especially to those fine pears, something happened—the process was so swift, you were never in time for them. It's not the flowers that are fleeting, Nina thought, it's the fruits—it's the time when things are ready that they don't stay. She even went through the rhyme, "Pear tree by the garden gate, How much longer must I wait?"—thinking it was the pears that asked it, not the picker. (*CS*, 355–56)

Without the context of the Adam and Eve myth, Nina's association of writing her name, finding strength, and pears might seem like a series of unconnected events. Because the myth lies beneath this passage, however, we can observe the structuring of events more clearly. The surprising aspect of Nina's thought is her ceding to the pear—the "forbidden fruit"—a kind of desire. Here, the pear desires to be picked and eaten at its moment of ideal ripeness, whereas usually desire is seated in the mind of Eve, who picks and eats the fruit. Welty clearly revises this placement of desire with Nina's reinterpretation of the rhyme, and this revision removes all guilt from Nina as Eve. Whatever the fruit represents—desire, forbidden knowledge—here, the object of desire desires to be desired. In Milton's terms, then, language, knowledge, power, all need Eve as much as she needs them. Welty offers in this reversal of agency the startling suggestion that things traditionally forbidden both have a strong pull for women and are well suited to a woman's possession. In other words, language, knowledge, and power need to be in a woman's life.

Nina awakens in "Moon Lake" to a world that is twice the size of the one she has known in Morgana, a world where she can have power and identity, where she can be fully herself in ways she never imagined. After the experience of writing her name, Nina wakes in the middle of the night and thinks about a new way of being:

> The orphan! she thought exultantly. The other way to live. There were secret ways. She thought, Time's really short, I've been only thinking like the others. It's only interesting, only worthy, to try for the fiercest secrets. To slip into them all—to change. To change for a moment into Gertrude, into Mrs. Gruenwald, into Twosie—into a boy. To *have been* an orphan. (*CS*, 361)

This ability to imagine herself even as a boy seems inevitable; Nina has, after all, co-opted the male privilege of writing and naming. Nina's desire "to try for the fiercest secrets" springs from her afternoon escape to the opposite shore of Moon Lake with Easter. Easter facilitates this awakening in Nina; described throughout the story in masculine terms, Easter announces as she writes her name in the sand that she has "named herself." This is true; she spells her name "E-S-T-H-E-R," but she deliberately calls herself "Easter." She has decided on her own identity: " 'I let myself name myself,' " she answers when Nina implores, " 'How could you? Who let you?' " (*CS*, 357).

While Easter may seem to represent an entirely self-sufficient masculinized female, Welty has Easter "fall" into her female identity at the end of the story. Easter cannot swim, and when Exum, the son of Elberta, one of the black maids, brushes her leg with a switch, she falls in the lake and almost drowns. Loch Morrison, "Boy Scout," resuscitates her vigorously:

> Astride Easter the Boy Scout lifted her up between his legs and dropped her. . . . On the table, the Boy Scout spat, and took a fresh appraisal of Easter. He reached for a hold on her hair and pulled her head back. No longer were her lips faintly parted—her mouth was open. It gaped. So did his. He dropped her, the head with its suddenness bowed again on its cheek, and he started again. (*CS*, 365; 368)

This is an important comic moment in Welty. The violence in "life-saving" startles the girl campers—"Life-saving was much worse than they had dreamed." The implied sexuality of it startles Miss Lizzie Stark, Jinny Love's mother, who "had arrived on her daily visit to see how the camp was running." No one tells her what is happening; Loch's grunts simply resonate across the lake. Miss Lizzie is horrified: " 'But what's *he* doing to her? Stop that.' . . . 'Why he ought to be—he ought to be—I can't stand it.' . . . 'He ought to be put out of business' ". Loch isn't put out of business; Miss Stark is subdued, and the rescue scene continues until "now the Boy Scout seemed for ever part of Easter and she part of him, he in motion on the up-and-down and she stretched across" (*CS*, 370). For Easter to be described in such sexual submission to Loch seems strange, given Easter's tomboyish flair—she has a pocketknife and plays mumblety-peg. But when she rises up from her temporary death—anyone named Easter would have to rise from the dead—she has a new demeanor, a new awareness of her female aspect: "Before their eyes, Easter got to her knees, sat up, and drew her legs up to her. She rested her head on her knees and looked out at them, while she slowly pulled her ruined dress downward. . . . 'Carry me.' Easter's words had no inflection. Again, 'Carry me' " (*CS*, 371–72). On one level, of course, Easter's new low-key effeminate personality rings true because she has just been through a death-defying experience. But Welty also underscores the symbolic with Easter, and with Loch, throughout the story, and together their encounter and its highly charged symbolism marks the important transformation—or confluence—in the story.

Both "moon" and "lake" are strongly identified with the female in mythic iconography. The moon represents the female because it is passive, it does not generate its own light or heat; it reflects both from the sun, the traditional symbol of maleness. The lake also is passive, a still vessel, in opposition to the more active, phallic river, which is a moving stream. When Easter falls into "Moon Lake," where she has not been able to swim before, she falls into her female identity. The descriptive passage ending this section emphasizes Easter's symbolic passage: "The lake grew darker, then gleamed, like the crater of a rimmed well. Easter was put to bed, they sat quietly on the ground outside the tent, and Miss Lizzie sipped water from Nina's cup. The sky's rising clouds lighted all over, like one spread-out blooming mimosa tree that could be seen from where the trunk itself should rise" (*CS*, 373). The entire scene suggests that nature looks down on Easter and affirms that "it is good."

We might view Loch's role in Easter's transformation as purely male if not for his name and the description of him after he saves Easter. "Loch" means lake, as in Loch Lomond. In name, then, he has a female association. In other ways, until the scene with Easter, Loch is the most male presence that the girls at camp can imagine: "Sometimes he swung in the trees. . . . He went through the air rocking and jerking like an engine, splashed in, climbed out, spat, climbed up again, dived off" (*CS*, 343). Loch's most important, and most male-identified, duty is to call the girls awake, asleep, and to every important daily event with his bugle: "Reveille was his. He harangued the woods. . . . And how lovely and altered the trees were then. . . . He blew his horn into their presence—trees' and girls'" (*CS*, 343). Throughout this story, Moon Lake takes on the aura of a contemporary paradise for women, but nowhere more so than with this establishment of Loch's role in this paradise. He is like a benign, omnipotent male deity, controlling time and nature with his phallic bugle: "The bugle blew for swimming" (*CS*, 350), and "they had to keep waiting till Loch Morrison blew his horn before they could come out of Moon Lake" (*CS*, 345).

Loch's transformation into a different kind of male presence begins as he is saving Easter. Miss Lizzie Stark diminishes considerably the size of Loch's bugle: "Under her gaze the Boy Scout's actions seemed to lose a good deal of significance. He was reduced almost to a nuisance—a mosquito, with a mosquito's proboscis. 'Get him off her,' Miss Lizzie repeated" (*CS*, 367). Loch's sign of maleness and control to this point in the story has been his bugle; Miss Lizzie shrinks it down to a "mosquito's proboscis." He does not remain emasculated, however; later in the evening, Jinny Love and Nina happen by Loch's tent.

> The Boy Scout, little old Loch Morrison, was undressing in his tent for the whole world to see. . . . His candle—for that was all it was—jumping a little now, he stood there studying and touching his case of sunburn in a Kress mirror like theirs. He was naked and there was his little tickling thing hung on him like the last drop on the pitcher's lip. He ceased or exhausted study and came to the tent opening again and stood leaning on one raised arm, with his weight on one foot—just looking out into the night, which was clamorous. (*CS*, 373)

Here is a deliberate role reversal. Instead of the male in control of the gaze, looking at the passive and nude woman, the two girls have sneaked up on Loch and see him naked. And his maleness may or may not be diminished; no longer a bugle or a mosquito's proboscis, "his little tickling thing" is "like the last the drop on the pitcher's lip." A more realistic and manageable size for the girls, perhaps. Just as important, Welty shows Loch here gazing into a mirror, another intertextual reference to *Paradise Lost* and to Eve's longing look at herself in the reflective pool. The mirror is "like theirs"; and in many ways Loch's identity by the end of "Moon Lake" shows strong female likeness. Nina and Jinny Love have a stereotype in mind when they find Loch: "Hadn't he surely, just before they caught him, been pounding his chest with his fists?" (*CS,* 373). Instead, he is looking at his sunburn in a mirror. As the narrator tells us, "By moonlight sometimes [Moon Lake] seemed to run like a river" (*CS,* 361); sometimes the female can seem male, and the male, female.

The exchange that occurs for Nina, Easter, and Loch suggests that Welty does not revise *Paradise Lost* and turn Milton's garden into a place for women only. Neither does Welty's reshaping of these three characters suggest that she surrenders the ideal of female agency to the stifling power of cultural myth. With "Moon Lake," Welty suggests that each gender and temperament can benefit from the other; we see her softening Easter and Loch, and giving an edge to Nina. In her novel *The Optimist's Daughter,* Welty talks about the marriage of Laurel and Phil in terms of "confluence"; they ride in a train over the "confluence of the waters, the Ohio and the Mississippi: . . . they themselves were a part of the confluence. Their own joint act of faith had brought them here at the very moment and matched its occurrence, and proceeded as it proceeded. Direction itself was made beautiful, momentous. They were riding as one with it, right up front." (*OD,* 159–60). "Confluence," the act of flowing together, combining to become one; these are marvelous terms in which to describe a marriage. But for Welty, "confluence" is not only descriptive of an ideal relationship; it also signifies her central use of myth. What we see in the characters of Nina, Loch, and Easter in "Moon Lake" is an example of confluence, the coming together within individuals of traits that society typically assigns to separate genders. Like a good marriage, individuals may be whole within themselves, and indeed we learn that in the marriage of Laural and Phil, each possesses traits typical of the other gender, and by possessing these traits is able to fill or complete the partner.

As Welty has said of herself, she has a positive view of life, and a moral view. Her revision of Milton's cultural myth shows both her positive side and her morality: the divisiveness that arises from the exclusion of one gender from the experience of the other appalls Welty, and she heals the division by making the genders confluent.

Virgie Rainey's New Myths

Virgie Rainey's story continues beyond Miss Eckhart's in *The Golden Apples.* In the final section of the book, fittingly entitled "The Wanderers," Welty brings many of her Wandering Aengus figures together for the funeral of Virgie Rainey's mother, Katie Rainey, who narrates the story opening *The Golden Apples,* "A Shower of Gold." Katie's death suggests a closing of the circle of stories, and in many ways this final story does offer some closure to the book. We learn, for instance, that Eugene's marriage to Emma does not, in the end, work out; he comes home to Morgana, never reconciles with his father, and is now dead. Ran, on the other hand, does solve his problems with Jinny Love, and he is now mayor of Morgana. King is home with Snowdie, having ceased his wandering. Loch Morrison has moved to New York, and his sister, Cassie, teaches piano in Morgana. The most significant closure that takes place in the story occurs because we are for the first time inside Virgie's head. Virgie has been the opaque figure throughout *The Golden Apples;* gifted as an artist, she seems defiant of her gifts and the expectations that go with them. Instead of continuing her music, as Miss Eckhart wishes, she gets a job playing piano accompaniment to silent films in the local movie theater. Cassie, rather than Virgie, seems to take on Miss Eckhart's role as artist; she is at least the piano teacher. Yet Cassie and Virgie have more in common than their piano teacher. What we learn of Cassie in "June Recital" we also learn about Virgie in "The Wanderers." Both understand the role of the artist, and both have the sensitivity to take it on. They have each been taught well by Miss Eckhart. Like Cassie's recalling the various verses of "Song of Wandering Aengus" and understanding, at least subconsciously, the meaning of the lines, Virgie in "The Wanderers" recalls the significant moment of Miss Eckhart's playing Beethoven for her students during the storm. And with this story she recalls another picture on Miss Eckhart's wall, not the sibyl that Eugene remembers but a more monstrous image of a woman, Medusa's beheading by Perseus:

> Miss Eckhart had had among the pictures from Europe on her walls a certain threatening one. It hung over the dictionary, dark as that book. It showed Perseus with the head of the Medusa. "The same thing as Siegfried and the Dragon," Miss Eckhart had occasionally said, as if

> explaining second-best. Around the picture—which sometimes blindly reflected by window by its darkness—was a frame enameled with flowers, which was always self-evident—Miss Eckhart's pride. In that moment Virgie had shorn it of its frame.
>
> The vaunting was what she remembered, that lifted arm.
>
> Cutting off the Medusa's head was the heroic act, perhaps, that made visible a horror in life, that was at once the horror in love, Virgie thought—the separateness. She might have seen heroism prophetically when she was young and afraid of Miss Eckhart. She might be able to see it now prophetically, but she was never a prophet. Because Virgie saw things in their time, like hearing them—and perhaps because she must believe in the Medusa equally with Perseus—she saw the stroke of the sword in three moments, not one. In the three was the damnation—no, only the secret, unhurting because not caring in itself—beyond the beauty and the sword's stroke and the terror lay their existence in time—far out and endless, a constellation which the heart could read over many a night. (*CS*, 459–60)

The myth of Perseus and Medusa that Virgie associates with Miss Eckhart's Beethoven also brings us full circle, back to "A Shower of Gold" where Snowdie's pregnancy by King evokes the myth of Zeus coming to rape Danae in a shower of gold. Perseus (the "hero" who kills Medusa) is born out of Zeus's rape. One key to the connection and convergence of these various mythical figures—Zeus, Perseus, Wandering Aengus, along with the sibyl that Eugene remembers hanging over Miss Eckhart's piano—is the mythic identity of Medusa. When Perseus kills her, Medusa's hair is made of slithering, hissing snakes. If a man looks at her, he is turned to stone. Symbolically, this myth represents the inherent danger to a man of a strong or masculinized woman—the snakes in the hair representing Medusa's co-opting of the male privilege of phallic strength. A strong woman unnatural, dangerous, must be slain. Perseus becomes the great hero for accomplishing this task by seeing a reflection of Medusa in his mirroring shield. Because he does not experience her dangerous gaze directly, Perseus is immune to her power. Like the myth of Adam and Eve, this myth teaches that women who take on male power—and the artist's role is one of those traditionally powerful roles—are unnatural and dangerous and must be destroyed. The sibyl that Virgie also evokes here, in her meditation on prophecy, while not a monstrous form of woman like the Medusa, is still a woman who serves the gods, filling the blank pages of her book with prophecies. A prototype of the woman who writes, the sybil, too, is difficult or impossible for mere mortal man to control.

Virgie sees Miss Eckhart's capacity to absorb the image of the female artist, independent of social dicta. Like her fellow Morganans, she sees Miss Eckhart as the ultimate outsider, an independent woman immune to the intricate social codes of a small southern town. This is an image with which Virgie—poor, socially ostracized at school, an outsider herself—can identify. But she also sees that Miss Eckhart represents a more complex figure; she is not purely the artist as outsider. Virgie remembers that Miss Eckhart frames the scene of Perseus and Medusa with pride, as if she were in control of both images, the slayer and the slain. In one sense, Miss Eckhart's capacity to represent at once both female and male, monster and slayer of monster, is the ideal that Welty sets up for the artist: the Spaniard also becomes both male and female in Eugene's vision of him in a moment of artistic inspiration. The image of the female he summons is of the prophetic sibyl. Yet for Virgie, becoming an artist, absorbing the hero and the monster at once, is for her, at this time in her life, unthinkable. When she was a young student of Miss Eckhart's, she understands now, she was willing to take on the role because Miss Eckhart wanted her to do so: "She might have seen heroism prophetically when she was young and afraid of Miss Eckhart. She might be able to see it now prophetically, but she was never a prophet." A prophet speaks for the divine, tells the future; Virgie realizes that she may be able to recognize the prophet—the artist—but she does not have the strength to be the artist in Miss Eckhart's terms.

Nor does Cassie have the strength. In Cassie's vision of Yeats's "Wandering Aengus," she cannot see the entire poem except in her dreams. In her dreams, the face in the poem looks out at her from the poem. "Face" is an ambiguous reference, since there are two faces in the poem: both the visage of Aengus and the "glimmering girl." The myths of Wandering Aengus and of Medusa and Perseus, as Welty revises them, suggest that the artist's vision is essentially a whole vision, both male and female, pursued and pursuant, hero and victim, gazer and object of the gaze, wanderer and that wandered after. When Cassie sees the face from the poem, it is the face of the whole, Aengus and the girl, not of one side or the other. Hers is not a vision that leaves her dreams, however. It is this wholeness of artistic vision that makes the artist the prophet, able to see all sides, just as a God would see. Miss Eckhart has the strength and what Virgie calls "pride" to encompass these two opposites within her psyche; "Miss Eckhart . . . had hung the picture on the wall for herself. She had absorbed the hero and the victim and then, stoutly, could sit down to the piano with all Beethoven ahead of her" (*CS*, 460). Virgie and Cassie both see the toll that "absorb[ing]" the dualistic life takes on Miss Eckhart. She must uphold the role of the female as artist, which goes against all cultural stories and myths, and consequently must fend off all male attacks against her and her art. Mr. Voight presents the greatest threat to Miss Eckhart's art; with his blatant show of phallic strength, he attempts to silence the female voice as he walks through the studio flashing Miss Eckhart and her students during their lessons: "It would be plain to Miss Eckhart or to anybody that [Mr. Voight] wanted, first, the music lesson to stop" (*CS*, 294). Miss Eckhart attempts to withstand Mr. Voight's assaults; she does just that, withstands them, but does not stop them. Instead she demands that her students remain silent about his antics, ensuring that Mr. Voight will be able to continue his assaults as long has he wants. Miss Eckhart can keep her art alive by upholding the role of the strong and artistic woman in most Morganan situations. In the face of Mr. Voight, however, she loses her power and becomes the victim. Virgie steps in for Miss Eckhart: "Virgie kept the upper hand over Miss Eckhart even at the moment when Mr. Voight came out to scare them. She only played on the stronger and clearer, and never pretended he had not come out and that she did not know it, or that she might not tell it, no matter how poor Miss Eckhart begged" (*CS*, 295). In this instance, as in many others, it is clear that Virgie is the natural and stronger heir of Miss Eckhart.

Virgie, like many heirs apparent, rejects her role. As Virgie understands, the myth of Perseus and Medusa, like the other cultural myths of Adam and Eve and Wandering Aengus, are as resilient in our culture as the constellations are. The myth of Perseus and Medusa for Virgie is "a constellation which the heart could read over many a night," both beautiful and terrible because the myth continues to exist as a cultural truth. Finally, Virgie must leave Miss Eckhart's dream for her behind, "perhaps because she must believe in the Medusa equally with Perseus"; if she believes that the artist is heroic, she must also believe that the artist is monstrous, and if she believes that the artist can seize what he desires, as Perseus does, then she must also believe that the artist can be pursued and destroyed, as is Medusa. Beyond the dualism of the artist, Virgie must also see the impossibility of being female and artistic in her society. The difference between Miss Eckhart and the Spaniard, the two artists in *The Golden Apples*, emphasizes the dangers for the woman artist. The Spaniard's female nature is expressed in the form of the sibyl, mythically an unapproachable female figure because she is prophetic, the voice of the divine. And the Spaniard is depicted as being vigorous and redemptive, giving Eugene a renewed sense of his life. Miss Eckhart, on the other hand, exudes the Medusa as the female side of her artistic whole, a destructive female presence that she must constantly destroy within herself, or be destroyed. And Miss Eckhart in the end is neither vigorous or redemptive. We see her at the end of her life trying to destroy her studio, the seat of her passion and art, and failing that, being led away presumably to a mental institution in Jackson where she dies, rejected by her star student, Virgie.

Yet Virgie as a young piano student at first accepted the legacy that Miss Eckhart offered her. In the final paragraphs of "The Wanderers," Virgie recalls her acceptance:

> With her hate, with her love, and with the small gnawing feelings that ate them, [Miss Eckhart] offered Virgie her Beethoven. . . . and when Virgie was young, in the strange wisdom of youth that is accepting of more than is given, she had accepted *the* Beethoven, as with the dragon's blood. That was the gift she had touched with her fingers that had drifted and left her.

Now she must transcend that legacy. Virgie and Cassie see what happens to a woman when she tries to break through the mythic barriers: Miss Eckhart is ostracized, laughed at, pitied, shunned, and, in the end, presumably driven mad. Eugene is dead, Ran and Jinny Love have reestablished their marriage. Cassie is the new piano teacher, but is quite absorbed with planting flowers in the shape of her mother's name, involved in maintaining the status quo of her mother's generation as well as the Eve-like role of the woman as domestic gardener. Loch is in New York. The burden falls on Virgie. Can roles be changed? Can myths be rewritten?

Virgie must leave Morgana to discover the answers to these questions. She has left once before, but was not, it seems, ready to leave. When she returns on the train from this first exodus, she leaps from the top step and "come[s] back to something—and she began to run toward it, with her suitcase as light as a shoebox, so little had she had to go away with and now to bring back—the lightness made it easier" (*CS*, 452). When she returns, she vows to give up the things she does best: "no music, no picture show job . . . no piano." Even in her dreams, her art metamorphoses into the practical work of the domestic household: "And if, as she dreamed one winter night, a new piano she had turned, after the one pristine moment, into a calling cow, it was by her own desire" (*CS*, 453). Returning after her first journey, she sticks to her resolve to become the domesticated woman that her society expects rather than the artist of Miss Eckhart's tutelage. Now that her mother is dead, her domestic ties seem broken; Virgie will leave with as few possessions as before—she gives away the cows and packs her mother's house in boxes—but with a new freedom and a knowledge and understanding of her past; when she returned before, it was "knowing herself not really, in her essence, yet hurt; and thus happy" (*CS*, 452–53). We are not told why Virgie left before—perhaps to go "out into the world," as Miss Eckhart wanted her to—but only that the journey was painful and empty. Unlike this time in her life, the description of Virgie during the few days surrounding her mother's funeral have primarily included scenes of Virgie unlocking herself, her body and her surroundings loosing their boundaries. As she lowers herself into the river near her house,

> she began to swim in the river, forcing it gently, as she would wish for gentleness to her body. Her breasts around which she felt the water curling were as sensitive at that moment as the tips of wings must feel to birds, or antennae to insects. She felt the sand, grains intricate as little cogged wheels, minute shells of old seas, and the many dark ribbons of grass and mud touch her and leave her, like suggestions and withdrawals of some bondage that might have been dear, now dismembering and losing itself. (*CS*, 440)

A part of this new freedom that Virgie feels is a result of putting her mother to rest, and with her the comparisons to her mother that Morganans always drew—Perdita Mayo tells Virgie as her mother's body is laid out, "Your mama was too fine for you, Virgie, too fine" (*CS*, 435)—as well as the duty to her mother's way of life. When the mourners leave the Rainey house before the funeral, Virgie feels that "They seemed to drag some *mythical* gates and barriers away from her view" (emphasis mine; *CS*, 438). The duty to Morgana's imperative of the womanly ideal has its basis in myth, and it is to these myths and imperatives that Virgie has not adhered, just as she did not adhere to the alternative available to her in the person and world of Miss Eckhart. The choices for Virgie have been grim: either conform—like her mother, cook, sew, (we learn in "The Wanderers" that Virgie, much to everyone's surprise, can do both), garden, marry—or become the monstrous woman and, like Miss Eckhart, follow passion, desire, art, and be ostracized, laughed at, crazy.

Virgie's choice between these two evils when she returns to Morgana after her first journey is to take on the domestic role, to rifle through a series of inappropriate candidates for marriage, and to hate Miss Eckhart. With her mother's death, Virgie is given a second chance, and she contemplates what this chance means as she sits gazing at Miss Eckhart's grave in the rain. In this meditative mode, she recalls Miss Eckhart's framing of Perseus holding Medusa's head. In the same instance, Virgie "shears it of its frame"—the pride of Miss Eckhart—and then focuses on one detail: "[I]t is the vaunting she remembered, that lifted arm." "Vaunting," from the Latin *vanitas,* means pride, arrogance. And it is at this moment, sitting in the rain, that Virgie allows an essential characteristic of herself to come to life: her modesty. Virgie realizes that there is a third choice for her—she doesn't have to be the prideful model of the "hero" artist that Miss Eckhart embodies, publicly defying all cultural mandates for women and turning herself into an outsider. Rather, Virgie can simply be herself, in her modesty, and can feel the dragon's blood just as palpably as did Miss Eckhart. Virgie, like her name, is on the verge of making her own way, neither conforming to the strictures of the closed domestic community of Morgana and of myth nor reversing the myth, and always being caught between roles of Perseus and Medusa, the hunter and the hunted.

In the final paragraph of "The Wanderers," Virgie has shed all of her ties to Morgana and her domestic duties; she remembers the "hideous and delectable face Mr. King MacLain had made at the funeral, and when they all knew he was next—even he" (*CS,* 461). Sitting down next to the old beggar woman underneath the shelter of "the big public tree," Virgie is free, free of things, free of the associations that objects have with them, and free of the legacy of King MacLain, the legacy of male power and privilege. Virgie and the beggar woman are free of all mental as well as physical baggage, and their imaginations run free together: "They head through falling rain the running of the horse and bear, the stroke of the leopard, the dragon's crusty slither, and the glimmer and the trumpet of the swan" (*CS,* 461). All of these animals are stock mythic characters, and they, too, have been set free from their entanglements in old, male myths. We are left to see that it will be Virgie, and the black beggar woman, who will make new myths.

We finish *The Golden Apples* on the verge. Welty has explored in this work the central myths about women that shaped her generation's expectations of what women should do. These myths dictated that women should be passive, beautiful objects of male vision. They tell us: Like Eve, a woman should shoulder the guilt for the fall of mankind. Like Yeats's "glimmering girl," a woman should be a beautiful, elusive, but pure object of male sexual desire. And like Medusa, if a woman should become aggressive, should step outside of her social role, then "the whole world knows" that she should be censured. As a woman and a writer, Welty cannot endorse these myths without destroying the artistic part of herself. Realistically, neither can she change the world in which she lives. The compromise that visionary writers such as Welty can strike is one of creating a fictional world as a laboratory of change. Welty creates a world that begins with her own world, and then creates a world in which she would like to live.

She says in *One Writer's Beginnings* that of all her characters, she feels closest to Miss Eckhart:

> [A]t last I realized that Miss Eckhart came from me. . . . What I have put into her is my passion for my own life work, my own art. Exposing yourself to risk is a truth Miss Eckhart and I had in common. What animates and possesses me is what drives Miss Eckhart, the love of her art and the love of giving it, the desire to give it until there is no more left. Even in the small and literal way, what I had done in assembling and connecting all the stories in *The Golden Apples*, and bringing them off as one, was not too unlike the June recital itself. (*OWB*, 101)

But Virgie represents the hope for real change. Welty identifies with Miss Eckhart, but she writes Virgie's story. We do not see what happens to Virgie—or to Loch, or to Easter—because the future is left up to us.

Notes to Part 1

1. All quotations from *One Writer's Beginnings* are from the first edition (Cambridge: Harvard University Press, 1984) and will be hereafter cited in the text as *OWB*. Excerpts from *One Writer's Beginnings* are reprinted in the third part of this volume.

2. Nicholas Dawidoff, "Only the Typewriter Is Silent," *New York Times* (10 August 1995): C1 and C10.

3. Essays by Porter, Warren, and Oates are reprinted in part 3 of this volume. See also Reynolds Price, "The Collected Stories of Eudora Welty," New

Republic 183 (1 November 1980): 31–34; Anne Tyler, "A Visit With Eudora Welty," *New York Times Book Review* (2 November 1980): 33–4.

4. Warren was responding in this essay to a negative and wrongheaded review by Diana Trilling. Originally published in the *Kenyon Review* 6 (Spring 1944): 446–59; Warren's essay has been reprinted many times. I cite from *Critical Essays on Eudora Welty,* ed. W. Craig Turner and Lee Emling Harding (Boston: G. K. Hall, 1989), 42–51.

5. Ruth M. Vande Kieft, *Eudora Welty,* rev. ed. (Boston: G. K. Hall, 1991).

6. Vande Kieft, "Eudora Welty: The Question of Meaning," *The Southern Quarterly* 20 (Summer 1982): 24–39.

7. Louise Westling, "The Loving Observer of *One Time, One Place,*" in *Welty: A Life in Literature,* ed. Albert J. Devlin (Jackson, University Press of Mississippi), 168–87.

8. Victor H. Thompson, *Eudora Welty: A Reference Guide* (Boston: G. K. Hall, 1976).

9. Warren French, " 'All Things Are Double': Eudora Welty as a Civilized Writer," in *Eudora Welty: Critical Essays,* ed. Peggy Whitman Prenshaw (Jackson: University Press of Mississippi, 1979), 179–88; rpt. *Eudora Welty: Thirteen Essays Selected from Eudora Welty: Critical Essays,* ed. Peggy Whitman Prenshaw (Jackson: University Press of Mississippi, 1983), 3–25.

10. French continues in this essay to give a valuable reading of *The Robber Bridegroom,* placing it in an American tradition of such works as F. Scott Fitzgerald's *The Great Gatsby,* William Faulkner's "The Bear," and Stephen Crane's "The Bride Comes to Yellow Sky" and finding an English predecessor in John Gay's eighteenth-century play *The Beggar's Opera.* I find French's use of Gay unconvincing; if he needs an English antecedent, why not Shakespeare? Welty certainly knows her Shakespeare, but it isn't at all clear that she knows her John Gay. Lear's speech to Gloucester about the imperceptible differences between judges and criminals, as well as Hal's shift in the *Henriad* from robber to king, seem more in line with the story Welty fashions about the imperceptible differences between the robber and his respectable life as a merchant.

11. Noel Polk, "Water, Wanderers, and Weddings: Love in Eudora Welty," in *Eudora Welty: A Form of Thanks,* ed. Lois Dollarhide and Ann J. Abadie (Jackson: University Press of Mississippi, 1979), 95–122.

12. Ruth Weston's recent *Gothic Traditions and Narrative Techniques in the Fiction of Eudora Welty* (Baton Rouge: Louisiana State University Press, 1994) again takes up the question of Welty and the gothic and argues that Welty's "connection to the Gothic tradition is far from tenuous" and connects the "mystery and magic" of Welty's work to a "core of gothic (lower case) materials—plots, settings, characters, image patterns, and vocabulary" (1–2).

13. Louise Bogan, "The Gothic South," *Nation* 153 (6 December 1941): 572.

14. "New Writer," *Time* (24 November 1941): 110–11.

15. Diana Trilling, "Fiction in Review," *Nation* (2 October 1943): 386–87.

16. Diana Trilling, "Fiction in Review," *Nation* (11 May 1946): 578.

17. Whitney Balliett, "Making the Jump," *New Yorker* (5 January 1981): 89.

18. Reynolds Price, "The Collected Stories of Eudora Welty," *New Republic* 183 (1 November 1980): 31–34. The full text of Price's review is reprinted in part 3 of this book.

19. Patricia S. Yaeger, " 'Because a Fire Was in My Head': Eudora Welty and the Dialogic Imagination," *PMLA* 99 (1984): 955–73. (Rpt. in Devlin, *A Life,* 139–67. Rev. and rpt. in *Mississippi Quarterly* 39.4 [1986]: 561–86). This essay is reprinted in part 3 of this book. Yaeger has also applied Lacan's psychoanalytic theories and Habermas's ideas about political power to Welty's work, helping to center it within contemporary critical issues and methods. See her "Case of the Dangling Signifier: Phallic Imagery in Eudora Welty's 'Moon Lake,' " *Twentieth Century Literature* 28 (Winter 1982): 431–52.

20. Peter Schmidt, *The Heart of the Story: Eudora Welty's Short Fiction* (Jackson: University Press of Mississippi, 1991).

21. Rebecca Mark, *The Dragon's Blood: Feminist Intertextuality in Eudora Welty's "The Golden Apples"* (Jackson: University Press of Mississippi, 1994). I offer in this brief survey only representative theoretical studies of the short fiction. Other studies bring Welty criticism into a contemporary mode while addressing Welty's novels along with the short fiction. For example, Gail Mortimer's guiding critical principle in *The Daughter of the Swan: Love and Knowledge in Eudora Welty's Fiction* (Athens: University of Georgia Press, 1994) is Nancy Chodorow's psychoanalytic object-relations theory, which she uses most directly to examine Welty's "love and separateness" dichotomy.

22. A selection of Welty's letters to her literary agent, Diarmuid Russell, is reproduced in Michael Kreyling, *Author and Agent* (New York: Farrar, Straus and Giroux, 1991). These letters primarily concern her early attempts to publish her stories, and the pressure she felt to write a longer, more mainstream work.

23. Welty's "Where Is the Voice Coming From?" is an interesting exception to this general rule; Welty talks about the story (in the preface to her *Collected Stories* and elsewhere) taking its generation from the murder of the civil rights activist Medgar Evers: "I wrote the [murderer's] story—my fiction—in the first person: about that character's point of view, I felt, through my shock and revolt, I could make no mistake" (preface, xi).

24. Eudora Welty, *The Collected Stories of Eudora Welty* (New York: Harcourt Brace Jovanovich, 1980); hereafter noted in the text as *CS*.

25. Suzanne Marrs's essay on Welty's photographs and photography in her *Welty Collection* (Jackson: University Press of Mississippi, 1988) details the various models of cameras that Welty used from graduate school until 1950. Marrs's bibliography of Welty also describes all of her negatives housed in the Mississippi State Archives. Excellent theoretical discussion of the art of photography appears in *Thinking Photography,* ed. Victor Burgin (London: Macmillan, 1982);

The Language of Images, ed. W. J. T. Mitchell (Chicago: University of Chicago Press, 1980); Roland Barthes's *Camera Lucida,* trans. Richard Howard (New York: Hill and Wang, 1981); and *Image-Music-Text,* trans. Steven Heath (New York: Hill and Wang, 1977).

26. The critical response to this story has overwhelmingly been just the opposite of what I argue about Ruby Fisher; readers concentrate on her as being weak and trapped in a "no exit" situation. I believe that her powers of imagination have been awakened by the news story. Welty's use of nature to signal emotional change is almost a signature of her style; here, crossing the bridge is a powerful emotional indicator. I argue further about Ruby's strength when I discuss in the following chapter the embedded myth of Eve in paradise. Patricia Yaeger, in her *Honey Mad Women* (New York: Columbia University Press, 1988), makes brief mention of Welty, and in that mention offers a reading of Ruby's empowerment against the dominant discourse; Dawn Trouard takes Yeager's reading and expands on it in her essay "Diverting Swine: The Magical Relevances of Eudora Welty's Ruby Fisher and Circe," in *The Critical Response to Eudora Welty's Fiction,* ed. Laurie Champion (Westport: Greenwood Press, 1994), 335–55.

27. Katherine Anne Porter, "Eudora Welty and *A Curtain of Green,* in *The Collected Essays and Occasional Writings of Katherine Anne Porter* (Boston: Houghton Mifflin, 1970), 284–90. This essay is reprinted in part 3 of this volume.

28. In Harry C. Morris, "Eudora Welty's Use of Mythology," *Shenandoah* 6 no. 2 (Spring 1955): 34–40. Morris also argues that Welty uses myth as a "movement toward structural control," though he does not offer compelling evidence to support this point. Danièle Pitavy-Souques discusses myth as structure in her "Technique as Myth: The Structure of *The Golden Apples,*" in *Eudora Welty: Critical Essays,* ed. Peggy Whitman Prenshaw (Jackson: University Press of Mississippi, 1979), 258–268; rpt. *Eudora Welty: Thirteen Essays Selected from Eudora Welty: Critical Essays,* ed. Peggy Whitman Prenshaw (Jackson: University Press of Mississippi, 1983), 146–56.

29. The French critic Julia Kristeva comes to a similar understanding of how writers use other texts with her term "intertextuality." Intertextuality offers critics a new way of viewing their relationship between texts and their predecessors. Arguing that texts are not closed, exclusive systems but rather depositories of various cultural signs and as well as of other texts, Kristeva suggests that intertextuality includes not only citations and references acknowledged by the author but also includes covert citations as well as the more slippery assimilation of features from earlier texts and textual participation in a common stock of conventions and codes of which the author may be unaware.

30. Rich, Adrienne. *On Lies, Secrets, and Silence* (New York: W. W. Norton & Co., 1979).

31. Alicia Suskin Ostriker, "Thieves of Language: Women Poets and Revisionist Mythology," in *Stealing the Language* (Boston: Beacon Press, 1986), 210–38.

32. As I have said, Welty does not want her work to be categorized with any political agenda, specifically a feminist agenda. When asked in a 1970 survey what she thought of "women's liberation," Welty gave a one-word answer: "Noisiness" (*Con,* 39).

33. Laurel Hand, the principal character in Welty's autobiographical novel *The Optimist's Daughter,* finds such a notebook as she goes through her mother's desk. Her response: to burn it. Welty describes this action quite simply: "She [Laurel] burned Milton's Universe" (p. 169). This is certainly one way to get rid of the myths casting women into weak or unflattering roles. The implication of Laurel's burning this notebook is usually read as her way of setting herself straight with her past and her personal history. (Peggy Whitman Prenshaw argues, for example, that "Laurel confronts the inevitable dilemma manifest in her early lessons: she must maintain her ties to the past, and yet she must constantly struggle to free herself sufficiently to create a separate self." See Peggy Whitman Prenshaw, "Southern Ladies and the Southern Literary Renaissance," in *The Female Tradition in Southern Literature,* ed. Carol S. Manning (Chicago: 1993), 87). It is that, certainly, since Laurel no longer lives in the South but in Chicago, and is a widower and has a career in fabric design. She is, in other words, far outside of her mother's southern world—"Milton's Universe"—which consisted of taking care of her husband and performing various domestic duties. Since the novel is autobiographical, written after the lengthy illness resulting in the death of Welty's mother, I think that we have to consider Laurel's burning the notebook that contained her mother's defining myth as deeply symbolic of Welty's laying to rest one of the defining myths of her mother's culture.

34. For further discussion see Christine Fruola, "When Eve Reads Milton: Undoing the Canonical Economy," in *Critical Inquiry* 10 (December 1983): 321–47. All quotations from *Paradise Lost* are from *John Milton: Complete Poems and Major Prose,* ed. Merritt Y. Hughes (Indianapolis: Bobbs-Merrill, 1957).

35. For those without ready access to a copy of *Paradise Lost,* I quote here the text:

> That day I oft remember, when from sleep
> I first awak't, and found myself repos'd
> Under a shade on flow'rs, much wond'ring where
> And what I was, whence thither brought, and how.
> Not distant far from thence a murmuring sound
> Of waters issu'd from a Cave and spread
> Into a liquid Plain, then stood unmov'd
> Pure as th' expanse of Heav'n; I thither went
> With unexperienc't thought, and laid me down
> On the green bank, to look into the clear
> Smooth Lake, that to me seem'd another Sky.
> As I bent down to look, just opposite,

A Shape within the wat'ry gleam appear'd
Bending to look on me, I started back,
It started back, but pleas'd I soon return'd,
Pleas'd it return'd as soon with answering looks
Of sympathy and love; there I had fixt
Mine eyes till now, and pin'd with vain desire,

. . . .

Till I espie'd thee [Adam], fair indeed and tall,
Under a Platan, yet methought less fair,
Less winning soft, less amiably mild,
Than that smooth wat'ry image; back I turn'd,
Thou following cri'd'st aloud, Return fair *Eve,*
Whom fli'st thou? whom thou fli'st, of him thou art,
His flesh, his bone; to give thee being I lent
Out of my side to thee, nearest my heart
Substantial Life, to have thee by my side
Henceforth an individual solace dear;
Part of my Soul I seek thee, and thee claim
My other half; with that thy gentle hand
Seiz'd mine, I yielded, and from that time see
How beauty is excell'd by manly grace
And wisdom, which alone is truly fair. (*PL,* 4.449–66; 477–91)

36. The rather simplistic scenario of her own death that Ruby imagines does not, however, show a powerful imagination at work; the scene is melodramatic. Yet the understated way in which the plot unrolls in Welty's narrative shows that Ruby has not been trapped inside the house with Clyde, as her timorous nature suggests; she is not physically as marginalized as one might expect a young married woman on a farm to be. The story opens as Ruby comes in, alone, from outdoors. Gradually we learn that the newspaper that is the vehicle of her self-discovery comes from her paramour, a coffee salesman whom she sneaks out to see during the day while Clyde tends his still. This mode of physical escape, though, is unsatisfactory; it is the device of a child running away from home. Clyde apparently spanks her each time he catches her; in the final scene "[h]e spank[s] her good-humoredly across her back side" (*CS,* 16). Clearly, Clyde's fatherly patronizing of Ruby will now need to address the more complex manner of her running away in the form of an interior narrative that Ruby constructs as her imagination and self-knowledge become more well-developed.

37. Most readers connect Clytie's experience with the mythic story of Narcissus, who worships his image in a reflective pool to such a degree that as punishment he is turned into a flower—a narcissus—that always grows next to water. This myth is what inspires Milton's version of Eve gazing into the pool,

so even though Clytie's story is Welty's version of the results of women's lack of self-knowledge, we could say that it is linked through Milton to Narcissus.

38. In Greek mythology, Clytie, originally a sea nymph, daughter of Oceanus (god of water), is changed into the plant *heliotropium,* a kind of flower that must always turn its head toward the sun, the traditional symbol of masculinity.

39. In Greek mythology, Comus is the son of Circe and Bacchus, and behaves accordingly. Milton's short play *Comus,* or *A Masque,* turns this mythological figure into a drunken seducer who lurks in the forest and tries to violate chaste young girls. Welty's Comus is habitually drunk, and he eventually takes a drunken stumble down a flight of stairs and dies. Welty seems to be having a bit of fun with the parallels to Milton's character.

40. Ruth Vande Kieft first argues that Welty's use of Yeats's poem creates a framework for *The Golden Apples* in her *Eudora Welty.* Franklin Carson adds to Vande Kieft's catalog of Welty's allusions to the poem in his " 'Song of Wandering Aengus': Allusions in Eudora Welty's *The Golden Apples,*" *Notes on Mississippi Writers* 6 no. 1 (Spring 1973): 14–17. Patricia Yaeger offers a reading of "The Song of Wandering Aengus" as one of the many dialogic voices in Welty's *The Golden Apples.* See Yaeger's essay in part 3 of this volume.

41. My discussion of Yeats and Welty owes much to Patricia Yaeger's " 'Because a Fire Was in My Head': Eudora Welty and the Dialogic Imagination;" reprinted in part 3 of this volume. I do part ways with Yaeger on several important issues, however, among them my conviction that Mattie Will's rape by King is as "real" an event in the story as the other episodes there.

42. Peter Schmidt discusses at length three passages in Welty's stories that contain references to sibyls: one from "Powerhouse," this one from "Music from Spain," and one in "The Wanderers." He argues that "The three quotations are points of descriptive excess or rupture in Welty's tales, points where the violence and strangeness of the tropes contrast strikingly with the language used before and after these passages." See Peter Schmidt, "Sibyls in Eudora Welty's Stories," in Trouard, p. 79. He discusses Welty's sibyls as symbols of the dominance of an oral, "female" text over the written male text. The sibyl has multiple and various representations in mythology, several of which Schmidt elides. It seems to me that Schmidt narrows the sibyl too radically in his reading, in the process oversignifying Welty's use of the myth.

Part 2

THE WRITER

Introduction

The language that Eudora Welty uses to describe her writing has remained consistent throughout her career. In the following three pieces, Welty discusses writing and her writing life in the familiar terms of family, place, and vision. Her conversation with critic Hermione Lee reveals the strength Welty gained from the sheltering love of her family, coupled with the guilt that she felt for breaking away from that family in order to find her independence as an artist. Love and guilt, as she tells us in *One Writer's Beginnings,* are "two of the springs, one bright, one dark, that feed the stream" of her stories (*OWB,* 20).

In the excerpt printed here from *One Writer's Beginnings* (1984), Welty describes the importance of the books her mother read to her as a child and that she read when she taught herself how to read before starting school. From the feel of the spoken word in the mouth as well as the visual representation of the word on the page, Welty tells us, she experienced a palpable sense of the word from earliest childhood: the word "moon" like a grape crushed against her palate, "held in [her] mouth . . . became a word." Her father's love of instruments—such as the telescope that brought the moon closer to Welty's eye, as well as the clock and the camera—developed in Welty two aptitudes that the fiction writer must have, an observing eye and a strong sense of time: "[A]ll of [my family] have been time-minded all of our lives. This was good. . . . For a future fiction writer, being able to learn so penetratingly, and almost first of all, about chronology" (*OWB,* 3). Love of words, highly attuned visual and temporal sensibilities, all legacies from Welty's attentive family.

In the third essay printed here, "Place in Fiction" (1956), Welty emphasizes the importance of a writer's region as a point of departure for her work. As she does with her family, Welty credits the richness of her region for offering her stability. More important, however, place gives not only the "validity" of the "raw materials of writing"—such tools as characters to develop and landscapes to describe—but a point of view: she tells us that "It is by knowing where you stand that you grow able to judge where you are" (*Eye,* 128). Even while ostensibly explaining how a sense of place informs the writing process, Welty cannot resist the urge to use visual metaphors; here, she speaks of framing, focus, and perspective as tools that the writer uses to clarify and communicate her vision. As I have shown, and as she indicates in this essay, visual techniques dictate the way that Welty constructs her narrative. While there is a consistency in Welty's discussion of her writing life, these selections also show that Welty's description of her work and of the people and places she believes make her work possible is rich and various.

Interview with Hermione Lee

E.W. I never in my wildest dreams thought I would write anything autobiographical. Of course, many things in my life were used in the stories, but they were very much transformed. I never expected to write about my mother, or anything like that. The unhappy fact is that usually by the time you're ready to think about your parents they're gone, and can't tell you anything. That happened with both my parents. But I'm awfully glad I did do this book [*One Writer's Beginnings*], because it made me explicitly know what I owed things to.

H.L. Was it a difficult book to write?

E.W. It was difficult mostly because it was a matter of choice. So many things crowded in—maybe to make the same point, and I was trying to use the one detail that would convey it in the most direct way. I think in terms of fiction, and it's awfully hard for me to think in terms of nonfiction, the explanatory. I tried to be selective, just to tell the things that I thought contributed to my being a writer. That's what I'd been asked to do. I threw away lots more stuff than is in there, other things that I thought best left out.

H.L. But there are certain things that obviously keep coming back to haunt you, like your grandmother coming in with her hands cold because she's been out breaking the ice . . .

E.W. Oh—my mother told me that again and again. She would put her own hands in front of her and say, "Her hands, she had such beautiful white hands, they were all bleeding from the ice on the well!"

H.L. You say in *One Writer's Beginnings* that you had a sheltered life, and that your mother and father were equally supportive of your wanting to become a writer, but in very different ways.

E.W. Very different ways. For a while I thought my father couldn't be supporting me because—oh, he was against fiction, because he thought

From *Writing Lives* (Virago, 1988, pp. 250–59). Reprinted with permission from Hermione Lee.

it wasn't true. He said, it's not the truth about life. And he thought I might be wasting my time, because he thought I was going to write the sort of things that came out in the *Saturday Evening Post,* and if I *didn't* write those things I couldn't earn a living. We never really talked about the kind of things I did want to write. I couldn't have done that, with either one of my parents, with anybody. And how did I know what I *could* do? But he did support me. All he wanted to do was to make sure that I could survive, make my living. And that was good advice. I was rather scornful at the time—"Live for art," you know.

H.L. He never said, "Don't do it"?

E.W. No, he never did. But when I was growing up there wasn't much a woman could do to make a living, except teach, or else go into a business office as a stenographer or something low down the scale. I knew I couldn't teach, so I decided to go into business, and he was all for that. He sent me to a business graduate school in Columbia, and that was wonderful, it gave me a year in New York. I went to the theatre every night. Almost no work, it was so easy. Anybody could do it.

H.L. Later on, did you show your mother things that you were writing?

E.W. Yes, but I never could show them to anyone until after I had sent them away, because I was too fearful of having them treated as a school paper—"I think that's awfully good, dear," you know. I wanted a professional, objective answer, so I would send them to magazines, and that way I could learn what professional editors thought. If they sent it back I took that as a proper judgement, as indeed it was. If they praised me I was elated, and only after that would I show them to my mother, or friends.

H.L. And did you feel that she understood what you were doing?

E.W. I think she did. I know she tried with all her generous imagination. She was very proud of my work, because she was a *reader.* She loved the written word.

H.L. Many of your stories and novels have very powerful women in them, strong matriarchs.

E.W. Yes, they do. But my mother wasn't really like that, except she was a very powerful schoolteacher. I'm a first-generation Mississippian and though my mother was Southern in her origins and birth—Virginia and West Virginia—she didn't come out of plantation life. Those were the real matriarchies, which sprang out of the South during and after the Civil War years. I don't know that first hand, but I've read it and seen the results down the generations, where the sexes seem to me really divided, with the men galloping around outside and the women running everything.

H.L. You say your mother was a powerful schoolteacher, and you've written about the importance of these women schoolteachers in the South. They come into your fiction a lot.

E.W. Oh, they played such a large part. Because of the poverty in the South, the teachers were dedicated people. They never made any money, they were people who gave their lives to it, like the new women who went into colleges in the Middle West. After the Civil War, when all the schools had been burned and the land was levelled and everything had to start over and there was no money, the churches had to try to raise the money for schools. That's why there are so many church-supported, small private colleges in the South still. It was the immediate need for education, and they were doing it the best way they could. Where my mother came from, in the mountains of West Virginia, there wasn't any money at all in teaching. I remember she told me she was paid 'thirty silver dollars' in salary for the first month she taught there, and she never was paid again. And just like in *Losing Battles*, she had to go across the river to teach. I told the real facts of that in this book [*One Writer's Beginnings*], how she went riding horseback over the mountain, with a little brother on the back to take the horse home, and would row herself across the river, and come back in the evening. And the little brother would meet her and ride home again. If you stayed the night you had to sleep with the family, with two or three children in the bed. They really were marvellous women . . . Of course the men were doing other things, they left the teaching to the women. But people who went to school with them almost never forget them. We had, if you can comprehend this, the fiftieth anniversary of my high school class—Jackson, Miss., Class of '25—and we all still remembered this Miss Duling who taught us in grade school. And some of our teachers were still alive. They remembered everything about us, and they would say, "Well, I never thought *you'd* amount to anything."

H.L. Do you think you had a good education?

E.W. Yes, I had a good basic education, because reading was respected, and writing too. We really had to learn those fundamental things.

H.L. You read a lot at home, from early on?

E.W. Yes, I did. Of course, you learn to read early when you want to. I went to school when I was five and I could read by then. I think that was common in those days.

H.L. Are there people that you read between the ages of say, twelve and sixteen, who still matter to you?

E.W. Oh yes, people like Mark Twain . . . Ring Lardner . . . the Brontës. Books I found in the house, and in the library. I didn't read, you know, Homer and all that lot, like people are supposed to. I always liked fiction. I'm not terribly well-read, I'm sure, I just always read for pleasure. Now, that counts Homer!

H.L. Was it difficult to move away from home? Did you feel a pull between wanting your independence and feeling guilty about the people who loved you?

E.W. Oh yes, I still feel it. It haunts me. I think about how I could have managed it better. And I realized later that both my parents must have felt exactly the same thing when they left home. My mother was especially torn. And distances were so far then. Communications were hard in those days unless you were rich. But daily letters travelled back and forth, and we always knew how each other was.

H.L. Did you know that in the end you were bound to come back to Jackson?

E.W. No, I didn't feel that. I wanted to, and I still do, regard it as a base, which helps me in writing. I feel it's some sort of touchstone. It's what I check up by, in the sense that I know it so well I don't have to wonder about whether I have got it right. Either I have to know everything about a place, so that I don't have to think, or else I must never have seen it before, so that I'm wide awake to everything as a stranger, and can write one thing out of what I see and feel, as I did once with a story about Ireland ["The Bride of the Innisfallen"]. I didn't know Ireland and I didn't mean to write a story about it, but it left an indelible impression on my mind.

H.L. Do you think it's especially true that Southern writers in America have to use the place they know as a base?

E.W. I feel that what is maybe kin to the Southerner is the New Englander, who has a sense of place. In urban life, that really isn't possible, in the way that I feel it, as a knowledge of seasons or changes or stability. Of course, the South now is full of people in motion, just like the rest of the country. But when I grew up it was so changeless that it was like a base you could touch and be sure you were accurate about something. But I think New Englanders and Southerners are alike in this, and it's odd how each had their flowering time in literature, New England first, and then the South in Faulkner's day.

H.L. Do you think you get your sense of narrative from the South?

E.W. I do feel that. Because of the pleasure that is taken in it in the South.

H.L. Is that a particularly female thing, do you think?

E.W. No. I think it's really more male. Women are supposed to be waiting on the men and bringing them food while they tell stories. That's the way it was in *Losing Battles*! And my mother's brothers in West Virginia were like that. They would gather and tell stories, and the women just kept bringing food so they'd keep talking and going on, and sometimes the women would scoff and say, "Oh now, don't tell it that way!" But mother loved it all.

H.L. But it's very often the women who tell the stories in your books.

E.W. Well, maybe what's according to my story wasn't quite true to life . . . I know when I was in William Faulkner's house a couple of times, I heard him and his cronies telling stories, and they were all men. But those would be the stories they would tell at hunting camp or out sailing. Or stories about crazy people in Oxford, Mississippi. Men know more stories, at least they did in those days, because they get out and live in the world more, and their stories are more adventurous and full of action. More to tell.

H.L. But it's women who make up the fabric of gossip, who know what's going on?

E.W. That's true—the gossip, the domestic kind . . . I think women tell their kind of story to women and men tell theirs to men. But when there's a reunion, and everybody comes together for an occasion, then the stories are mingled. Everyone's in one company, they tell them together. It's like a set of voices joining one after the other, sometimes. I made this seem like a chorus in *Losing Battles*, to give the crowd effect.

Part 2

Story-telling is *part* of life in the South, it's a social activity, always arising in family gatherings. Stories are told not to teach or learn from—everybody knows them already—but to participate in, to enjoy all over again. Their character is the thing. "Wasn't that exactly like Aunt Maggie?"

H.L. Do any of your stories come out of the photographs you took in the Depression years in Mississippi?

E.W. I am an observer, and I would notice the same thing, I would look for the same kind of thing, whether I was carrying a camera or just watching. But I didn't make up stories from my pictures. The odd thing is that some of the photographs turned out almost to illustrate stories that I wrote later on.

H.L. Did you ever find that it was a disadvantage to be a woman journalist in those days, travelling around Mississippi?

E.W. The only thing that annoyed me was that I was called junior publicity agent, and I was working with somebody called senior publicity agent, who was a man. We did exactly the same work, and of course he got a lot more money. I sort of wondered about that. But I was so happy to get a job that it didn't bother me any then. Otherwise, I never had difficulties. I would go into the poorest parts of the State, in the depths of the Depression, and I would say to people, a lot of them black people, "Do you mind if I take a picture?" and some of them would say, "Never had a picture taken in my life." And I'd say, "Just stay the way you are." They'd be in some wonderful pose, a woman on a porch, leaning forward from the hips, like this, her elbows on here and her hands crossed, with this wonderful curve of buttocks and legs, bare-footed on the porch. Beautiful woman. I would say, "Do you mind if I take your picture like that?" "No," she'd say, "if that's what you want to do, I don't care!" . . . It taught me so much, about coming upon people I didn't know and taking this minute of their lives. But I had to go on to fiction from photographing. That's the only way you can really part the veil between people, not in images but in what comes from inside, in both subject and writer.

H.L. When you started publishing your stories, I believe Katherine Anne Porter was very important to you?

E.W. She was indeed. I suppose Katherine Anne was the first living writer I'd ever seen. I published almost my first story in the *Southern*

Review, which was published by Louisiana State University Press and edited by Robert Penn Warren and Cleanth Brooks. Katherine Anne was living in Baton Rouge, and she was married to Albert Erskine, who was also on the *Southern Review*. She wrote me a letter and said that she thought my work was good, and would I like to come and see her. That petrified me. I thought, how *can* I go! It was a long time before I did it. I was really scared to go. But I did, and she was so supportive, as she was to many young writers. If it had not been for *her* work, we couldn't ever have published, because she had such a hard time winning her place as a writer. Indeed it took *me* six years to be published in a national magazine, and that would be about average.

H.L. Do you think that was partly because you were a woman?

E.W. I don't know. I never did think of that. I don't think it was that, I think it was the short story form.

H.L. Do you think the short story, as practised by Katherine Anne Porter, and Flannery O'Connor, and Elizabeth Bowen, and yourself—with a very vivid sense of place, and a lot of close detail, and a strong narrative voice—is a particularly female art form?

E.W. I just don't know. I suppose Mary Lavin would be another example of that kind of writing? But then there's Frank O'Connor and Sean O'Faolain, and they're not female. No, I can't express an opinion about that. But it sounds rather interesting.

H.L. Do you think of yourself as an objective writer?

E.W. That's what I try to be, but I know I'm not. In my work I try to be objective, and I can't really feel a story is finished until I can stand off from it and see it objectively. But in fact I'm sure I'm an absolutely exposed and naked writer. I mean in the way I feel and think about the world. I feel very exposed to it, and I've probably learned from that. But your work has to be objective.

H.L. But are you moved by your own writing?

E.W. I'm afraid I am! That is, there has to be some criterion of whether or not you brought it off. It has to meet that emotional test. You feel that only you yourself can judge it. Something tells me when I have not been objective enough, and I've got a story now that I won't let go for that reason. I know that it's not controlled enough.

H.L. Is there a moment when you know, when you can say to yourself, "I've got it"?

E.W. Yes. Or so I say.

H.L. And then you're completely confident?

E.W. Well—as near as you can be. I have a friend who's a writer—I won't tell you his name because he might not want me to, I mean it's his story, not mine. He kept all the versions of a story he'd written in a drawer, till he'd written about thirteen versions, and then he opened the drawer much later, and found that number seven was it. I think that's a wonderful lesson.

H.L. Do you revise a great deal?

E.W. Yes, I do.

H.L. And do you work quite slowly?

E.W. I revise very slowly, and I like to revise. I like to write the first draft quickly, to do it in one sitting if it were only possible, and I would like to write the last version all in one sitting. That's hard to do! But revision, I don't care how long it takes. I love it.

H.L. Do you think a writer's life is a lonely life?

E.W. No. I feel in touch. I like doing things, you know, privately. But I like to write with a window that looks out on to the street. I don't feel that I'm in a cell. Some people like that feeling—to be a monk or a nun or something. But I like to be part of my world. No, writing is solitary. But I don't feel lonely.

Hermione Lee teaches English at the University of York and reviews books for the Observer. *Her published works include* The Mulberry Tree: Selected Writings of Elizabeth Bowen *(Virago, 1986) and introductions to* Bowen's Court *(Virago, 1984) and Willa Cather's* Sapphira and the Slave Girl *and* One of Ours *(Virago, 1987), as well as books on Elizabeth Bowen, Virginia Woolf and Philip Roth, and two anthologies of short stories by women,* The Secret Self 1 & 2.

From *One Writer's Beginnings*

In our house on North Congress Street in Jackson, Mississippi, where I was born, the oldest of three children, in 1909, we grew up to the striking of clocks. There was a mission-style oak grandfather clock standing in the hall, which sent its gong-like strokes through the livingroom, diningroom, kitchen, and pantry, and up the sounding board of the stairwell. Through the night, it could find its way into our ears; sometimes, even on the sleeping porch, midnight could wake us up. My parents' bedroom had a smaller striking clock that answered it. Though the kitchen clock did nothing but show the time, the diningroom clock was a cuckoo clock with weights on long chains, on one of which my baby brother, after climbing on a chair to the top of the china closet, once succeeded in suspending the cat for a moment. I don't know whether or not my father's Ohio family, in having been Swiss back in the 1700s before the first three Welty brothers came to America, had anything to do with this; but we all of us have been time-minded all our lives. This was good at least for a future fiction writer, being able to learn so penetratingly, and almost first of all, about chronology. It was one of a good many things I learned almost without knowing it; it would be there when I needed it.

My father loved all instruments that would instruct and fascinate. His place to keep things was the drawer in the "library table" where lying on top of his folded maps was a telescope with brass extensions, to find the moon and the Big Dipper after supper in our front yard, and to keep appointments with eclipses. There was a folding Kodak that was brought out for Christmas, birthdays, and trips. In the back of the drawer you could find a magnifying glass, a kaleidoscope, and a gyroscope kept in a black buckram box, which he would set dancing for us on a string pulled tight. He had also supplied himself with an assortment of puzzles composed of metal rings and intersecting links and keys chained together, impossible for the rest of us, however patiently shown, to take apart; he had an almost childlike love of the ingenious.

In time, a barometer was added to our diningroom wall; but we didn't really need it. My father had the country boy's accurate knowledge of the weather and its skies. He went out and stood on our front steps first thing in the morning and took a look at it and a sniff. He was a pretty good weather prophet.

"Well, I'm *not,*" my mother would say with enormous self-satisfaction.

He told us children what to do if we were lost in a strange country. "Look for where the sky is brightest along the horizon," he said. "That reflects the nearest river. Strike out for a river and you will find habitation." Eventualities were much on his mind. In his care for us children he cautioned us to take measures against such things as being struck by lightning. He drew us all away from the windows during the severe electrical storms that are common where we live. My mother stood apart, scoffing at caution as a character failing. "Why, I always loved a storm! High winds never bothered me in West Virginia! Just listen at that! I wasn't a bit afraid of a little lightning and thunder! I'd go out on the mountain and spread my arms wide and *run* in a good big storm!"

So I developed a strong meteorological sensibility. In years ahead when I wrote stories, atmosphere took its influential role from the start. Commotion in the weather and the inner feelings aroused by such a hovering disturbance emerged connected in dramatic form. (I tried a tornado first, in a story called "The Winds.")

I learned from the age of two or three that any room in our house, at any time of day, was there to read in, or to be read to. My mother read to me. She'd read to me in the big bedroom in the mornings, when we were in her rocker together, which ticked in rhythm as we rocked, as though we had a cricket accompanying the story. She'd read to me in the diningroom on winter afternoons in front of the coal fire, with our cuckoo clock ending the story with "Cuckoo," and at night when I'd got in my own bed. I must have given her no peace. Sometimes she read to me in the kitchen while she sat churning, and the churning sobbed along with *any* story. It was my ambition to have her read to me while *I* churned; once she granted my wish, but she read off my story before I brought her butter. She was an expressive reader. When she was reading "Puss in Boots," for instance, it was impossible not to know that she distrusted *all* cats.

It had been startling and disappointing to me to find out that story books had been written by *people,* that books were not natural wonders, coming up of themselves like grass. Yet regardless of where they came from, I cannot remember a time when I was not in love with them—

with the books themselves, cover and binding and the paper they were printed on, with their smell and their weight and with their possession in my arms, captured and carried off to myself. Still illiterate, I was ready for them, committed to all the reading I could give them.

I live in gratitude to my parents for initiating me—and as early as I begged for it, without keeping me waiting—into knowledge of the word, into reading and spelling, by way of the alphabet. They taught it to me at home in time for me to begin to read before starting to school. I believe the alphabet is no longer considered an essential piece of equipment for traveling through life. In my day it was the keystone to knowledge. You learned the alphabet as you learned to count to ten, as you learned "Now I lay me" and the Lord's Prayer and your father's and mother's name and address and telephone number, all in case you were lost.

My love for the alphabet, which endures, grew out of reciting it but, before that, out of seeing the letters on the page. In my own story books, before I could read them for myself, I fell in love with various winding, enchanted-looking initials drawn by Walter Crane at the heads of fairy tales. In "Once upon a time," an "O" had a rabbit running it as a treadmill, his feet upon flowers. When the day came, years later, for me to see the Book of Kells, all the wizardry of letter, initial, and word swept over me a thousand times over, and the illumination, the gold, seemed a part of the word's beauty and holiness that had been there from the start.

Learning stamps you with its moments. Childhood's learning is made up of moments. It isn't steady. It's a pulse.

In my sensory education I include my physical awareness of the *word.* Of a certain word, that is; the connection it has with what it stands for. At around age six, perhaps, I was standing by myself in our front yard waiting for supper, just at that hour in a late summer day when the sun is already below the horizon and the risen full moon in the visible sky stops being chalky and begins to take on light. There comes the moment, and I saw it then, when the moon goes from flat to round. For the first time it met my eyes as a globe. The word "moon" came into my mouth as though fed to me out of a silver spoon. Held in my mouth the moon became a word. It had the roundness of a Concord grape Grandpa took off his vine and gave me to suck out of its skin and swallow whole, in Ohio.

Ever since I was first read to, then started reading to myself, there has never been a line read that I didn't *hear.* As my eyes followed the sentence, a voice was saying it silently to me. It isn't my mother's voice, or the voice of any person I can identify, certainly not my own. It is human, but inward, and it is inwardly that I listen to it. It is to me the voice of the story or the poem itself. The cadence, whatever it is that asks you to believe, the feeling that resides in the printed word, reaches me through the reader-voice. I have supposed, but never found out, that this is the case with all readers—to read as listeners—and with all writers, to write as listeners. It may be part of the desire to write. The sound of what falls on the page begins the process of testing it for truth, for me. Whether I am right to trust so far I don't know. By now I don't know whether I could do either one, reading or writing, without the other.

My own words, when I am at work on a story, I hear too as they go, in the same voice that I hear when I read in books. When I write and the sound of it comes back to my ears, then I act to make my changes. I have always trusted this voice.

Long before I wrote stories, I listened for stories. Listening *for* them is something more acute than listening *to* them. I suppose it's an early form of participation in what goes on. Listening children know stories are *there.* When their elders sit and begin, children are just waiting and hoping for one to come out, like a mouse from its hole.

My instinct—the dramatic instinct—was to lead me, eventually, on the right track for a storyteller: the *scene* was full of hints, pointers, suggestions, and promises of things to find out and know about human beings. I had to grow up and learn to listen for the unspoken as well as the spoken—and to know a truth, I also had to recognize a lie.

I never dreamed I could learn as long as I was away from the schoolroom, and that bits of enlightenment far-reaching in my life went on as ever in their own good time. After they'd told me goodnight and tucked me in—although I knew that after I'd finally fallen asleep they'd pick me up and carry me away—my parents draped the lampshade with a sheet of the daily paper, which was tilted, like a hatbrim, so that they could sit in their rockers in a lighted part of the room and I could supposedly go to sleep in the protected dark of the bed. They sat talking. What was thus dramatically made a present of to me was the secure sense of the hidden observer. As long as I could make myself keep awake, I was free to listen to every word my parents said between them.

I suppose I was exercising as early as then the turn of mind, the nature of temperament, of a privileged observer; and owing to the way I became so, it turned out that I became the loving kind.

A conscious act grew out of this by the time I began to write stories: getting my distance, a prerequisite of my understanding of human events, is the way I begin work. Just as, of course, it was an initial step when, in my first journalism job, I stumbled into making pictures with a camera. Frame, proportion, perspective, the values of light and shade, all are determined by the distance of the observing eye.

I have always been shy physically. This in part tended to keep me from rushing into things, including relationships, headlong. Not rushing headlong, though I may have wanted to, but beginning to write stories about people, I drew near slowly; noting and guessing, apprehending, hoping, drawing my eventual conclusions out of my own heart, I *did* venture closer to where I wanted to go. As time and my imagination led me on, I did plunge.

The best college in the state was very possibly the private liberal-arts one right here in Jackson, but I was filled with desire to go somewhere away and enter a school I'd never passed on the street. My parents thought that I was too young at sixteen to live for my first year too far from home. Mississippi State College for Women was well enough accredited and two hundred miles to the north.

Mr. Lawrence Painter, the only man teacher in the college, spent his life conducting the MSCW girls in their sophomore year through English Survey, from "Summer is y-comen in" to "I have a rendezvous with Death." In my time a handsome, learned, sandy-haired man—wildly popular, of course, on campus—he got instant silence when he would throw open the book and begin to read aloud to us.

In high-school freshman English, we had committed to memory "Whan that Aprille with his shoures soote . . ." which as poetry was not less remote to our ears than "Arma virumque cano . . ." I had come unprepared for the immediacy of poetry.

I felt the shock closest to this a year later at the University of Wisconsin when I walked into my art class and saw, in place of the bowl of fruit and the glass bottle and ginger jar of the still life I used to draw at MSCW, a live human being. As we sat at our easels, a model, a young woman, lightly dropped her robe and stood, before us and a little above us, holding herself perfectly contained, in her full self and naked. Often that year in Survey Course, as Mr. Painter read, poetry came into the room where we could see it and all around it, free-standing poetry. As we listened, Mr. Painter's, too, was a life class.

Part 2

After I transferred, in my junior year, to the University of Wisconsin, I made in this far, new place a discovery for myself that has fed my life ever since. I express a little of my experience in a story, one fairly recent and not yet completed. It's the story of a middle-aged man who'd come from a farm in the Middle West, who's taciturn and unhappy as a teacher of linguistics and now has reached a critical point in his life. The scene is New Orleans; he and a woman are walking at night (they are really saying goodbye) and he speaks of himself without reserve to her for the first time.

He'd put himself through the University of Wisconsin, he tells her:

> "And I happened to discover Yeats, reading through some of the stacks in the library. I read the early and then the later poems all in the same one afternoon, standing up, by the window . . . I read 'Sailing to Byzantium,' standing up in the stacks, read it by the light of falling snow. It seemed to me that if I could stir, if I could move to take the next step, I could go out into the poem the way I could go out into that snow. That it would be falling on my shoulders. That it would pelt me on its way down—that I could move in it, live in it—that I could die in it, maybe. So after that I had to *learn* it," he said. "And I told myself that I would. That I accepted the invitation."

The experience I describe in the story had indeed been my own, snow and all; the poem that smote me first was "The Song of Wandering Aengus"; it was the poem that turned up, fifteen years or so later, in my stories of *The Golden Apples* and runs all through that book.

At length too, at Wisconsin, I learned the word for the nature of what I had come upon in reading Yeats. Mr. Riccardo Quintana lecturing to his class on Swift and Donne used it in its true meaning and import. The word is *passion.*

My first full-time job was rewarding to me in a way I could never have foreseen in those early days of my writing. I went to work for the state office of the Works Progress Administration as junior publicity agent. (This was of course one of President Roosevelt's national measures to combat the Great Depression.) Traveling over the whole of Mississippi, writing news stories for county papers, taking pictures, I saw my home state at close hand, really for the first time.

With the accretion of years, the hundreds of photographs—life as I found it, all unposed—constitute a record of that desolate period; but most of what I learned for myself came right at the time and directly out of the *taking* of the pictures. The camera was a hand-held auxiliary of wanting-to-know.

It had more than information and accuracy to teach me. I learned in the doing how *ready* I had to be. Life doesn't hold still. A good snapshot stopped a moment from running away. Photography taught me that to be able to capture transience, by being ready to click the shutter at the crucial moment, was the greatest need I had. Making pictures of people in all sorts of situations, I learned that every feeling waits upon its gesture; and I had to be prepared to recognize this moment when I saw it. These were things a story writer needed to know. And I felt the need to hold transient life in *words*—there's so much more of life that only words can convey—strongly enough to last me as long as I lived. The direction my mind took was a writer's direction from the start, not a photographer's, or a recorder's.

My first good story began spontaneously, in a remark repeated to me by a traveling man—our neighbor—to whom it had been spoken while he was on a trip into North Mississippi: "He's gone to borry some fire." The words, which carried such lyrical and mythological and dramatic overtones, were real and actual—their hearer repeated them to me.

As usual, I began writing from a distance, but "Death of a Traveling Salesman" led me closer. It drew me toward what was at the center of it, to a cabin back in the red clay hills—perhaps just such a house as I used to see from far off on a train at night, with the firelight or lamplight showing yellow from its open doorway. In writing the story I approached and went inside with my traveling salesman, and had him, pressed by imminent death, figure out what was there:

> Bowman could not speak. He was shocked with knowing what was really in this house. A marriage, a fruitful marriage. That simple thing. Anyone could have had that.

Writing "Death of a Traveling Salesman" opened my eyes. And I had received the shock of having touched, for the first time, on my real subject: human relationships. Daydreaming had started me on the way; but story writing, once I was truly in its grip, took me and shook me awake.

My temperament and my instinct had told me alike that the author, who writes at his own emergency, remains and needs to remain at his private remove. I wished to be, not effaced, but invisible—actually a powerful position. Perspective, the line of vision, the frame of vision—these set a distance.

What discoveries I've made in the course of writing stories all begin with the particular, never the general. They are mostly hindsight: arrows that I now find I myself have left behind me, which have shown me some right, or wrong, way I have come. What one story may have pointed out to me is of no avail in the writing of another. But "avail" is not what I want; freedom ahead is what each story promises—beginning anew. And all the while, as further hindsight has told me, certain patterns in my work repeat themselves without my realizing. There would be no way to know this, for during the writing of any single story, there is no other existing. Each writer must find out for himself, I imagine, on what strange basis he lives with his own stories.

It is our inward journey that leads us through time—forward or back, seldom in a straight line, most often spiraling. Each of us is moving, changing, with respect to others. As we discover, we remember; remembering, we discover; and most intensely do we experience this when our separate journeys converge. Our living experience at those meeting points is one of the charged dramatic fields of fiction.

Place in Fiction

Place is one of the lesser angels that watch over the racing hand of fiction, perhaps the one that gazes benignly enough from off to one side, while others, like character, plot, symbolic meaning, and so on, are doing a good deal of wing-beating about her chair, and feeling, who in my eyes carries the crown, soars highest of them all and rightly relegates place into the shade. Nevertheless, it is this lowlier angel that concerns us here. There have been signs that she has been rather neglected of late; maybe she could do with a little petitioning.

What place has place in fiction? It might be thought so modest a one that it can be taken for granted: the location of a novel; to use a term of the day, it may make the novel "regional." The term, like most terms used to pin down a novel, means little; and Henry James said there isn't any difference between "the English novel" and "the American novel," since there are only two kinds of novels at all, the good and the bad. Of course Henry James didn't stop there, and we all hate generalities, and so does place. Yet as soon as we step down from the general view to the close and particular, as writers must and readers may and teachers well know how to, and consider what good writing may be, place can be seen, in her own way, to have a great deal to do with that goodness, if not to be responsible for it. How so?

First, with the goodness—validity—in the raw material of writing. Second, with the goodness in the writing itself—the achieved world of appearance, through which the novelist has his whole say and puts his whole case. There will still be the lady, always, who dismissed *The Ancient Mariner* on grounds of implausibility. Third, with the goodness—the worth—in the writer himself: place is where he has his roots, place is where he stands; in his experience out of which he writes, it provides the base of reference; in his work, the point of view. Let us consider place in fiction in these three wide aspects.

Wide, but of course connected—vitally so. And if in some present-day novels the connection has apparently slipped, that makes a fresh reason for us to ponder the subject of place. For novels, besides being the pleasantest things imaginable, are powerful forces on the side. Mutual understanding in the world being nearly always, as now, at low ebb, it is comforting to remember that it is through art that one country can nearly always speak reliably to another, if the other can hear at all. Art, though, is never the voice of a country; it is an even more precious thing, the voice of the individual, doing its best to speak, not comfort of any sort, indeed, but truth. And the art that speaks it most unmistakably, most directly, most variously, most fully, is fiction; in particular, the novel.

Why? Because the novel from the start has been bound up in the local, the "real," the present, the ordinary day-to-day of human experience. Where the imagination comes in is in directing the use of all this. That use is endless, and there are only four words, of all the millions we've hatched, that a novel rules out: "Once upon a time." They make a story a fairy tale by the simple sweep of the remove—by abolishing the present and the place where we are instead of conveying them to us. Of course we shall have some sort of fairy tale with us always—just now it is the historical novel. Fiction is properly at work on the here and now, or the past made here and now; for in novels *we* have to be there. Fiction provides the ideal texture through which the feeling and meaning that permeate our own personal, present lives will best show through. For in his theme—the most vital and important part of the work at hand—the novelist has the blessing of the inexhaustible subject: you and me. You and me, here. Inside that generous scope and circumference—who could ask for anything more?—the novel can accommodate practically anything on earth; and has abundantly done so. The novel so long as it be *alive* gives pleasure, and must always give pleasure, enough to stave off the departure of the Wedding Guest forever, except for that one lady.

It is by the nature of itself that fiction is all bound up in the local. The internal reason for that is surely that *feelings* are bound up in place. The human mind is a mass of associations—associations more poetic even than actual. I say, "The Yorkshire Moors," and you will say, "*Wuthering Heights,*" and I have only to murmur, "If Father were only alive—" for you to come back with "We could go to Moscow," which certainly is not even so. The truth is, fiction depends for its life on place. Location is the crossroads of circumstance, the proving ground of "What happened? Who's here? Who's coming?"—and that is the heart's field.

Unpredictable as the future of any art must be, one condition we may hazard about writing: of all the arts, it is the one least likely to cut the cord that binds it to its source. Music and dancing, while originating out of place—groves!—and perhaps invoking it still to minds pure or child-like, are no longer bound to dwell there. Sculpture exists out in empty space: that is what it commands and replies to. Toward painting, place, to be so highly visible, has had a curious and changing relationship. Indeed, wasn't it when landscape invaded painting, and painting was given, with the profane content, a narrative content, that this worked to bring on a revolution to the art? Impressionism brought not the likeness-to-life but the mystery of place onto canvas; it was the method, not the subject, that told this. Painting and writing, always the closest two of the sister arts (and in ancient Chinese days only the blink of an eye seems to have separated them), have each a still closer connection with place than they have with each other; but a difference lies in their respective requirements of it, and even further in the way they use it—the written word being ultimately as different from the pigment as the note of the scale is from the chisel.

One element, which has just been mentioned, is surely the underlying bond that connects all the arts with place. All of them celebrate its mystery. Where does this mystery lie? Is it in the fact that place has a more lasting identity than we have, and we unswervingly tend to attach ourselves to identity? Might the magic lie partly, too, in the *name* of the place—since that is what *we* gave it? Surely, once we have it named, we have put a kind of poetic claim on its existence; the claim works even out of sight—may work forever sight unseen. The Seven Wonders of the World still give us this poetic kind of gratification. And notice we do not say simply "The Hanging Gardens"—that would leave them dangling out of reach and dubious in nature; we say "The Hanging Gardens of Babylon," and there they are, before our eyes, shimmering and garlanded and exactly elevated to the Babylonian measurement.

Edward Lear tapped his unerring finger on the magic of place in the limerick. There's something unutterably convincing about that Old Person of Sparta who had twenty-five sons and one darta, and it is surely beyond question that he fed them on snails and weighed them in scales, because we know where that Old Person is *from*—Sparta! We certainly do not need further to be told his *name.* "Consider the source." Experience has ever advised us to base validity on point of origin.

Being shown how to locate, to place, any account is what does most toward *making* us believe it, not merely allowing us to, may the account be the facts or a lie; and that is where place in fiction comes in. Fiction is a lie. Never in its inside thoughts, always in its outside dress.

Some of us grew up with the china night-light, the little lamp whose lighting showed its secret and with that spread enchantment. The outside is painted with a scene, which is one thing; then, when the lamp is lighted, through the porcelain sides a new picture comes out through the old, and they are seen as one. A lamp I knew of was a view of London till it was lit; but then it was the Great Fire of London, and you could go beautifully to sleep by it. The lamp alight is the combination of internal and external, glowing at the imagination as one; and so is the good novel. Seeing that these inner and outer surfaces do lie so close together and so implicit in each other, the wonder is that human life so often separates them, or appears to, and it takes a good novel to put them back together.

The good novel should be steadily alight, revealing. Before it can hope to be that, it must of course be steadily visible from its outside, presenting a continuous, shapely, pleasing and finished surface to the eye.

The sense of a story when the visibility is only partial or intermittent is as endangered as Eliza crossing the ice. Forty hounds of confusion are after it, the black waters of disbelief open up between its steps, and no matter which way it jumps it is bound to slip. Even if it has a little baby moral in its arms, it is more than likely a goner.

The novel must get Eliza across the ice; what it means—the way it proceeds—is always in jeopardy. It must be given a surface that is continuous and unbroken, never too thin to trust, always in touch with the senses. Its world of experience must be at every step, through every moment, within reach as the world of appearance.

This makes it the business of writing, and the responsibility of the writer, to disentangle the significant—in character, incident, setting, mood, everything—from the random and meaningless and irrelevant that in real life surround and beset it. It is a matter of his selecting and, by all that implies, of changing "real" life as he goes. With each word he writes, he acts—as literally and methodically as if he hacked his way through a forest and blazed it for the word that follows. He makes choices at the explicit demand of this one present story; each choice implies, explains, limits the next, and illuminates the one before. No two stories ever go the same way, although in different hands one story might possibly go any one of a thousand ways; and though the woods may look the same from outside, it is a new and different labyrinth every time. What tells the author his way? Nothing at all but what he knows inside himself: the same thing that hints to him afterward how far he has missed it, how near he may have come to the heart of it. In a working sense, the novel and its place have become one: work has made them, for the time being, the same thing, like the explorer's tentative map of the known world.

The reason why every word you write in a good novel is a lie, then, is that it is written expressly to serve the purpose; if it does not apply, it is fancy and frivolous, however specially dear to the writer's heart. Actuality, it is true, is an even bigger risk to the novel than fancy writing is, being frequently even more confusing, irrelevant, diluted and generally far-fetched than ill-chosen words can make it. Yet somehow, the world of appearance in the novel has got to *seem* actuality. Is there a reliable solution to the problem? Place being brought to life in the round before the reader's eye is the readiest and gentlest and most honest and natural way this can be brought about, I think; every instinct advises it. The moment the place in which the novel happens is accepted as true, through it will begin to glow, in a kind of recognizable glory, the feeling and thought that inhabited the novel in the author's head and animated the whole of his work.

Besides furnishing a plausible abode for the novel's world of feeling, place has a good deal to do with making the characters real, that is, themselves, and keeping them so. The reason is simply that, as Tristram Shandy observed, "We are not made of glass, as characters on Mercury might be." Place *can* be transparent, or translucent: not people. In real life we have to express the things plainest and closest to our minds by the clumsy word and the half-finished gesture; the chances are our most usual behavior makes sense only in a kind of daily way, because it has become familiar to our nearest and dearest, and still demands their constant indulgence and understanding. It is our describable outside that defines us, willy-nilly, to others, that may save us, or destroy us, in the world; it may be our shield against chaos, our mask against exposure; but whatever it is, the move we make in the place we live has to signify our intent and meaning.

Then think how unprotected the poor character in a novel is, into whose mind the author is inviting us to look—unprotected and hence surely unbelievable! But no, the author has expressly seen to believability. Though he must know all, again he works with illusion. Just as the world of a novel is more highly selective than that of real life, so character in a novel is much more definite, less shadowy than our own, in order that we may believe in it. This is not to say that the character's scope must be limited; it is our vision of it that is guided. It is a kind of phenomenon of writing that the likeliest character has first to be enclosed inside the bounds of even greater likelihood, or he will fly to pieces. Paradoxically, the more narrowly we can examine a fictional character, the greater he is likely to loom up. We must see him set to scale in his proper world to know his size. Place, then, has the most delicate control over character too: by confining character, it defines it.

Place in fiction is the named, identified, concrete, exact and exacting, and therefore credible, gathering spot of all that has been felt, is about to be experienced, in the novel's progress. Location pertains to feeling; feeling profoundly pertains to place; place in history partakes of feeling, as feeling about history partakes of place. Every story would be another story, and unrecognizable as art, if it took up its characters and plot and happened somewhere else. Imagine *Swann's Way* laid in London, or *The Magic Mountain* in Spain, or *Green Mansions* in the Black Forest. The very notion of moving a novel brings ruder havoc to the mind and affections than would a century's alteration in its time. It is only too easy to conceive that a bomb that could destroy all trace of places as we know them, in life and through books, could also destroy all feelings as we know them, so irretrievably and so happily are recognition, memory, history, valor, love, all the instincts of poetry and praise, worship and endeavor, bound up in place. From the dawn of man's imagination, place has enshrined the spirit; as soon as man stopped wandering and stood still and looked about him, he found a god in that place; and from then on, that was where the god abided and spoke from if ever he spoke.

Feelings are bound up in place, and in art, from time to time, place undoubtedly works upon genius. Can anyone well explain otherwise what makes a given dot on the map come passionately alive, for good and all, in a novel—like one of those novae that suddenly blaze with inexplicable fire in the heavens? What brought a *Wuthering Heights* out of Yorkshire, or a *Sound and the Fury* out of Mississippi?

If place does work upon genius, how does it? It may be that place can focus the gigantic, voracious eye of genius and bring its gaze to point. Focus then means awareness, discernment, order, clarity, insight—they are like the attributes of love. The act of focusing itself has beauty and meaning; it is the act that, continued in, turns into mediation, into poetry. Indeed, as soon as the least of us stands still, that is the moment something extraordinary is seen to be going on in the world. The drama, old beyond count as it is, is no older than the first stage. Without the amphitheatre around it to persuade the ear and bend the eye upon a point, how could poetry ever have been spoken, how have been heard? Man is articulate and intelligible only when he begins to communicate inside the strict terms of poetry and reason. Symbols in the end, both are permanent forms of the act of focusing.

Surely place induces poetry, and when the poet is extremely attentive to what is there, a meaning may even attach to his poem out of the spot on earth where it is spoken, and the poem signify the more because it does spring so wholly out of its place, and the sap has run up into it as into a tree.

But we had better confine ourselves here to prose. And then, to take the most absolutely unfanciful novelist of them all, it is to hear him saying, "*Madame Bovary—c'est moi.*" And we see focusing become so intent and aware and conscious in this most "realistic" novel of them all as to amount to fusion. Flaubert's work is indeed of the kind that is embedded immovably as rock in the country of its birth. If, with the slicers of any old (or new) criticism at all, you were to cut down through *Madame Bovary,* its cross section would still be the same as the cross section of that living earth, in texture, color, composition, all; which would be no surprise to Flaubert. For such fusion always means accomplishment no less conscious than it is gigantic—effort that must exist entirely as its own reward. We all know the letter Flaubert wrote when he had just found, in the morning paper, in an account of a minister's visit to Rouen, a phrase in the Mayor's speech of welcome

> which I had written the day before, textually, in my *Bovary* . . . Not only were the idea and the words the same, but even the rhythm of the style. It's things like this that give me pleasure . . . Everything one invents is true, you may be perfectly sure of that! Poetry is as precise as geometry . . . And besides, after reaching a certain point, one no longer makes any mistakes about the things of the soul. My poor Bovary, without a doubt, is suffering and weeping this very instant in twenty villages of France.

And now that we have come to the writer himself, the question of place resolves itself into the point of view. In this changeover from the objective to the subjective, wonderful and unexpected variations may occur.

Place, to the writer at work, is seen in a frame. Not an empty frame, a brimming one. Point of view is a sort of burning-glass, a product of personal experience and time; it is burnished with feelings and sensibilities, charged from moment to moment with the sun-points of imagination. It is an instrument—one of intensification; it acts, it behaves, it is temperamental. We have seen that the writer must accurately choose, combine, superimpose upon, blot out, shake up, alter the outside world for one absolute purpose, the good of his story. To do this, he is always seeing double, two pictures at once in his frame, his and the world's, a fact that he constantly comprehends; and he works best in a state of constant and subtle and unfooled reference between the two. It is his clear intention—his passion, I should say—to make the reader see only one of the pictures—the author's—under the pleasing illusion that it is the world's; this enormity is the accomplishment of a good story. I think it likely that at the moment of the writer's highest awareness of, and responsiveness to, the "real" world, his imagination's choice (and miles away it may be from actuality) comes closest to being infallible for his purpose. For the spirit of things is what is sought. No blur of inexactness, no cloud of vagueness, is allowable in good writing; from the first seeing to the last putting down, there must be steady lucidity and uncompromise of purpose. I speak, of course, of the ideal.

One of the most important things the young writer comes to see for himself is that point of view *is* an instrument, not an end in itself, that is useful as a glass, and not as a mirror to reflect a dear and pensive face. Conscientiously used, point of view will discover, explore, see through—it may sometimes divine and prophesy. Misused, it turns opaque almost at once and gets in the way of the book. And when the good novel is finished, its cooled outside shape, what Sean O'Faoláin has called "the veil of reality," has all the burden of communicating that initial, spontaneous, overwhelming, driving charge of personal inner feeling that was the novel's reason for being. The measure of this representation of life corresponds most tellingly with the novel's life expectancy: whenever its world of outside appearance grows dim or false to the eye, the novel has expired.

Establishing a chink-proof world of appearance is not only the first responsibility of the writer; it is the primary step in the technique of every sort of fiction: lyric and romantic, of course; the "realistic," it goes without saying; and other sorts as well. Fantasy itself must touch ground with at least one toe, and ghost stories must have one foot, so to speak, in the grave. The black, squat, hairy ghosts of M. R. James come right out of Cambridge. Only fantasy's stepchild, poor science-fiction, does not touch earth anywhere; and it is doubtful already if happenings entirely confined to outer space are ever going to move us, or even divert us for long. Satire, engaged in its most intellectual of exercises, must first of all establish an impeccable *locus operandi;* its premise is the kingdom where certain rules apply. The countries Gulliver visits are the systems of thought and learning Swift satirizes made visible one after the other and set in operation. But while place in satire is a purely artificial construction, set up to be knocked down, in humor place becomes its most revealing and at the same time is itself the most revealed. This is because humor, it seems to me, of all forms of fiction, entirely accepts place for what it is.

"Spotted Horses," by William Faulkner, is a good case in point. At the same time that this is just about Mr. Faulkner's funniest story, it is the most thorough and faithful picture of a Mississippi crossroads hamlet that you could ever hope to see. True in spirit, it is also true to everyday fact. Faulkner's art, which often lets him shoot the moon, tells him when to be literal too. In all its specification of detail, both mundane and poetic, in its complete adherence to social fact (which nobody knows better than Faulkner, surely, in writing today), by its unerring aim of observation as true as the sights of a gun would give, but Faulkner has no malice, only compassion; and even and also in the joy of those elements of harlequinade-fantasy that the spotted horses of the title bring in—in all that shining fidelity to place lies the heart and secret of this tale's comic glory.

Faulkner is, of course, the triumphant example in America today of the mastery of place in fiction. Yoknapatawpha County, so supremely and exclusively and majestically and totally itself, is an everywhere, but only because Faulkner's first concern is for what comes first—Yoknapatawpha, his own created world. I am not sure, as a Mississippian myself, how widely it is realized and appreciated that these works of such marvelous imaginative power can also stand as works of the carefulest and purest representation. Heightened, of course: their specialty is they are twice as true as life, and that is why it takes a genius to write them. "Spotted Horses" may not have happened yet; if it had, some others might have tried to make a story of it; but "Spotted Horses" could happen tomorrow—that is one of its glories. It could happen today or tomorrow at any little crossroads hamlet in Mississippi; the whole combination of irresistibility is there. We have the Snopses ready, the Mrs. Littlejohns ready, nice Ratliff and the Judge ready and sighing, the clowns, sober and merry, settled for the evening retrospection of it in the cool dusk of the porch; and the Henry Armstids armed with their obsessions, the little periwinkle-eyed boys armed with their indestructibility; the beautiful, overweening spring, too, the moonlight on the pear trees from which the mockingbird's song keeps returning; and the little store and the fat boy to steal and steal away at its candy. There are undoubtedly spotted horses too, in the offing—somewhere in Texas this minute, straining toward the day. After Faulkner has told it, it is easy for one and all to look back and see it.

Faulkner, simply, knew it already; it is a different kind of knowledge from Flaubert's, and proof could not add much to it. He was born knowing, or rather learning, or rather prophesying, all that and more; and having it all together at one time available while he writes is one of the marks of his mind. If there *is* any more in Mississippi than is engaged and dilated upon, and made twice as real as it used to be and applies now to the world, in the one story "Spotted Horses," then we would almost rather not know it—but I don't bet a piece of store candy that there is. In Faulkner's humor, even more measurably than in his tragedy, it is all there.

It may be going too far to say that the exactness and concreteness and solidity of the real world achieved in a story correspond to the intensity of feeling in the author's mind and to the very turn of his heart; but there lies the secret of our confidence in him.

Making reality real is art's responsibility. It is a practical assignment, then, a self-assignment: to achieve, by a cultivated sensitivity for observing life, a capacity for receiving its impressions, a lonely, unremitting, unaided, unaidable vision, and transferring this vision without distortion to it onto the pages of a novel, where, if the reader is so persuaded, it will turn into the reader's illusion. How bent on this peculiar joy we are, reader and writer, willingly to practice, willingly to undergo, this alchemy for it!

What is there, then, about place that is transferable to the pages of a novel? The best things—the explicit things: physical texture. And as place has functioned between the writer and his material, so it functions between the writer and reader. Location is the ground conductor of all the currents of emotion and belief and moral conviction that charge out from the story in its course. These charges need the warm hard earth underfoot, the light and lift of air, the stir and play of mood, the softening bath of atmosphere that give the likeness-to-life that life needs. Through the story's translation and ordering of life, the unconvincing raw material becomes the very heart's familiar. Life *is* strange. Stories hardly make it more so; with all they are able to tell and surmise, they make it more believably, more inevitably so.

I think the sense of place is as essential to good and honest writing as a logical mind; surely they are somewhere related. It is by knowing where you stand that you grow able to judge where you are. Place absorbs our earliest notice and attention, it bestows on us our original awareness; and our critical powers spring up from the study of it and the growth of experience inside it. It perseveres in bringing us back to earth when we fly too high. It never really stops informing us, for it is forever astir, alive, changing, reflecting, like the mind of man itself. One place comprehended can make us understand other places better. Sense of place gives equilibrium; extended, it is sense of direction too. Carried off we might be in spirit, and should be, when we are reading or writing something good; but it is the sense of place going with us still that is the ball of golden thread to carry us there and back and in every sense of the word to bring us home.

What can place *not* give? Theme. It can present theme, show it to the last detail—but place is forever illustrative: it is a picture of what man has done and imagined, it is his visible past, result. Human life is fiction's only theme.

Should the writer, then, write about home? It is both natural and sensible that the place where we have our roots should become the setting, the first and primary proving ground, of our fiction. Location, however, is not simply to be used by the writer—it is to be discovered, as each novel itself, in the act of writing, is discovery. Discovery does not imply that the place is new, only that we are. Place is as old as the hills. Kilroy at least has been there, and left his name. Discovery, not being a matter of writing our name on a wall, but of seeing what that wall is, and what is over it, is a matter of vision.

One can no more say, "To write stay home," than one can say, "To write leave home." It is the writing that makes its own rules and conditions for each person. And though place is home, it is for the writer writing simply *locus*. It is where the particular story he writes can be pinned down, the circle it can spin through and keep the state of grace, so that for the story's duration the rest of the world suspends its claim upon it and lies low as the story in peaceful extension, the *locus* fading off into the blue.

Naturally, it is the very breath of life, whether one writes a word of fiction or not, to go out and see what is to be seen of the world. For the artist to be unwilling to move, mentally or spiritually or physically, out of the familiar is a sign that spiritual timidity or poverty or decay has come upon him; for what is familiar will then have turned into all that is tyrannical.

One can only say: writers must always write best of what they know, and sometimes they do it by staying where they know it. But not for safety's sake. Although it is in the words of a witch—or all the more because of that—a comment of Hecate's in *Macbeth* is worth our heed: "Security / Is mortal's chiefest enemy." In fact, when we think in terms of the spirit, which are the terms of writing, is there a conception more stupefying than that of security? Yet writing of what you know has nothing to do with security: what is more dangerous? How can you go out on a limb if you do not know your own tree? No art ever came out of not risking your neck. And risk—experiment—is a considerable part of the joy of doing, which is the lone, simple reason all writers of serious fiction are willing to work as hard as they do.

The open mind and the receptive heart—which are at last and with fortune's smile the informed mind and the experienced heart—are to be gained anywhere, any time, without necessarily moving an inch from any present address. There must surely be as many ways of seeing a place as there are pairs of eyes to see it. The impact happens in so many different ways.

It may be the stranger within the gates whose eye is smitten by the crucial thing, the essence of life, the moment or act in our long-familiar midst that will forever define it. The inhabitant who has taken his fill of a place and gone away may look back and see it for good, from afar, still there in his mind's eye like a city over the hill. It was in the New Zealand stories, written eleven thousand miles from home and out of homesickness, that Katherine Mansfield came into her own. Joyce transplanted not his subject but himself while writing about it, and it was as though he had never left it at all: there it was, still in his eye, exactly the way he had last seen it. From the Continent he wrote the life of Dublin as it was then into a book of the future, for he went translating his own language of it on and on into a country of its own, where it set up a kingdom as renowned as Prester John's. Sometimes two places, two countries, are brought to bear on each other, as in E. M. Forster's work, and the heart of the novel is heard beating most plainly, most passionately, most personally when two places are at meeting point.

There may come to be new places in our lives that are second spiritual homes—closer to us in some ways, perhaps, than our original homes. But the home tie is the blood tie. And had it meant nothing to us, any other place thereafter would have meant less, and we would carry no compass inside ourselves to find home ever, anywhere at all. We would not even guess what we had missed.

It is noticeable that those writers who for their own good reasons push out against their backgrounds nearly always passionately adopt the new one in their work. Revolt itself is a reference and tribute to the potency of what is left behind. The substitute place, the adopted country, is sometimes a very much stricter, bolder, or harsher one than the original, seldom more lax or undemanding—showing that what was wanted was structure, definition, rigidity—perhaps these were wanted, and understanding was not.

Hemingway in our time has sought out the formal and ruthless territories of the world, archaic ones often, where there are bullfight arenas, theatres of hunting and war, places with a primitive, or formidable, stripped-down character, with implacable codes, with inscrutable justices and inevitable retributions. But whatever the scene of his work, it is the *places* that never are hostile. People give pain, are callous and insensitive, empty and cruel, carrying with them no pasts as they promise no futures. But place heals the hurt, soothes the outrage, fills the terrible vacuum that these human beings make. It heals actively, and the response is given consciously, with the ardent care and explicitness, respect and delight of a lover, when fishing streams or naming over streets becomes almost something of the lover's secret language—as the careful conversations between characters in Hemingway bear hints of the secret language of hate. The response to place has the added intensity that comes with the place's not being native or taken for granted, but found, chosen; thereby is the rest more heavily repudiated. It is the response of the aficionado; the response, too, is adopted. The title "A Clean Well Lighted Place" is just what the human being is not, for Hemingway, and perhaps it is the epitome of what man would like to find in his fellow-man but never has yet, says the author, and never is going to.

We see that point of view is hardly a single, unalterable vision, but a profound and developing one of great complexity. The vision itself may move in and out of its material, shuttle-fashion, instead of being simply turned on it, like a telescope on the moon. Writing is an expression of the writer's own peculiar personality, could not help being so. Yet in reading great works one feels that the finished piece transcends the personal. All writers great and small must sometimes have felt that they have become part of what they wrote even more than it still remains a part of them.

Part 2

When I speak of writing from where you have put down roots, it may be said that what I urge is "regional" writing. "Regional," I think, is a careless term, as well as a condescending one, because what it does is fail to differentiate between the localized raw material of life and its outcome as art. "Regional" is an outsider's term; it has no meaning for the insider who is doing the writing, because as far as he knows he is simply writing about life. Jane Austen, Emily Brontë, Thomas Hardy, Cervantes, Turgenev, the authors of the books of the Old Testament, all confined themselves to regions, great or small—but are they regional? Then who from the start of time has not been so?

It may well be said that all work springing out of such vital impulse from its native soil has certain things in common. But what signifies is that these are not the little things that it takes a fine-tooth critic to search out, but the great things, that could not be missed or mistaken, for they are the beacon lights of literature.

It seems plain that the art that speaks most clearly, explicitly, directly and passionately from its place of origin will remain the longest understood. It is through place that we put out roots, wherever birth, chance, fate or our traveling selves set us down; but where those roots reach toward—whether in America, England or Timbuktu—is the deep and running vein, eternal and consistent and everywhere purely itself, that feeds and is fed by the human understanding. The challenge to writers today, I think, is not to disown any part of our heritage. Whatever our theme in writing, it is old and tried. Whatever our place, it has been visited by the stranger, it will never be new again. It is only the vision that can be new; but that is enough.

Part 3

The Critics

Introduction

The critical essays reprinted here represent a multiplicity of approaches to Eudora Welty's short fiction. Her earliest admirers were also her fellow writers. Katherine Anne Porter's introduction to *A Curtain of Green* launched Welty's first collection, and Porter's perspicacity still serves readers well, both in the introduction to the volume of stories and as a guide to Welty's oeuvre. Robert Penn Warren first identified the paradox at the center of Welty's imagination; his essay "The Love and Separateness in Miss Welty" remains an influential discussion of the aesthetic design of Welty's stories. "The Art of Eudora Welty," as Joyce Carol Oates describes it, is to baffle our expectations with her ability to insinuate "horror" within stories gentle and comic in tone. This, too, is a paradox at work in Welty's stories, which "def[y] analysis." In his review of *The Collected Stories of Eudora Welty*, Reynolds Price also remarks on the difficulty that critics have shown in coming to terms with the "breadth of Welty's offering" in the genre of the short story, because "every tale" represents "as complete and unassailable an image of human relations as any in our art, tragic of necessity but also comic." Price suggests that Welty's stories must be reread for the complex vision at work to be understood.

Taking up the challenge of Price's 1980 review, Danièle Pitavy-Souques, Patricia Yaeger, and Nancy K. Butterworth reassess Welty's achievement. Pitavy-Souques places Welty's stories within the modernist movement, even as she points out Welty's anticipation of postmodernist techniques. For Pitavy-Souques, Welty "has a much more advanced and complex position than her moment in time would lead one to expect." Yaeger places Welty's use of Yeats's "Song of Wandering Aengus" in the context of Mikhail Bakhtin's theories about language in fiction, which is disruptive, open to change, and in short, "dialogic." *The Golden Apples*, for Yaeger, is Welty's dialogue with Yeats's poem in which she transforms his male discourse with her own distinctly female tradition and expression. Noting that Welty's "black characters frequently have evoked [discussion in terms of mythological and cultural archetypes]," Butterworth reopens the complicated question of "race relations" in Welty, finding that Welty's use of myth allows readers both to comprehend black characters as whole individuals and understand that those around them see them only in part.

These essays and the issues they represent show both the areas of discussion that have proved fruitful for critics in the past as well as the rich ground that remains in Welty's short fiction for critics to come.

Katherine Anne Porter

Friends of us both first brought Eudora Welty to visit me two and a half years ago in Louisiana. It was hot midsummer, they had driven over from Mississippi, her home state, and we spent a pleasant evening together talking in the cool old house with all the windows open. Miss Welty sat listening, as she must have done a great deal of listening on many such occasions. She was and is a quiet, tranquil-looking, modest girl, and unlike the young Englishman of the story, she has something to be modest about, as *A Curtain of Green* proves.

She considers her personal history as hardly worth mentioning, a fact in itself surprising enough, since a vivid personal career of fabulous ups and downs, hardships and strokes of luck, travels in far countries, spiritual and intellectual exile, defensive flight, homesick return with a determined groping for native roots, and a confusion of contradictory jobs have long been the mere conventions of an American author's life. Miss Welty was born and brought up in Jackson, Mississippi, where her father, now dead, was president of a Southern insurance company. Family life was cheerful and thriving; she seems to have got on excellently with both her parents and her two brothers. Education, in the Southern manner with daughters, was continuous, indulgent, and precisely as serious as she chose to make it. She went from school in Mississippi to the University of Wisconsin, thence to Columbia, New York, and so home again where she lives with her mother, among her lifelong friends and acquaintances, quite simply and amiably. She tried a job or two because that seemed the next thing, and did some publicity and newspaper work; but as she had no real need of a job, she gave up the notion and settled down to writing.

She loves music, listens to a great deal of it, all kinds; grows flowers very successfully, and remarks that she is "underfoot locally," meaning that she has a normal amount of social life. Normal social life in a medium-sized Southern town can become a pretty absorbing occupation, and the only comment her friends make when a new story appears is, "Why, Eudora, when did you write that?" Not how, or even why, just when. They see her about so much, what time has she for writing? Yet she spends an immense amount of time at it. "I haven't a literary life at all," she wrote once, "not much of a confession, maybe. But I do feel that the people and things I love are of a true and human world, and there is no clutter about them. . . . I would not understand a literary life."

We can do no less than dismiss that topic as casually as she does. Being the child of her place and time, profiting perhaps without being aware of it by the cluttered experiences, foreign travels, and disorders of the generation immediately preceding her, she will never have to go away and live among the Eskimos, or Mexican Indians; she need not follow a war and smell death to feel herself alive: she knows about death already. She shall not need even to live in New York in order to feel that she is having the kind of experience, the sense of "life" proper to a serious author. She gets her right nourishment from the source natural to her—her experience so far has been quite enough for her and of precisely the right kind. She began writing spontaneously when she was a child, being a born writer; she continued without any plan for a profession, without any particular encouragement, and, as it proved, not needing any. For a good number of years she believed she was going to be a painter, and painted quite earnestly while she wrote without much effort.

Nearly all the Southern writers I know were early, omnivorous, insatiable readers, and Miss Welty runs reassuringly true to this pattern. She had at arm's reach the typical collection of books which existed as a matter of course in a certain kind of Southern family, so that she had read the ancient Greek and Roman poetry, history and fable, Shakespeare, Milton, Dante, the eighteenth-century English and the nineteenth-century French novelists, with a dash of Tolstoy and Dostoievsky, before she realized what she was reading. When she first discovered contemporary literature, she was just the right age to find first W. B. Yeats and Virginia Woolf in the air around her; but always, from the beginning until now, she loved folk tales, fairy tales, old legends, and she likes to listen to the songs and stories of people who live in old communities whose culture is recollected and bequeathed orally.

She has never studied the writing craft in any college. She has never belonged to a literary group, and until after her first collection was ready to be published she had never discussed with any colleague or older artist any problem of her craft. Nothing else that I know about her could be more satisfactory to me than this; it seems to me immensely right, the very way a young artist should grow, with pride and independence and the courage really to face out the individual struggle; to make and correct mistakes and take the consequences of them, to stand firmly on his own feet in the end. I believe in the rightness of Miss Welty's instinctive knowledge that writing cannot be taught, but only learned, and learned by the individual in his own way, at his own pace and in his own time, for the process of mastering the medium is part of a cellular growth in a most complex organism; it is a way of life and a mode of being which cannot be divided from the kind of human creature you were the day you were born, and only in obeying the law of this singular being can the artist know his true directions and the right ends for him.

Miss Welty escaped, by miracle, the whole corrupting and destructive influence of the contemporary, organized tampering with young and promising talents by professional teachers who are rather monotonously divided into two major sorts: those theorists who are incapable of producing one passable specimen of the art they profess to teach; or good, sometimes first-rate, artists who are humanly unable to resist forming disciples and imitators among their students. It is all well enough to say that, of this second class, the able talent will throw off the master's influence and strike out for himself. Such influence has merely added new obstacles to an already difficult road. Miss Welty escaped also a militant social consciousness, in the current radical-intellectual sense, she never professed communism, and she has not expressed, except implicitly, any attitude at all on the state of politics or the condition of society. But there is an ancient system of ethics, an unanswerable, indispensable moral law, on which she is grounded firmly, and this, it would seem to me, is ample domain enough; these laws have never been the peculiar property of any party or creed or nation, they relate to that true and human world of which the artist is a living part; and when he dissociates himself from it in favor of a set of political, which is to say, inhuman, rules, he cuts himself away from his proper society—living men.

There exist documents of political and social theory which belong, if not to poetry, certainly to the department of humane letters. They are reassuring statements of the great hopes and dearest faiths of mankind and they are acts of high imagination. But all working, practical political systems, even those professing to originate in moral grandeur, are based upon and operate by contempt of human life and the individual fate; in accepting any one of them and shaping his mind and work to that mold, the artist dehumanizes himself, unfits himself for the practice of any art.

Not being in a hurry, Miss Welty was past twenty-six years when she offered her first story, "The Death of a Traveling Salesman," to the editor of a little magazine unable to pay, for she could not believe that anyone would buy a story from her; the magazine was *Manuscript,* the editor John Rood, and he accepted it gladly. Rather surprised, Miss Welty next tried the *Southern Review,* where she met with a great welcome and the enduring partisanship of Albert Erskine, who regarded her as his personal discovery. The story was "A Piece of News" and it was followed by others published in the *Southern Review,* the *Atlantic Monthly,* and *Harper's Bazaar.*

She has, then, never been neglected, never unappreciated, and she feels simply lucky about it. She wrote to a friend: "When I think of Ford Madox Ford! You remember how you gave him my name and how he tried his best to find a publisher for my book of stories all that last year of his life; and he wrote me so many charming notes, all of his time going to his little brood of promising writers, the kind of thing that could have gone on forever. Once I read in the *Saturday Review* an article of his on the species and the way they were neglected by publishers, and he used me as the example chosen at random. He ended his cry with 'What is to become of both branches of Anglo-Saxondom if this state of things continues?' Wasn't that wonderful, really, and typical? I may have been more impressed by that than would other readers who knew him. I did not know him, but I knew it was typical. And here I myself have turned out to be not at all the martyred promising writer, but have had all the good luck and all the good things Ford chided the world for withholding from me and my kind."

But there is a trap lying just ahead, and all short-story writers know what it is—The Novel. That novel which every publisher hopes to obtain from every short-story writer of any gifts at all, and who finally does obtain it, nine times out of ten. Already publishers have told her, "Give us first a novel, and then we will publish your short stories." It is a special sort of trap for poets, too, though quite often a good poet can and does write a good novel. Miss Welty has tried her hand at novels, laboriously, dutifully, youthfully thinking herself perhaps in the wrong to refuse, since so many authoritarians have told her that was the next step. It is by no means the next step. She can very well become a master of the short story, there are almost perfect stories in *A Curtain of Green.* The short story is a special and difficult medium, and contrary to a widely spread popular superstition it has no formula that can be taught by correspondence school. There is nothing to hinder her from writing novels if she wishes or believes she can. I only say that her good gift, just as it is now, alive and flourishing, should not be retarded by a perfectly artificial demand upon her to do the conventional thing. It is a fact that the public for short stories is smaller than the public for novels; this seems to me no good reason for depriving that minority. I remember a reader writing to an editor, complaining that he did not like collections of short stories because, just as he had got himself worked into one mood or frame of mind, he was called upon to change to another. If that is an important objection, we might also apply it to music. We might compare the novel to a symphony, and a collection of short stories to a good concert recital. In any case, this complainant is not our reader, yet our reader does exist, and there would be more of him if more and better short stories were offered.

The stories in *A Curtain of Green* offer an extraordinary range of mood, pace, tone, and variety of material. The scene is limited to a town the author knows well; the farthest reaches of that scene never go beyond the boundaries of her own state, and many of the characters are of the sort that caused a Bostonian to remark that he would not care to meet them socially. Lily Daw is a half-witted girl in the grip of social forces represented by a group of earnest ladies bent on doing the best thing for her, no matter what the consequences. Keela, the Outcast Indian Maid, is a crippled little Negro who represents a type of man considered most unfortunate by W. B. Yeats: one whose experience was more important than he, and completely beyond his powers of absorption. But the really unfortunate man in this story is the ignorant young white boy, who had innocently assisted at a wrong done the little Negro, and for a most complex reason, finds that no reparation is possible, or even desirable to the victim. . . . The heroine of "Why I live at the P.O." is a terrifying family poltergeist, when one reconsiders it. While reading, it is gorgeously funny. In this first group—for the stories may be loosely classified on three separate levels—the spirit is satire and the key grim comedy. Of these, "The Petrified Man" offers a fine clinical study of vulgarity—vulgarity absolute, chemically pure, exposed mercilessly to its final subhuman depths. Dullness, bitterness, rancor, self-pity, baseness of all kinds, can be most interesting material for a story provided these are not also the main elements in the mind of the author. There is nothing in the least vulgar or frustrated in Miss Welty's mind. She has simply an eye and an ear sharp, shrewd, and true as a tuning fork. She has given to this little story all her wit and observation, her blistering humor and her just cruelty; for she has none of that slack tolerance or sentimental tenderness toward symptomatic evils that amounts to criminal collusion between author and character. Her use of this material raises the quite awfully sordid little tale to a level above its natural habitat, and its realism seems almost to have the quality of caricature, as complete realism so often does. Yet, as painters of the grotesque make only detailed reports of actual living types observed more keenly than the average eye is capable of observing, so Miss Welty's little human monsters are not really caricatures at all, but individuals exactly and clearly presented: which is perhaps a case against realism, if we cared to go into it.

She does better on another level—for the important reason that the themes are richer—in such beautiful stories as "Death of a Traveling Salesman," "A Memory," "A Worn Path." Let me admit a deeply personal preference for this particular kind of story, where external act and the internal voiceless life of the human imagination almost meet and mingle on the mysterious threshold between dream and waking, one reality refusing to admit or confirm the existence of the other, yet both conspiring toward the same end. This is not easy to accomplish, but it is always worth trying, and Miss Welty is so successful at it, it would seem her most familiar territory. There is no blurring at the edges, but evidences of an active and disciplined imagination working firmly in a strong line of continuity, the waking faculty of daylight reason recollecting and recording the crazy logic of the dream. There is in none of these stories any trace of autobiography in the prime sense, except as the author is omnipresent, and knows each character she writes about as only the artist knows the thing he has made, by first experiencing it in imagination. But perhaps in "A Memory," one of the best stories, there might be something of early personal history in the story of the child on the beach, estranged from the world of adult knowledge by her state of childhood, who hoped to learn the secrets of life by looking at everything, squaring her hands before her eyes to bring the observed thing into a frame—the gesture of one born to select, to arrange, to bring apparently disparate elements into harmony within deliberately fixed boundaries. But the author is freed already in her youth from self-love, self-pity, self-preoccupation, that triple damnation of too many of the young and gifted, and has reached an admirable objectivity. In such stories as "Old Mr. Marblehall," "Powerhouse," "The Hitch-Hikers," she combines an objective reporting with great perception of mental or emotional states, and in "Clytie" the very shape of madness takes place before your eyes in a straight account of actions and speech, the personal appearance and habits of dress of the main character and her family.

In all of these stories, varying as they do in excellence, I find nothing false or labored, no diffusion of interest, no wavering of mood—the approach is direct and simple in method, though the themes and moods are anything but simple, and there is even in the smallest story a sense of power in reserve which makes me believe firmly that, splendid beginning that this is, it is only the beginning.

> But now that so much is being changed, is it not time that we should change? Could we not try to develop ourselves a little, slowly and gradually take upon ourselves our share in the labor of love? We have been spared all its hardship . . . we have been spoiled by easy enjoyment. . . . But what if we despised our successes, what if we began from the beginning to learn the work of love which has always been done for us? What if we were to go and become neophytes, now that so much is changing?
>
> Rainer Marie Rilke

Robert Penn Warren

> He could understand God's giving Separateness first and then giving Love to follow and heal in its wonder; but God had reversed this, and given Love first and then Separateness, as though it did not matter to Him which came first.
>
> —"A Still Moment"

If we put *The Wide Net,* Eudora Welty's second collection of stories, up against her first collection, *A Curtain of Green,* we can immediately observe a difference: the stories of *The Wide Net* represent a specializing, an intensifying, of one of the many strains which were present in *A Curtain of Green.* All of the stories in *A Curtain of Green* bear the impress of Miss Welty's individual talent, but there is a great variety among them in subject matter and method and, more particularly, mood. It is almost as if the author had gone at each story as a fresh start in the business of writing fiction, as if she had had to take a new angle each time out of a joy in the pure novelty of the perspective. We find the vindictive farce of "The Petrified Man," the nightmare of "Clytie," the fantasy and wit of "Old Mr. Marblehall," the ironic self-revelation of "Why I Live at the P.O.," the nearly straight realism of "The Hitch-Hikers," the macabre comedy and pathos of "Keela, the Outcast Indian Maiden." The material of many of the stories was sad, or violent, or warped, and even the comedy and wit were not straight, but if read from one point of view, if read as a performance, the book was exhilarating, even gay, as though the author were innocently delighted not only with the variety of the world but with the variety of ways in which one could look at the world and the variety of things that stories could be and still be stories. Behind the innocent delight of the craftsman, and of the admirer of the world, there was also a seriousness, a philosophical cast of mind, which gave coherence to the book, but on the surface there was the variety, the succession of surprises. In *The Wide Net* we do not find the surprises. The stories are more nearly cut to one pattern.

We do not find the surprises. Instead, on the first page, with the first sentence of the first story, "First Love," we enter a special world: "Whatever happened, it happened in extraordinary times, in a season of dreams . . ." And that is the world in which we are going to live until we reach the last sentence of the last story. "Whatever happened," the first sentence begins, as though the author cannot be quite sure what did happen, cannot quite undertake to resolve the meaning of the recorded event, cannot, in fact, be too sure of recording all of the event. This is coyness, of course; or a way of warning the reader that he cannot expect quite the ordinary direct light on the event. For it is "a season of dreams"—and the faces and gestures and events often have something of the grave retardation, the gnomic intensity, the portentous suggestiveness of dreams. The logic of things here is not quite the logic by which we live, or think we live, our ordinary daylight lives. In "The Wide Net," for example, the young husband, who thinks his wife has jumped into the river, goes out with a party of friends to dredge for the body, but the sad occasion turns into a saturnalian fish-fry which is interrupted when the great King of the Snakes raises his hoary head from the surface of the river. But usually, in *The Wide Net*, the wrenching of logic is not in terms of events themselves, though "The Purple Hat" is a fantasy, and "Asphodel" moves in the direction of fantasy. Usually the events as events might be given a perfectly realistic treatment (Dreiser could take the events of "The Landing" for a story). But in these cases where the events and their ordering are "natural" and not supernatural or fantastic, the stories themselves finally belong to the "season of dreams" because of the special tone and mood, the special perspective, the special sensibility with which they are rendered.

Some readers, in fact, who are quite aware of Miss Welty's gifts, have recently reported that they are disturbed by the recent development of her work. Diana Trilling, in her valuable and sobering comments on current fiction, which appear regularly in the *Nation*, says that the author "has developed her technical virtuosity to the point where it outweighs the uses to which it is put, and her vision of horror to the point of nightmare." There are two ideas in this indictment, and let us take the first one first and come to the second much later. The indictment of the technique is developed along these lines: Miss Welty has made her style too fancy—decorative, "falsely poetic" and "untrue," "insincere." ("When an author says 'look at me' instead of 'look at it,' there is insincerity. . . .") This insincerity springs from "the extreme infusion of subjectivism and private sensibility." But the subjectivism, Mrs. Trilling goes on to say, leads not only to insincerity and fine writing but to a betrayal of the story's obligation to narrative and rationality. Miss Welty's stories take off from a situation, but "the stories themselves stay with their narrative no more than a dance, say, stays with its argument." That is the summary of the indictment.

The indictment is, no doubt, well worth the close attention of Miss Welty's admirers. There is, in fact, a good deal of the falsely poetic in Miss Welty's present style, metaphors that simply pretend to an underlying logic, and metaphors (and descriptions) that, though good themselves, are irrelevant to the business in hand. And sometimes Miss Welty's refusal to play up the objective action—her attempt to define and refine the response rather than to present the stimulus—does result in a blurred effect. But the indictment treats primarily not of such failures to fulfill the object the artist has set herself but of the nature of that object. The critic denies, in effect, that Miss Welty's present kind of fiction is fiction at all: "It is a book of ballets, not of stories."

Now is it possible that the critic is arguing from some abstract definition of "story," some formalistic conception which does not accommodate the present exhibit, and is not concerning herself with the question of whether or not the present exhibit is doing the special job which it proposes for itself, and, finally, the job which we demand of all literature? Perhaps we should look at a new work first in terms of its effect and not in terms of a definition of type, because every new work is in some degree, however modest, wrenching our definition, straining its seams, driving us back from the formalistic definition to the principles on which the definition was based. Can we say this, therefore, of our expectation concerning a piece of literature, new or old: That it should intensify our awareness of the world (and of ourselves in relation to the world) in terms of an idea, a "view." This leads us to what is perhaps the key statement by Diana Trilling concerning *The Wide Net:* she grants that the volume "has tremendous emotional impact, despite its obscurity." In other words, she says, unless I misinterpret her, that the book does intensify the reader's awareness—but *not* in terms of a presiding idea.

This has led me to reread Miss Welty's two volumes of stories in the attempt to discover the issues which are involved in the "season of dreams." To begin with, almost all of the stories deal with people who, in one way or another, are cut off, alienated, isolated from the world.

There is the girl in "Why I Live at the P.O."—isolated from her family by her arrogance, meanness, and sense of persecution; the half-witted Lily Daw, who, despite the efforts of "good" ladies, wants to live like other people; the deaf-mutes of "The Key," and the deaf-mute of "First Love"; the people of "The Whistle" and "A Piece of News," who are physically isolated from the world and who make their pathetic efforts to re-establish something lost; the traveling salesman and the hitch-hikers of "The Hitch-Hikers," who, for their different reasons, are alone, and the traveling salesman of "Death of a Traveling Salesman" who, in the physically and socially isolated backwoods cabin, discovers that he is the one who is truly isolated; Clytie, isolated in family pride and madness and sexual frustration, and Jennie of "At the Landing," and Mrs. Larkin of "A Curtain of Green," the old women of "A Visit of Charity" and the old Negro woman of "A Worn Path"; the murderer of "Flowers for Marjorie," who is cut off by an economic situation and the pressure of a great city; Mr. Marblehall in his secret life; Livvie, who, married to an old man and trapped in his respectable house, is cut off from the life appropriate to her years; Lorenzo, Murrell, and Audubon in "A Still Moment," each alone in his dream, his obsession; the old maids of "Asphodel," who tell the story of Miss Sabina and then are confronted by the naked man and pursued by the flock of goats. In some of the cases, the matter is more indirectly presented. For instance, in "Keela, the Outcast Indian Maiden," we find, as in *The Ancient Mariner*, the story of a man who, having committed a crime, must try to re-establish his connection with humanity; or in the title story of *The Wide Net*, William Wallace, because he thinks his wife has drowned herself, is at the start of the story cut off from the world of natural joy in which he had lived.

We can observe that the nature of the isolation may be different from case to case, but the fact of isolation, whatever its nature, provides the basic situation of Miss Welty's fiction. The drama which develops from this basic situation is of either of two kinds: first, the attempt of the isolated person to escape into the world; or second, the discovery by the isolated person, or by the reader, of the nature of the predicament.

As an example of the first type, we can remember Clytie's obsessed inspection of faces ("Was it possible to comprehend the eyes and the mouth of other people, which concealed she knew not what, and secretly asked for still another unknown thing?") and her attempt to escape, and to solve the mystery, when she lays her finger on the face of the terrified barber who has come to the ruinous old house to shave her father. Or there is Jennie, of "At the Landing," or Livvie, or the man of

"Keela." As an example of the second type, there is the new awareness on the part of the salesman in "The Hitch-Hikers," or the new awareness on the part of the other salesman in the back-country cabin.

Even in "A Still Moment" we have this pattern, though in triplicate. The evangelist Lorenzo, the outlaw Murrell, and the naturalist and artist Audubon stand for a still moment and watch a white heron feeding. Lorenzo sees a beauty greater than he can account for (he had earlier "accounted for" the beauty by thinking, "Praise God, His love has come visible"), and with the sweat of rapture pouring down from his forehead, shouts into the marshes, "Tempter!" He has not been able to escape from his own obsession, or in other words, to make his definition of the world accommodate the white heron and the "natural" rapture which takes him. Murrell, looking at the bird, sees "only whiteness ensconced in darkness," and thinks that "if it would look at him a dream penetration would fill and gratify his heart"—the heart which Audubon has already defined as belonging to the flinty darkness of a cave. Neither Lorenzo nor Murrell can "love" the bird, and so escape from their own curse as did, again, the Ancient Mariner. But there remains the case of Audubon himself, who does "love" the bird, who can innocently accept nature. There is, however, an irony here. To paint the bird he must "know" the bird as well as "love" it, he must know it feather by feather, he must have it in his hand. And so he must kill it. But having killed the bird, he knows that the best he can make of it now in a painting would be a dead thing, "never the essence, only a sum of parts," and that "it would always meet with a stranger's sight, and never be one with beauty in any other man's head in the world." Here, too, the fact of the isolation is realized: as artist and lover of nature he had aspired to a communication, a communion, with other men in terms of the bird, but now "he saw his long labor most revealingly at the point where it met its limit" and he is forced back upon himself.

"A Still Moment," however, may lead us beyond the discussion of the characteristic situation, drama, and realization in Miss Welty's stories. It may lead us to a theme which seems to underlie the stories. For convenience, though at the risk of incompleteness, or even distortion, we may call it Innocence and Experience. Let us take Audubon in relation to the heron. He loves the bird, innocently, in its fullness of being. But he must subject this love to knowledge; he must kill the bird if he is to commemorate its beauty, if he is to establish his communion with other men in terms of the bird's beauty. There is in the situation an irony of limit and contamination.

Let us look at this theme in relation to other stories. "A Memory," in *A Curtain of Green,* gives a simple example. Here we have a young girl lying on a beach and looking out at the scene through a frame made by her fingers, for the girl can say of herself, "To watch everything about me I regarded grimly and possessively as a need." (As does Audubon, in "A Still Moment.") And further: "It did not matter to me what I looked at; from any observation I would conclude that a secret of life had been nearly revealed to me. . . ." Now the girl is cherishing a secret love, a love for a boy at school about whom she knows nothing, to whom she has never even spoken, but whose wrist her hand had once accidentally brushed. The secret love had made her watching of the world more austere, had sharpened her demand that the world conform to her own ideas, and had created a sense of fear. This fear had seemed to be realized one day when, in the middle of a class, the boy had a fit of nosebleed. But that is in the past. This morning she suddenly sees between the frame of her fingers a group of coarse, fat, stupid, and brutal people disporting themselves on the sand with a maniacal, aimless vigor which comes to climax when the fat woman, into the front of whose bathing suit the man had poured sand, bends over and pulls down the cloth so that the lumps of mashed and folded sand empty out. "I felt a peak of horror, as though her breasts themselves had turned to sand, as though they were of no importance at all and she did not care." Over against this defilement (a defilement which implies that the body, the breasts which turn to sand, has no meaning), there is the refuge of the dream, "the undefined austerity of my love."

"A Memory" presents the moment of the discovery of the two poles—the dream and the world; the idea and nature; innocence and experience; individuality and the anonymous, devouring life-flux; meaning and force; love and knowledge. It presents the contrast in terms of horror (as do "The Petrified Man" and "Why I Live at the P.O." when taken in the context of Miss Welty's work) and with the issue left in suspension, but other stories present it with different emphases and tonalities.

For instance, when William Wallace, in "The Wide Net," goes out to dredge the river, he is presumably driven by the fear that his wife has jumped in, but the fear is absorbed into the world of the river, and in a saturnalian revel he prances about with a great catfish hung on his belt, like a river-god laughing and leaping. But he had also dived deep down into the water: "Had he suspected down there, like some secret, the real true trouble that Hazel had fallen into, about which words in a letter could not speak . . . how (who knew?) she had been filled to the brim with that elation that they all remembered, like their own secret, the elation that comes of great hopes and changes, sometimes simply of the harvest time, that comes with a little course of its own like a tune to run in the head, and there was nothing she could do about it, they knew—and so it had turned into this? It could be nothing but the old trouble that William Wallace was finding out, reaching and turning in the gloom of such depths."

This passage comes clear when we recall that Hazel, the wife who is supposed to have committed suicide by drowning, is pregnant: she had sunk herself in the devouring life-flux, has lost her individuality there, just as the men hunting for the body have lost the meaning of their mission. For the river is simply force, which does not have its own definition; in it are the lost string of beads to wind around the little Negro boy's head, the catfish for the feast, the baby alligator that looks "like the oldest and worst lizard," and the great King of the Snakes. As Doc, the wise old man who owns the net, says: "The outside world is full of endurance." And he also says: "The excursion is the same when you go looking for your sorrow as when you go looking for your joy." Man has the definition, the dream, but when he plunges into the river he runs the risk of having it washed away. But it is important to notice that in this story, there is not horror at the basic contrast, but a kind of gay acceptance of the issue: when William Wallace gets home he finds that his wife had fooled him, and spanks her, and then she lies smiling in the crook of his arm. "It was the same as any other chase in the end."

As "The Wide Net," unlike "A Memory," does more than merely present the terms of contrast, so do such stories as "Livvie" and "At the Landing." Livvie, who lives in the house of wisdom (her infirm husband's name is Solomon) and respectability (the dream, the idea, which has withered) and Time (there is the gift of the silver watch), finally crosses into the other world, the world of the black buck, the field hand, in his Easter clothes—another god, not a river-god but a field god. Just after Solomon's death, the field hand in his gorgeous Easter clothes takes Livvie in his arms, and she drops the watch which Solomon had given her, while outside "the redbirds were flying and crisscrossing, the sun was in all the bottles on the prisoned trees, and the young peach was shining in the middle of them with the bursting light of spring."

If Livvie's crossing into the world of the field god is joyous, the escape of Jennie, in "At the Landing," is rendered in a different tonality. This story assimilates into a new pattern many of the elements found in "A Memory," "The Wide Net," "Livvie," and "Clytie." As in the case of

Clytie, Jennie is caught in the house of pride, tradition, history, and as in the case of Livvie, in a house of death. The horror which appears in "A Memory," in "Clytie," reappears here. The basic symbolism of "Livvie" and of "The Wide Net" is again called into play. The river, as in "The Wide Net," is the symbol of that world from which Jennie is cut off. The grandfather's dream at the very beginning sets up the symbolism which is developed in the action:

> The river has come back. That Floyd came to tell me. The sun was shining full on the face of the church, and that Floyd came around it with his wrist hung with a great long catfish. . . . That Floyd's catfish has gone loose and free. . . . And all of a sudden, my dears—my dears, it took its river life back, and shining so brightly swam through the belfry of the church, and downstream.

Floyd, the untamed creature of uncertain origin, is like William Wallace, the river-god dancing with the great catfish at his belt. But he is also, like the buck in "Livvie," a field god, riding the red horse in a pasture full of butterflies. He is free and beautiful, and Jennie is drawn after him, for "she knew that he lived apart in delight." But she also sees him scuffling playfully with the hideous old Mag: the god does not make nice distinctions. When the flood comes over the Landing (upsetting the ordered lives, leaving slime in the houses), Floyd takes her in his boat to a hill (significantly the cemetery hill where her people are buried), violates her, feeds her wild meat and fish (field and river), and when the flood is down, leaves her. She has not been able to talk to him, and when she does say, "I wish you and I could be far away. I wish for a little house," he only stares into the fire as though he hasn't heard a word. But after he has gone she cannot live longer in the Landing; she must find him.

Her quest leads her into the dark woods (which are like an underwater depth) and to the camp of the wild river people, where the men are throwing knives at a tree. She asks for Floyd, but he is not there. The men put her in a grounded houseboat and come in to her. "A rude laugh covered her cry, and somehow both the harsh human sounds could easily have been heard as rejoicing, going out over the river in the dark night." Jennie has crossed into the other world to find violence and contamination, but there is not merely the horror as in "Clytie" and "A Memory." Jennie has acted out a necessary role: she has moved from the house of death, like Livvie, and there is "gain" as well as "loss." We must not forget the old woman who looks into the dark houseboat, at the very end of the story, and understands when she is told that the strange girl is "waiting for Billy Floyd." The old woman nods "out to the flowing river, with the firelight following her face and showing its dignity."

If this general line of interpretation is correct, we find that the stories represent variations on the same basic theme, on the contrasts already enumerated. It is not that there is a standard resolution for the contrasts which is repeated from story to story; rather, the contrasts, being basic, are not susceptible of a single standard resolution, and there is an implicit irony in Miss Welty's work. But if we once realize this, we can recognize that the contrasts are understood not in mechanical but in vital terms: the contrasts provide the terms of human effort, for the dream must be carried to, submitted to, the world, innocence to experience, love to knowledge, knowledge to fact, individuality to communion. What resolution is possible is, if I read the stories with understanding, in terms of the vital effort. The effort is a "mystery," because it is in terms of the effort, doomed to failure but essential, that the human manifests itself as human. Again and again, in different forms, we find what we find in Joel of "First Love": "Joel would never know now the true course, or the true outcome of any dream: this was all he felt. But he walked on, in the frozen path into the wilderness, on and on. He did not see how he could ever go back and still be the boot-boy at the Inn."

It is possible that, in trying to define the basic issue and theme of Miss Welty's stories, I have made them appear too systematic, too mechanical. I do not mean to imply that her stories should be read as allegories, with a neat point-to-point equating of image and idea. It is true that a few of her stories, such as "The Wide Net," do approach the limit of allegory, but even in such cases we find rather than the system of allegory a tissue of symbols which emerge from, and disappear into, a world of scene and action which, once we discount the author's special perspective, is recognizable in realistic terms. The method is similar to the method of much modern poetry, and to that of much modern fiction and drama, but at the same time it is a method as old as fable, myth, and parable. It is a method by which the items of fiction (scene, action, character, etc.) are presented not as document but as comment, not as a report but as a thing made, not as history but as idea. Even in the most realistic and reportorial fiction, the social picture, the psychological analysis, and the pattern of action do not rest at the level of mere report; they finally operate as expressive symbols as well.

Fiction may be said to have two poles, history and idea, and the emphasis may be shifted very far in either direction. In the present collection the emphasis has been shifted very far in the direction of idea, but at the same time there remains a sense of the vividness of the actual world: the picnic of "The Wide Net" is a real picnic as well as a "journey," Cash of "Livvie" is a real field hand in his Easter clothes as well as a field god. In fact, it may be said that when the vividness of the actual world is best maintained, when we get the sense of one picture superimposed upon another, different and yet somehow the same, the stories are most successful.

The stories which fail are stories like "The Purple Hat" and "Asphodel," in which the material seems to be manipulated in terms of an idea, in which the relation between the image and the vision has become mechanical, in which there is a strain, in which we do find the kind of hocus-pocus deplored by Diana Trilling.

And this brings us back to the criticism that the volume "has tremendous emotional impact, despite its obscurity," that the "fear" it engenders is "in inverse ratio to its rational content." Now it seems to me that this description does violence to my own experience of literature, that we do not get any considerable emotional impact unless we sense, at the same time, some principle of organization, some view, some meaning. This does not go to say that we have to give an abstract formulation to that principle or view or meaning before we can experience the impact of the work, but it does go to say that it is implicit in the work and is having its effect upon us in immediate aesthetic terms. Furthermore, in regard to the particular work in question, I do not feel that it is obscure. If anything, the dreamlike effect in many of the stories seems to result from the author's undertaking to squeeze meaning from the item which, in ordinary realistic fiction, would be passed over with a casual glance. Hence the portentousness, the retardation, the otherworldliness. For Miss Welty is like the girl in "A Memory":

> . . . from any observation I would conclude that a secret of life had been nearly revealed to me, and from the smallest gesture of a stranger I would wrest what was to me a communication or a presentiment.

In many cases, as a matter of fact, Miss Welty has heavily editorialized her fiction. She wants us to get that smallest gesture, to participate in her vision of things as intensely meaningful. And so there is almost always a gloss to the fable.

One more word: It is quite possible that Miss Welty has pushed her method to its most extreme limit. It is also possible that the method, if pursued much farther, would lead to monotony and self-imitation and merely decorative elaboration. Perhaps we shall get a fuller drama when her vision is submitted more daringly to fact, when the definition is plunged into the devouring river. But meanwhile Miss Welty has given us stories of brilliance and intensity; and as for the future, Miss Welty is a writer of great resourcefulness, sensitivity, and intelligence, and can probably fend for herself.

Joyce Carol Oates

What shocks us about this art is its delicate blending of the casual and the tragic, the essential femininity of the narration and the subject, the reality, which is narrated. How can the conversational and slightly arch tone of her fiction give way to such amazing revelations? That horror may evolve out of gentility—and, even in stories dealing with the very poor or the very unenlightened, Miss Welty is always "genteel"—is something we are not prepared to accept. Our natural instinct is to insist that horror be emphasized, underlined, somehow exaggerated so that we may absorb it in a way satisfying to our sensibilities. Fiction about crime and criminals suggests always the supreme importance of crime and criminals; it is a statement of moral value. The kind of black comic-naturalism that has descended from Celine also insists, heavily, upon a moral point, about the crazy depravity of the world and the endless combinations and permutations in which it may be located . . . and this too, though it is constructed as a kind of joke or a series of jokes, may be related to a sense of proportion, a feeling that outrages certainly deserve more attention than normal events.

Eudora Welty baffles our expectations. Like Kafka, with whom she shares a number of traits, she presents the distortions of life in the context of ordinary, even chatty life; she frightens us. I have no doubt that her intentions are not to frighten anyone, or to make particular judgments on life, but the effect of her fiction is indeed frightening. It is the bizarre combination of a seemingly boundless admiration for feminine nonsense—family life, food, relatives, conversations, eccentric old people—and a sharp, penetrating eye for the seams of this world, through which a muderous light shines. Flannery O'Connor, who was certainly indebted to Miss Welty's stories, abandons entirely the apparatus of "realism"; she has no patience for, no interest in, real people. Amazing as some of Flannery O'Connor's stories are, they are ultimately powerless to move us seriously—like the beautiful plays of Yeats, they are

Reprinted from *Shenandoah:* The Washington and Lee University Review, 20 (Spring 1969), with the permission of the Editor.

populated with beings not quite human. Eudora Welty's people are always human.

The most impatient and unsympathetic of readers will find himself drawn in gradually, even charmed, by the Fairchild clan of *Delta Wedding.* They are indeed a "capricious and charming Southern family" (quote from paperback edition cover). That the foundation of their charm, the leisure in which to develop their charm, is something wholly ugly and unacceptable—the obvious exploitation of Negroes, inside an accidental economic structure in which the Fairchilds are, certainly, American nobility in spite of their lack of real wealth—is something one comes to accept, just the same as one comes to accept the utter worthlessness of certain characters of James and Proust, in social and human terms, but maintains an interest in their affairs. And then it is stunning to realize, as one nears the conclusion of *Delta Wedding,* that in spite of the lovingly detailed story, in spite of her seemingly insatiable generosity toward these unexceptional people, Miss Welty understands clearly their relationship with the rest of the world. So much cute nonsense about a wedding!—and then the photographer announces, making conversation, that he has also taken a picture of a girl recently hit by a train. "Ladies, she was flung off in the blackberry bushes," he says; and Aunt Tempe says what every aunt will say, "Change the subject." The dead girl may have been as pretty and flighty and exasperating as the young bride, but her human value is considerably less. She is on the outside; she is excluded from society. Her existence is of no particular concern to anyone. So, a member of this claustrophobic and settled world may well venture into hers, make love to her, leave her, and her death is a kind of natural consequence of her being excluded from the "delta wedding" and all its bustling excitement. It is more disturbing for the mother of all those children to be told, by her Negro servant, that he quite seriously wishes all the roses were out of the world—"If I had my way, wouldn't be a rose in de world. Catch your shirt and stick you and prick you and grab you. Got thorns." Ellen trembles at this remark "as at some imprudence." Protected by her social position, her family, her condition of being loved, protected by the very existence of the Negro servant who must brave the thorns for her, it is only imprudence of one kind or another that she must tremble at.

In "The Demonstrators"—the O. Henry First Prize story of 1968—the lonely consciousness of an ordinary, good man is seen in a context of greater, more violent loneliness, the terrible general failure of mankind. The demonstrators themselves, the civil rights agitators, do not appear in the story and need not appear; their intrusion into the supposedly placid racist society of this small Southern town is only symbolic. They too are not to be trusted, idealistic as they sound. Another set of demonstrators—demonstrating our human powerlessness as we disintegrate into violence—are the Negroes of the town, a choral and anonymous group with a victim at their theatrical center, one of themselves and yet a curious distance from them, in her death agony.

The story begins with the semi-colloquial "Near eleven o'clock" and concerns itself at first with the forceful, colorful personality of an aged woman, Miss Marcia Pope. Subject to seizures as she is, crotchety and wise in the stereotyped manner of such old dying ladies, she is nevertheless the only person in town "quite able to take care of herself," as the doctor thinks at the conclusion of the story; a great deal has happened between the first and last paragraphs. The doctor's mission is to save a young Negro woman, who has been stabbed by her lover with an ice pick; his attempt is hopeless, the woman is bleeding internally, too much time has been wasted. And so she dies. The doctor goes home and we learn that he himself is living a kind of death, since his wife has left him; his wife left him because their thirteen-year-old daughter, an idiot, had died . . . everything is linked to everything else, one person to another, one failure to another, earlier, equally irremediable failure. The doctor is "so increasingly tired, so sick and even bored with the bitterness, intractability that divided everybody and everything." The tragedy of life is our permanence of self, of Ego: but this is also our hope, in Miss Welty's phrase our "assault of hope," throwing us back into life.

The next morning he reads of the deaths of the Negro lovers, who managed to kill each other. The homespun newspaper article concludes, "No cause was cited for the fracas." The doctor had not failed to save the Negro woman and man because there was never the possibility of their being saved. There was never the possibility of his daughter growing up. Of the strange failure of his marriage nothing much is said, yet it too seems irreparable. But, as he looks into the garden, he distinguishes between those flowers which are "done for" and those which are still "bright as toys." And two birds pick in the devastation of leaves, apparently permanent residents of the garden, "probing and feeding."

"The Demonstrators" resists analysis. It is a small masterpiece of subtlety, of gentleness—a real gentleness of tone, a reluctance to exaggerate or even to highlight drama, as if sensing such gestures alien to life. We are left with an unforgettable sense of the permanence and the impermanence of life, and especially of the confused web of human relationships that constitute most of our lives. The mother of the dying Negro girl warns her, "*I* ain't going to raise him," speaking of the girl's baby. Of course she is going to raise him. There is no question about it. But the warning itself, spoken in that room of unfocussed horror, is horrible; the grotesque has been assimilated deftly into the ordinary, the natural.

It is an outstanding characteristic of Miss Welty's genius that she can write a story that seems to me, in a way, about "nothing"—Flaubert's ideal, a masterpiece of style—and make it mean very nearly everything.

Reynolds Price

American letters may still lack a novelist whose life work matches in weight the achievement of Dickens or Tolstoy, but our 20th-century masters of the short story bow to no one for for stylistic elegance or emotional penetration. The past decade has brought in stout collections from three of the best—Flannery O'Connor, John Cheever, Paul Bowles—and of the certified living masters of the form, only Eudora Welty has resisted collection (though all but two of the stories were continuously available in separate volumes). A change of publisher stymied the project for several years, but finally here they are—41 stories, the entire contents of her four individual collections plus two stories previously uncollected.

The best news is the availability, in a single package, of stories as good in themselves and as influential on the aspirations of other stories as any since Hemingway's. Second best—a quick check indicates that Welty has avoided the worst temptation of collectors, the revision of old work in hindsight. Thus some of the early stories are still clouded by a compulsively metaphoric prose (virtually everything is compared to, equated with, some other thing). And even an untypically hollow story like "The Purple Hat" or a misfire like "A Visit of Charity" has been perpetuated with the successes. Far better though to have them in the forms of their initial occurrence than obscured by a forged technical gloss or uselessly suppressed.

Only one sizable question may be asked. Would it have been better to break up the sequence of the original volumes and print the stories in order of composition (with an exception for *The Golden Apples*, whose stories are connected)? Such an arrangement would at least have made possible the inclusion of a few never-collected early stories as viable as two or three now canonized, and it would have clarified the reader's legitimate search for evolving themes and repetitions in a writer whose concerns have dived and surfaced in unusually patient cycles. But Welty presumably chose in favor of her first, chiefly musical placement; and she of all contemporary writers since Auden has spoken out most sternly against the bald historical-biographical curiosity of readers and critics. In any case, the original appearances of the components of the four volumes were closely grouped. Those in *A Curtain of Green* were published in magazines from 1936 to 1941, those in *The Wide Net* from 1941 to 1943, *The Golden Apples* from 1947 to 1949, *The Bride of the Innisfallen* from 1949 to 1954, and the two latest stories in 1963 and 1966. (Each of these volumes was followed by a novel—*The Robber Bridegroom* in 1942, *Delta Wedding* in 1946, *The Ponder Heart* in 1954, and the two late stories by *Losing Battles* in 1970 and *The Optimist's Daughter* in 1972.)

A long performance then and one which, though it has never lacked praise and devoted readers, has presented critics with the kind of fearless emotional intensity, the fixed attention to daily life, and the technical audacity that have mercilessly revealed the poverty of scholastic critical methods. In the 1940s the lucid early stories and *Delta Wedding* were automatically accused of gothicism and indifference to the plight of southern blacks. The connected stories of *The Golden Apples* set off a dismal and apparently endless hunt for mythological underpinning (a curse that the stories innocently brought on themselves). The internalized experiments of the long stories of the 1950s met with general bafflement. Though prizes descended and though a handful of stories were rushed into most anthologies while Welty fans round the land stood ready to burst into recitations from "Petrified Man" or "A Shower of Gold," it was only with Ruth Vande Kieft's discerning *Eudora Welty* in 1962 that the size of the achievement began to be acknowledged and mapped—the size and the peculiar pitfalls of the stories as objects for contemplation, guides to action.

The difficulties are big, both of matter and of manner. As the center of critical power shifted in the 1950s from the south to the northeast, a vestigial resistance to southern fiction quickly enlarged and hardened. The south had had too long an inning as Literary Central; its writers were obsessed with the ruling classes of a society rotten with greed and racist inhumanity (as though Tolstoy, Flaubert, or Bellow had more exemplary subjects). Thus Welty's Christian white ladies and their ineffectual mates, her resigned fieldhands and maids, her garrulous white trash, were obstacles for a high proportion of trained readers. And no native southern critics of distinction rose in succession to Ransom, Tate, and Warren to mediate such work to the nation. But even more daunting than the unabashed southern grounding of the work was the statement at its center, a quiet reiterated statement that declared two polar yet indissoluble things. Most disturbing of all, the statement proved itself by locating characters and actions of recognizable solidity and pursuing them with a gaze that occasionally seemed serpentine in its steadiness—or angelic (as in angel of judgment). On first acquaintance one might be tempted to link the Welty of the stories with an apparent progenitor and paraphrase the statement by quoting D. H. Lawrence's essay on Poe—"A ghastly disease love. Poe telling us of his disease: trying to make his disease fair and attractive. Even succeeding."

If we substitute *Homo sapiens* for Poe we do have a crucial beam for the scaffolding of any of Welty's stories. The fact was realized in other terms in Robert Penn Warren's important early essay, "The Love and the Separateness in Miss Welty." For the stories from first to last do say this clearly: "Human creatures are compelled to seek one another in the hope of forming permanent bonds of mutual service, not primarily from an instinct to continue the species" (children are only minor players in her cast), "but from a profound hunger, mysterious in cause, for individual gift and receipt of mutual care." ("Tenderness" is Welty's most sacred word.) "So intense is the hunger however that, more often than not, it achieves no more than its own frustration—the consumption and obliteration of one or both of the mates." (The words "bitter" and "shriek" occur as frequently, and weightily, as "tenderness.")

To that extent, Poe or even Strindberg is a truer ancestor to the stories than Virginia Woolf or E. M. Forster, who have often been mentioned. But such whimsical genealogies are of interest only to literary historians. They give little help to a reader whose aim is the enjoyment of and kinetic response to fiction that is so obviously the report of a particular pair of eyes on a particular place. For the dense matrix of observed life—mineral, bestial, human—which surrounds Welty's statement of the doomed circularity of love is the source of her originality, the flavor which quickly distinguishes a stretch of her prose from any other writer's.

> She knew that now at the river, where she had been before on moonlit nights in autumn, drunken and sleepless, mist lay on the water and filled the trees, and from the eyes to the moon would be a cone, a long silent horn, of white light. It was a connection visible as the hair is in air, between the self and the moon, to make the self feel the child, a daughter far, far back. Then the water, warmer than the night air or the self that might be suddenly cold, like any other arms, took the body under too, running without visibility into the mouth. As she would

> drift in the river, too alert, too insolent in her heart in those days, the mist might thin momentarily and brilliant jewel eyes would look out from the water-line and the bank. Sometimes in the weeds a lightning bug would lighten, on and off, on and off, for as long in the night as she was there to see.
>
> Out in the yard, in the coupe, in the frayed velour pocket next to the pistol was her cache of cigarettes. She climbed inside and shielding the matchlight, from habit, began to smoke cigarettes. All around her the dogs were barking. ["The Wanderers"]

Her monitoring senses record two main strands of data—the self-sufficient splendor of the natural world (in a number of American and European places) and the enciphered poetry of human thought and speech which rises, sometimes through fits of laughter, to moments of eloquently plain truth-telling. The first-written of the stories provides a pure example. In "Death of a Traveling Salesman," the lost itinerant shoe-salesman comes suddenly to understand the fertile union of a couple in whose home he has harbored after an automobile accident.

> Bowman could not speak. He was shocked with knowing what was really in this house. A marriage, a fruitful marriage. That simple thing. Anyone could have had that.
>
> Somehow he felt unable to be indignant or protest, although some sort of joke had certainly been played upon him. There was nothing remote or mysterious here—only something private.

Such yearning for love is found in numerous other mouths in the stories, as character after character (male and female indifferently) reaches the boundary of illusion. But the second half of their repeated discovery is almost never spoken, by character or author. Only at the solitary ends of fated action do the characters perceive an inexorably closing circle. Having earned his vision, the salesman flees the scene of care and continuance and dies of heart failure, literally felled by his knowledge. Virgie Rainey at the end of "The Wanderers" is driven from her home and all she has known by the collapse of her dream of transcending love; and her first stopping place—perhaps her final destination—is a heightened awareness of the gorgeous nonhuman world that coils round our species (the only species, so far as we know, capable of contemplating that world). The casual pair who nearly connect in "No Place for You, My Love" are actually prevented by a watchful and judging world, the sunstruck land below New Orleans.

> At length he stopped the car again, and this time he put his arm under her shoulders and kissed her—not knowing ever whether gently or harshly. It was the loss of that distinction that told him this was now. Then their faces touched unkissing, unmoving, dark, for a length of time. The heat came inside the car and wrapped them still, and the mosquitoes had begun to coat their arms and even their eyelids.
>
> Later, crossing a large open distance, he saw at the same time two fires. He had the feeling that they had been riding for a long time across a face—great, wide, and upturned. In its eyes and open mouth were those fires they had had glimpses of, where the cattle had drawn together: a face, a head, far down here in the South—south of South, below it. A whole giant body sprawled downward then, on and on, always, constant as a constellation or an angel. Flaming and perhaps falling, he thought.

Similar ambush awaits the characters of her novels, though the greater length of a novel generally results in a more ambiguous, if not truer, statement. The stories preserve the naked cry—as sane, inevitable, and unaswerable as the evening call of a solitary beast from the edge of a wood.

No wonder that admirers of Welty's fiction have concentrated most of their scrutiny and affection on comic stories like "Why I Live at the P.O." or the numerous others that richly summon atmospheres of serene nature and the warm conglomerations of family life—weddings, funerals, reunions. The choice has been instinctive, a normal reflex of narrative hunger (which craves consolation, with small side-orders of fright or sadistic witness).

The favorites are certainly worthy. In previous American fiction, only Mark Twain displays as skillfully poised a comic gift, poised on the razor that divides compassion and savagery (Faulkner's comedy is oddly gentler). Welty's power over loving and tussling groups of kin gathered on magnetized family ground is matched only by the 19th-century Russians, as is her courage for the plain declaration of loyalty and duty. A story like "A Worn Path" is unimaginable in any hands but hers or Chekhov's (and it is only illustrative of my point that this uncomplicated tale of duty has evoked a blizzard of nutty mytho-symbolist explications). And her effortless entry into masculine minds as various as the traveling salesman, the younger salesman in "The Hitch-Hikers," the young husband of "The Wide Net," the black jazz-pianist of "Powerhouse," and the majestically thoughtless King MacLain of *The Golden Apples* is a sustaining assurance (in the presently gory gender wars) that the sexes can occasionally comprehend and serve one another if they choose to.

But such selective attention—and the popular anthologies have been as monotonous as her admirers—has resulted in a partial, even distorted, sense of Welty as the mild, sonorous, "affirmative" kind of artist whom America loves to clasp to its bosom and crush with belated honors (Robert Frost endured a similar reputation, but he had handmade it assiduously). It is one of the qualities of genius to provide wares for almost any brand of shopper—it has taken ages to wrestle Jane Austen from the chaste grip of the Janeites or Dickens from the port-and-Stilton set—and Welty's stories have, without calculation, stocked most departments. But such an embarrassment of choice endangers understanding.

One can hope then that this first display of the whole supply in a single place will encourage readers not only to sample the random colors and harmonies of 20-odd masterpieces but to read all the stories in the roughly chronological order of their arrangement. I've already suggested the chief discovery or rediscovery to be made—a contemporary American genius of range as well as depth.

The breadth of Welty's offering is finally most visible not in the variety of types—farce, satire, horror, lyric, pastoral, mystery—but in the clarity and solidity and absolute honesty of a lifetime's vision. That it's a Janus-faced or, Argus-eyed vision, I've also suggested—even even at times a Gorgon stare. Yet its findings are not dealt out as one more of the decks of contradictory and generally appalling polaroids so prevalent in our fiction and verse. A slow perusal here—say a story a night for six weeks—will not fail to confirm a granite core in every tale: as complete and unassailable an image of human relations as any in our art, tragic of necessity but also comic (even the latest story, a chilling impersonation of the white assassin of a black civil rights leader, jokes to its end). As real a gift in our legacy as any broad river or all our lost battles.

Danièle Pitavy-Souques

> . . . be dreams that he is a great blazing butterfly stitching up a net; which doesn't make sense.
>
> —Eudora Welty, "Old Mr. Marblehall"

> —Vous moquez-vous de nous, Monsieur, avec une pareille histoire?
>
> —Est-ce qu'il n'y a pas, Madame, une espèce de tulle qu'on appelle du tulle illusion.
>
> —Barbey d'Aurévilly

To the late-twentieth-century reader, Eudora Welty appears an adventurer of the mind. A spirit of challenge, of pure exhilaration, lifts the fiction of a writer who taught her readers how to "creep out on the shimmering bridge of the tree," and whose figure of the artist in its protean garb is the wanderer, defiant and heroic, brave and vain—Loch Morrison, the young rebel, hanging upside down in the hackberry tree to see better, thus reestablishing the truth through his subversive vision; or Miss Eckhart, the foreign musician, devoured by a passion for her "life work," her "own art"; or else, Perseus the mythic hero. These examples are all taken from *The Golden Apples* (1949), that central book in Eudora Welty's work.

In "The Wanderers," Virgie Rainey meditates upon an engraving of "Perseus with the head of the Medusa" that hung above the piano in Miss Eckhart's studio: "The vaunting was what she remembered."[1] Nearly thirty years later, writing in praise of two American writers with whom she feels some spiritual kinship—Willa Cather and Mark Twain—Eudora Welty emphatically dwells on that same word "vaunt":

Material first printed in Fall 1986 issue of the *Mississippi Quarterly*, Vol. 39, No. 4 pp. 532–560. Reprinted by permission of Robert Phillips.

> Who can move best but the inspired child of his times? Whose story should better be told than that of the youth who has contrived to cut loose from ties and go flinging himself might and main, in every bit of his daring, in joy of life not to be denied, to vaunt himself in the love of vaunting, in the marvelous curiosity to find out everything, over the preposterous length and breadth of an opening new world, and in so doing to be one with it?[2]

The term is more ambiguous than it seems. Applied to Perseus, "vaunt" expresses the legitimate pride of the slayer of Medusa; to Twain and Cather, it links creative joy to ostentatious victory. And indeed there runs throughout her work evidence of Welty's secret fascination with appearances. She creates characters who delight in flaunting and shocking, from Virgie Rainey with her daredevil behavior and dress, to the "middle-aged lady" in "The Bride of the Innisfallen" who parades in a striped raincoat; or those who adore staging their response to life's drama: Fay dressed in glistening black satin, playing the part of the disconsolate widow in *The Optimist's Daughter*, or the narrator so magnificently "building up" a stage for *Losing Battles* in the first few pages. The very excess of such scenes betrays the ambiguity of Welty's feelings, the sense of ridicule that makes her laugh at the gesture while she cannot help admiring it. Etymology throws some light; the allied terms "vaunt" and "vain" are both stamped with vacuity, their common Latin origin meaning "empty" or "hollow." We come close to vainglory, at least to the idea of taking excess pride, when a more modest attitude is required.

To grasp the complex connotations of "vaunt" for Welty, consider how she uses the word "vain" in a later work, *The Optimist's Daughter*. When Laurel McKelva comes upon a photograph of her dead mother, she remembers Becky's pride in the blouse she wears in the picture: " 'The most beautiful blouse I ever owned in my life—I made it. Cloth from Mother's own spinning, and dyed a deep, rich, American Beauty color with pokeberries,' her mother had said with the gravity in which she spoke of 'up home.' 'I'll never have anything to wear that to me is as satisfactory as that blouse.' How *darling* and *vain* she was when she was *young!* Laurel thought now" (italics added).[3] The association "young-vain" is that of Perseus himself, and here "darling" softens the blame and asserts the right to glory. As for the garment itself, it is the symbol for the undaunted pioneering spirit that defied every obstacle that nature put in its way. Reflexively, Eudora Welty's praise of Twain and Cather comes to mean the celebration of two writers who wrote of

America's challenge to the wilderness—not mere recorders but adventurers too in the fresh province of Western literature. But behind the very necessity and nobleness of the conquest looms its costly aftermath, as Clement Musgrove, the cotton planter in *The Robber Bridegroom,* suspects. The reverse side of the success story weighs heavily and deserves examination. Just as, figuratively speaking, on his return journey the triumphant Perseus wore the mask of the slain Medusa, which he put on the better to be seen—not the other way round—so Welty's fiction also explores the inside of the mask, examines the figure observing the other: Perseus behind the face of Medusa watching reflexively this arrogant vaunting other self that moves behind a mask. The artist is both performer and audience, watched and watching. Hence those paired characters that people her fiction, one of whom acts—often with bravado and ostentation—while the other watches. And in this onlooker's gaze (character, narrator, or the writer herself) there passes the awareness of the futility of it all, the weariness and restlessness that Eudora Welty inscribed at the very beginning of her work in a brilliant story whose trope is a key, that of the title, which functions in many ways as trope for her entire fiction. In "The Key," the stance that she gives to the red-haired man reveals a writer singularly ahead of her time:

> . . . in his eyes, all at once wild and searching, there was certainly, besides the simple compassion in his regard, a look both restless and weary, very much used to the comic. You could see that he despised and saw the uselessness of the thing he had done. (p. 37)

To complete this imaginary figure by which Welty's fiction can be represented, I should add the other two elements of the myth: the mirror-shield and the Medusa, with corresponding mirror effects in the writing, fascination and death as themes. We know how those elements, which have always been present in serious fiction, became tropes of the modernist novel, the fiction of James, Conrad, Joyce, or Virginia Woolf.

I choose to single out Perseus because he stands for "the inspired child of his times," what could be called *modernity,* and with this word we are sent traveling down the twentieth century. Eudora Welty, although influenced by and heir to the aesthetic principles of the great modernist writers—like all other writers in this century—has a much more advanced and complex position than her moment in time would lead one to expect. As early as the mid-1930s, all alone and brave, she was already displaying that new spirit and experimenting with techniques that have since become accepted as postmodernist. I will not make her a postmodernist, though, for several reasons, perhaps the chief one being that she never fails to achieve, in William Gass's phrase, "the full responsive reach of her readers."

The word *modernity* was first used by the nineteenth-century French poet Charles Baudelaire, who in many respects was one of the founding fathers of modern thinking (and a great admirer of another Southerner, Edgar Allan Poe). "Modernity," he wrote, "is what is transitory, fugitive and contingent—one half of art, whose other half is the eternal and immutable." As a corollary, he insisted on "the dual composition of the Beautiful though it is experienced as one."[4]

To Baudelaire modernity meant, even more than receptiveness to the new ideas of one's time and immersion in one's own present, a spirit of challenge, the desire to question the "given," for the truly innovative artist is he who tries to capture and represent in his work what he perceives as a new *rapport* of the human mind with the created world. This involves altering known modes of representation since any new questioning of the reality of things and the way the self perceives its position in the universe necessarily affects mimesis. For instance, Baudelaire admired Eugène Delacroix because, alone in his time, he opposed the prevalent realism of such official painters as David or Ingres, and was already trying new techniques to express the slowly emerging tendency toward abstraction. To the rendering of surface reality Delacroix preferred the suggestion of the hidden truth, to the realistic painting of a brawny sinewy arm the suggestion of *tension* produced by a new use of color and shadow. Moreover, those "brilliant modern discoveries," which somehow acknowledged the inadequacy of painting to represent, resulted in a pervasive *mood of melancholy*, that "most remarkable quality which truly signals Delacroix as *the* nineteenth-century painter." While writing this, Baudelaire was quite aware of the near impossibility of the artistic endeavor: a mood is perhaps the closest that an artist can come to modernity.

There are many moods in Eudora Welty, as Ruth Vande Kieft brilliantly stressed some twenty years ago.[5] Earlier, Robert Penn Warren had taught us how to read this "serious fiction": "the items of fiction (scene, action, character, etc.) are presented not as document but as comment, not as a report but as a thing made, not as history, but as idea." Rather than develop this symbolic aspect of Welty's writing, a "method . . . similar to the method of much modern poetry,"[6] I want to examine, first, how Welty's challenge to mimesis expresses a radical fracture of the self, then, how in the organization of experience she moves further away from modernist writers by favoring a conceptual mode of thinking that leads toward abstraction and structure rather than pattern.

The theory of representation—a word I prefer to mimesis because the Aristotelian term does not imply possible negation—rests on the human faculties of recollection and imagination. Whereas recollection dominated narrative literature in the eighteenth and nineteenth centuries, imagination rules in the present one. There has been, in Gablik's words, "a gradual shift in art from iconic modes of representation (which are essentially figurative and are linked to immediate perceptual experience, where the image closely resembles the concrete objects to which it refers) towards non-representational, non-mimetic modes which are conceptual in organization." Here she follows Piaget, who writes: "The object only exists . . . in its relations with the subject and, if the mind always advances more toward the conquest of things, this is because it organizes experience more and more actively, instead of mimicking, from without, a ready-made reality."[7] At the same time, Sartre posits irreality in his theory of the imagination. His phenomenological psychology leads him to reject the three classical theories of associationism, continuity between the different modes of knowledge (i.e., between image and idea), and strict separation of image from idea, a disjunction that takes the image for a thing and dismisses its fallacy.[8] Conversely, Sartre says, the image is "a certain type of consciousness. The image is an act, not a thing. The image is awareness of something." He thus states the dissociation between the faculty of producing images and the world of reality, then goes further when he postulates as a prerequisite for the image "the possibility to posit irreality" ("la possibilité de poser une thèse d'irréalité"). For Sartre, the negative action is constituent of the image ("l'acte négatif est constitutif de l'image").[9]

Such theories throw needed light on the more experimental side of Welty's fiction, that side which the generous, inspired tone of her criticism tends to blur. She herself, in her work, is far more daring than her literary tastes would have us believe. As early as her first collection, *A Curtain of Green* (1941), she showed her preoccupation with uncertainty. Not the modernist sense of ambiguity or the technical device of a variety of narrators each telling or recreating the truth, nor the Chekhovian juxtaposition of events or delayed exposure—rather what Ruth Vande Kieft has called "the mysteries of Eudora Welty." These mysteries lead Welty to explore the borderline situations, the reversals, shifts and crossings of borders; to attempt to submerge the frame, "to render problematical what is, as it were, inside a text and what is outside it," as Tanner says of postmodernist writers.[10] Or she twists the narrative and lets in new narrative possibilities, as in "Death of a Traveling Salesman," "Powerhouse," "A Piece of News," or "Flowers for Marjorie," one of the more accomplished stories in this respect. However, "A Memory" is most daring as an instance of Welty's exploration—it belongs to those remarkable stories in *A Curtain of Green* that are metaphors, stories whose form is the dramatization of their meaning. "A Memory" is about representation and the process of seeing and writing. Or it is a story about "the familiar and its ghostly other," as Regis Durand puts it. Durand also quotes a paper entitled "On Aspects of the Familiar World," in which Walter Abish uses the idea of the familiar and its representations to make a distinction between fictional modes:

> The need to see the world *familiarly* is a result of a preoccupation with the "self" rather than with the world. The "familiar" is to be equated with "self" preoccupation.[11]

This preoccupation with the self, supreme in a self-centered world, is what we find in the modernist novel, in James or Proust. When Proust describes the experience of the madeleine, he is dealing with an "Effet de Réel," as Barthes says; in other words, he is representing "reality," trying to see the world familiarly. The reader who has had a similar experience will identify with Marcel and be reassured in the belief they both belong to the same world, share the same reality. Proust's fiction represents the self trying to come to terms with the world.

On the other hand, a postmodernist text, according to Walter Abish, "must disavow a self-centered world in which the self continues to reign supreme," for it is essentially

> a novel of disfamiliarization, a novel that has ceased to concern itself with the mapping of the "familiar" world, for to do so would compel the characters to adopt a perception of the everyday predicated on an unquestioning affirmation of the function and role of the "self" in society, as rigidly governed by the "reality principle" and as subsumed by the logic of everyday existence as we are.[12]

Let us look closely at "A Memory." We have a first "picture" or "representation" of reality, but what do we see? Certainly not a realistic painting, not even a "virtually pastoral"[13] one:

> The water shone like *steel,* motionless except for the feathery curl behind a distant swimmer. From my position I was looking at a rectangle brightly lit, actually *glaring* at me, with sun, sand, water, a little pavilion, a few solitary people in *fixed* attitudes, and *around* it all a border of dark rounded oak trees, like the engraved thunderclouds *surrounding* illustrations in the *Bible.* Ever since I had begun taking painting lessons, I had made small frames with my fingers, to look out at everything.
>
> .... I was at an age when I formed a judgment upon every person and every event which came under my eye, although I was easily frightened. (p. 75; my italics)

What is shown here is not reality as it is experienced directly in everyday life, but a *conventional representation of a public park,* a descriptive discourse acknowledged by a group at a given time. At the same time, *this description is extremely hostile,* as the words "steel," "glaring," and "thunderclouds" imply. Third, *this picture is framed,* and framed by the Bible, so to speak.

This first picture, which the young girl sees in her innocence, will be soon shattered. In other words, Eudora Welty rejects it, and she does so for reasons that seem to me very much postmodernist. First, we are confronted with a general suspicion of the myth of reality, i.e., "the consensual discourse describing the official representation of the world in a given cultural community at a given time."[14] Then, the picture raises the problem of frames and framing. This the young girl learned when she began taking painting lessons as part of the conventional way of dealing with representation. A frame is a way of delimiting her subject, of imposing restraint and cutting out all that might crop up unexpectedly. In this context, especially with reference to the thunderclouds in the Bible, the frame represents the law, the repressive law of Jehovah. When writing about the "problematic of judicial framing and the jurisdiction of frames," Jacques Derrida refers to "all organized narration" as "a matter for the police," that is, subjected to some kind of law which, in a written work, may be simply "language," not this or that discourse, but language itself.[15] Barthes speaks too of the "fascism" of language: "fascism is not the power to prevent from saying but the power to force to say." In "A Memory" the picture is "dictated" for the child, who in placing and judging people is somehow "framed" herself, i.e., held in a false position by the oppressive prejudice of her parents that makes her feel guilty when she asserts her rights to see and know. "Breaking frames" is also what the story is about, which is as old as the novel, and it is one of the first things that Welty as a user of language learned. Heidegger envisioned the possibility of inverting this "relation of dominance":

> Man acts as though he were the shaper and master of language, while in fact language remains the master of man. When this relation of dominance gets inverted, man hits upon strange manoeuvers. Language becomes the means for expression. . . .

Eudora Welty expresses much the same view in her beautiful essay "Words into Fiction": "We start from scratch, and words don't." And just as Heidegger hoped for "strange manoeuvres," Welty speaks of a "leap in the dark,"[16] or, in a superb image that reflects Heidegger's proposition, "in the boat":

> . . . it was not so much that they drifted, as that in the presence of a boat the world drifted, forgot. The dreamed-about changed places with the dreamer. ("Moon Lake," p. 360)

The third reason is linked to the deceiving quality of language—or vision. This picture is traditionally modernist, for in it "the *need* to see the world familiarly is a result of the preoccupation with the self rather than with the world." The narrator of "A Memory" says nothing else:

> To watch everything about me I regarded grimly and possessively as a *need.* All through this summer I had lain on the sand beside the small lake, with my hands squared over my eyes, finger tips touching, looking out by this device to see everything: which appeared as a kind of projection. It did not matter to me what I looked at; from any observation I would conclude that a secret of life had been nearly revealed to me—(pp. 75–76)

Framing and the need to see the world familiarly combine and represent the efforts of the self to master the world. The young girl feels such control because she can produce at will the memory of a brief encounter with a young boy, her first love:

> I still would not care to say which was more *real*—the dream I could make blossom at will, or the sight of the bathers. I am presenting them, you see, only as simultaneous. (p. 77; my italics)

At this first stage, otherness is defined as the not-self, the "world." Here the not-self is what is most familiar, the world she inhabits, the "real" society. "The paradox," Regis Durand remarks, "is that the familiar world is most familiar to us when it is least seen as it is, for what it is, but simply as the need of the self to see things familiarly: the real world treated familiarly." Modernist writers stop at this point, showing the self (as Walter Abish says) "forever striving to reach an agreement with the desirable otherness." Welty goes a step further, not only investigating the familiar, but also *looking at it for what it is.* We should perhaps bear in mind Freud's definition of the "uncanny" or *Unheimlich:* "The 'uncanny' is that class of the terrifying which leads back to something long known to us, once very familiar."[17]

The second picture presented in "A Memory" is one of violence and distortion as the child sees "a group of loud, squirming, ill-assorted people who seemed thrown together only by the most confused accident, and who seemed driven by foolish intent to insult each other, all of which they enjoyed with a hilarity which astonished my heart" (p. 77). The pleasantly controlled circle of the first picture becomes "wobbly ellipses" as the little boys chase each other. The trim white pavilion is replaced by the shapeless mound of sand built around the ugly woman. This is a painful initiation into the contingency of life as it is: in order to be true, the artist must be able to see all the violence and rage and ugliness that is part of life. But it is more than that, for in the culminating point of "A Memory," the little girl has a true vision of death. All of the images referring to the woman point to a petrified landscape. "Fat hung upon her upper arms like an arrested earthslide on a hill," her legs looked like "shadowed bulwarks" (p. 78), and when she pulled down the front of her bathing suit to empty out the "mashed and folded sand," the child "felt a peak of horror, as though her breasts themselves had turned to sand" (p. 79). This petrified landscape is the intrusion into the narrative of the face of the Medusa, the swoon into which the narrator falls, a sort of death. In "A Memory" the only escape from this "framed" condition seems to be through death; in other stories it will be through diffusion or dispersal, as in "Old Mr. Marblehall."

We see how petrifaction functions here as a strange maneuver by which Welty indicates that the girl's experience is not one of appropriation, as all her preceding ones were, but of disavowal. More important, it is one of intensification, an intensification of the radical otherness of the other, a recognition of the difference, of the unaccountable. But this disavowal, which is precisely the word used by Walter Abish, has a more complex meaning than just negation; it is, in a Freudian sense, something that involves the negation of the reality of a perception, usually a traumatic one, and it concerns itself with *the presence of an absence.* It is, as Freud has shown, the principle behind the cleavage of the self. Yet, in "A Memory" this deconstructive gesture is confronted by a very strong impulse to reestablish order, unity:

> I tried to withdraw to my most inner dream, that of touching the wrist of the boy I loved on the stair; I felt the shudder of my wish shaking the darkness like leaves where I had closed my eyes; I felt the heavy weight of sweetness which always accompanied this memory; but the memory itself did not come to me. (p. 79)

The world, the familiar world, is still present in a way, the same and not quite the same; but since the new experience is that of an *absence,* there is a fracture: "I did not know, any longer, the meaning of my happiness; it held me unexplained" (p. 79).

The third picture is that of the devastated beach. The narrator confesses: "for the object which met my eye, the small worn white pavilion, I felt pity suddenly overtake me, and I burst into tears" (p. 79). Those very tears are what Serge Leclaire, in *Rompre les charmes,* has called "the compulsion to referentiality," the illusions and displacements which the self creates to conceal the fracture, to uphold the fiction of a narcissistic whole, of an interior space. But we see how very precarious this new picture is, how pitiful our poor attempts at creating images are. It seems our lot in the end to accept the cleavage of the self, for what is the "other" but the revelation of the non-identify of self to self. This is the lesson taught in "A Still Moment."

In this story, which belongs to the second collection (*The Wide Net,* 1943), Welty pursues her reflection on representation—a reflection on the visible as it is affected by the presence of an absence. The obvious figure of the artist is Audubon, naturalist and painter. But the other two characters—Murrell, the murderer devoured by a dream of domination and the will to wrench the secret of life from his dying victims, and Lorenzo Dow, the preacher convinced in his teleological vision of the world that his fate is to save all souls—stand for the artist's darker selves or tempters. Their passion is the artist's and so is their awareness of "the object," the white heron, perceived by Murrell as a projection of himself, by Lorenzo as a part of God's creation, and by Audubon as a thing of beauty to be painted.

Just as the artist is seen in three, so is the creative process. In the first stage there must be a deep immersion in the sensible world, which prevails over the world of ideas, and an intimate knowledge of its workings. We note Welty's (or Perseus's) joy in the created world because it holds wonder, but this does not mean, however, that evil of all manner is not forever present, as "A Still Moment" reveals. The mirror surface of the story functions very much like one of those mirrors used by painters after the fashion of Claude Lorrain, framing and reflecting what is not seen directly—control and indirection in technique. In the second stage the artist must accomplish some form of severance; he must acknowledge the inevitable fracture, which is symbolized in "A Still Moment" by the killing of the heron. The third stage is that of representation. It states the impossibility of drawing from memory and restoring to wholeness an instant's vision of absolute beauty. Instead, the artist will reconstruct that vision through fragments, which is a deconstructive gesture:

> [Audubon] knew that the best he could make would be, after it was apart from his hand, a dead thing and not a live thing, never the essence, only a sum of parts; and that it would always meet with a stranger's sight, and never be one with the beauty in any other man's head in the world. (p. 198)

The artist faced with the impossibility of representing pure essence has become a cliché, as Welty, the avid reader of Virginia Woolf's fiction and diaries, knows all too well. But I think Welty departs from her modernist predecessors when she shows how representation involves a fracture, a construction which amounts to deconstruction ("never the essence, only a sum of parts"), and, still more pointedly, when she acknowledges the presence of an absence through the symbolism of the dead bird used to represent a live one. I would even suggest that "separateness" in this context—that of Lorenzo's dismay—means "an endeavour to dispose of causality," in Claude Richard's phrase. Let me quote again that well-known passage in "A Still Moment":

> He could understand God's giving Separateness first and then giving Love to follow and heal in its wonder; but God had reversed this, and given Love first and then Separateness, as though it did not matter to Him which came first. Perhaps it was that God never counted the moments of Time; Lorenzo did that, among his tasks of love. Time did not occur to God. Therefore—did He even know of it? How to explain Time and Separateness back to God, Who had never thought of them, Who could let the whole world come to grief in a scattering moment? (p. 198)

If time no longer ordains, the whole logically organized sequence of a narrative no longer matters. And indeed, the text is about a "still moment." Moreover, as the necessities of likeness or unlikeness disappear, representation may move further away from the original object. It becomes, in effect, a reflection on the distorting power of absence over presence, an absence which is a sort of echo but not the thing itself. This is the crux of Audubon's method: to represent a bird alive, the painter must kill it.

This experience of "otherness" in the familiar occurs again in *The Golden Apples.* "Moon Lake" is a story about the other (whether he be a boy for the girls, a grownup or an orphan for Nina and Jinny Love), a story about disavowing a self-centered world, with a lesson similar to that of "A Memory." To discover the other is to acknowledge one's own mortality, to become aware of the other side of the mirror, of the self.

The story begins with an exploration of differences, which, in our need to see the world familiarly, we tend to categorize. This is deeply ironic since the camp at Moon Lake was intended to abolish all differences, especially between the orphans and the respectable little girls of Morgana, but it has only succeeded in making them more bitterly felt. Nina's initiation consists in renouncing her own system of differentiation to acknowledge true "separateness." Her first intimation of the presence of the other *as presence* comes of a denial, when she realizes that Easter will not return or acknowledge her gaze—that is to say, when Easter refuses to be *seen,* possessed by Nina; in other words, when Nina's need to see the world familiarly fails. For although Nina has already "placed" the orphans, it is not without ambiguity—as the "not answerable" already hints with disquieting otherness:

> The reason orphans were the way they were lay first in nobody's watching them, Nina thought. . . . They, they were not answerable.

> Even on being watched, Easter remained not answerable to a soul on earth. Nobody cared! And so, in this beatific state, something came out of *her*. (p. 352)

Then, for the first time, Nina is able to enter Easter's mind and know what she thinks after they have played together in the boat. To signify this development in the narration (told from Nina's point of view), all "as if" and "it seemed" constructions are dropped; we have pure affirmative sentences, as the following modulation suggests:

> A dragonfly flew about their heads. Easter only waited in her end of the boat, not *seeming* to care about the disappointment either. If this was their ship, she was their figurehead, turned on its back, sky-facing. She wouldn't be their passenger. (p. 356; my italics)

For the first time, the voice we hear is no longer Nina's but Easter's.

The next step occurs through writing when Nina becomes capable of seeing herself as an object, just as she has seen Easter as the other. She writes side by side "Nina," then "Easter." The fine point made later about the spelling of Easter's name is that this *other* is totally unaccountable, not "wholly calculable," as Henry James said. It lives its own life and escapes our power of naming it; this is why *Easter* can spell her name *Esther*, which is at least a real name, not a nickname, and can proudly say in a world defying all laws of causation—that new world which Welty's fiction ceaselessly explores—"I let myself name myself" (p. 357).

I will not insist on Nina's education as a writer, which implies the experience of death and, ultimately, becoming the other. Yet, I wish to make one more point in this exploration of the unfamiliar: somehow, Easter's proud declaration brings us close to "A Still Moment." The reflexive pronoun becomes warped on the way back. "I let myself name myself" does not describe the same/identical, i.e., what Nina expected—Easter. Instead, there rises from the depth of time the Other—Esther. Duration and time are challenged as Nina is brought face to face with the mirror of writing: it reflects the person whom we call but his true character is never spelled correctly. Instead of the foundling, the Biblical heroine faces Nina. The silvering is now *before* the mirror, not behind, thus turning it into a medal (a coin). What is sent back to Nina is no longer her own image but that of other women unknown to her:

> Easter's eyes . . . were neither brown nor green nor cat; they had something of metal, flat ancient metal, so that you could not see into them. Nina's grandfather had possessed a box of coins from Greece and Rome. Easter's eyes could have come from Greece or Rome that day. (pp. 347–348)

The fine quality of Welty's writing comes from this dual texture. Beneath the apparently familiar world—shall we say realistic?—spreads the huge territory of the never quite known or mapped, the wholly elusive. Here I mean more than the unconscious, which has always been explored by writers; I mean the very questioning of the possibilities of the human mind to conceive and represent the world. In work after work, Welty tries to represent the functioning of the human mind, to evoke the duality between an extreme susceptibility to the sensuousness of the created world and the desire to grasp it and show it through figures. This abstracting tendency in her fiction I would now like to examine in relation to the way she constructs her stories. This will be a discussion of structure as opposed to pattern.

In the modernist aesthetics of the earlier part of this century, the formal and symbolic resources of the novel were emphasized; "form," "pattern," and "myth" were of paramount importance. Traces of this can be seen in *The Wide Net,* but we see in a later story such as "Circe" (1955) how Welty has decisively broken new paths. Let me quote from both a postmodern writer and a postmodern critic to make my point. John Hawkes writes in 1965:

> I began to write fiction on the assumption that the true enemies of the novel were plot, character, setting and theme, and having once abandoned these familiar ways of thinking about fiction, totality of vision or structure was really all that remained. And structure—verbal and psychological coherence—is still my largest concern as a writer.[18]

And Robert Scholes in 1967:

> Fabulation, then, means a return to a more verbal kind of fiction. It also means a return to a more fictional kind. By this I mean a less realistic and more artistic kind of narrative: more shapely, more evocative; more concerned with ideas and ideals, less concerned with things.[19]

This could be compared with what Welty writes in "Words into Fiction," where we note her essential preoccupation with form, the "totality of vision and structure":

> The novel or story ended, shape must have made its own impression on the reader, so that he feels that some *design* in life (by which I mean esthetic pattern, not purpose) has just been discovered there. And this pattern, shape, form that emerges for you then, a reader at the end of the book, may do the greatest thing that fiction does: it may move you. And however you have been moved by the parts, this still has to happen from *the whole* before you know what indeed you have met with in that book.[20] (my italics)

The important words, of course, are *design* and *whole.* In this deep awareness of form, what matters is the ultimate shape of the finished work, the concern for the *figures* that graphically represent the written work, just as a building is represented by the blueprint of an architect. In this can be traced Welty's surest right to innovation. Claude Simon in *Les Georgiques,* his latest novel, points out this fictional mode and insists on the fact that to read the blueprint correctly one must be aware of the code; otherwise the design is indecipherable. This is somewhat akin to Welty's story of the caves in "Words into Fiction." We need an interpretation.

The difficulty of her work comes from the fact that Eudora Welty used those codes at a time when few could decipher them. The reading of more avant-garde fiction has since taught the public how to look for another representation beneath or behind the story, how to seize, hidden in the visible broken pattern, a more secret pattern. Out of the wide range of figures by which this fiction reveals itself, I will select two, equally beautiful, although the more daring and brilliant may well be the earlier one. Both show, however, the extremely lucid and original way in which Eudora Welty deals with the South—I mean "Old Mr. Marblehall" and "Kin."

"Old Mr. Marblehall" is a story about the imposture of writing; it shows the creation, the "fabrication," of a character, and its limitations. Once again, the surface is deceptive; the apparent subject of the narration is a picture of the decadent society of the Old South, the South seen as myth, if you prefer, and consequently reduced to staging with sets and costumes. In reality, the story shows what Genette argues in *Figures III* about the *recit,* the narrative, which is related both to the story as story and to the act of telling a story. In other words, "Old Mr. Marblehall" stages the specificity of the literary act, the questioning of the very nature of poetical invention and what happens at the moment invention becomes a narrative. In large measure, Eudora Welty's innovative art rests upon this constant shifting towards narration: the *telling* of the story as opposed to the story proper. In "Old Mr. Marblehall," the story is always shown as something elusive, uncertain, in great danger of complete dissolution. Along with this postmodernist tendency to destroy all certainties and reduce the story to its mere constituent parts, we have another well-known trope, constant in Welty's fiction, which I shall call "narrative reversal." Apparently, we shift from what is seen to what is written, but this is pure illusion for it is just the reverse.

To create her character, Eudora Welty raises the two basic questions at the same time: How do we define a character? How do we give him a fictional existence? For this, she relies entirely on a stylistic device often adopted by later writers (William Gass, for instance), that of stylization or the use of stereotypes. It enables her to satirize a number of clichés about the South, to expose hypocritical attitudes, and to insure the active critical participation of her reader. This discourse, founded on a number of infallible and reiterated signs, aims at producing all the marks of what is conventionally known as the Old South, *including its reverse.* The two possible dangers of stylization, imitation and parody (i.e., excessive admiration for one's model or harsh criticism), are brilliantly avoided. This results in Eudora Welty's inimitable tone—her unique voice—which transmutes into poetry the displacement inherent in parody. No labored effects, rather arabesques and flights of the imagination. Writing becomes "a great blazing butterfly" (p. 97).

Character as it appears in the nineteenth-century novel and still quite often in the twentieth-century English novel is defined by family, house, and social life. In "Old Mr. Marblehall," Welty plays on doubles that are not quite identical in order to deconstruct such traditional conception of character. Thus, instead of drawing a portrait of Mr. Marblehall as a Southern gentleman, she paints a full-scale portrait of Mrs. Marblehall as a Southern gentlewoman—hyperbolic if not hysterical. The reality of the couple is denied by the deliberately Balzacian effect of the portrait, doubled by the poor histrionic origins of the husband on another level, and also by the fabricated existence of their child, whose portrait is a series of collages from nineteenth- and twentieth-century writers. For Mr. Marblehall's other more common family Welty follows the same process in the reverse. The whole story, then, is based on the deconstruction of the characters; by stressing their unimportance and artificiality, Welty presents them as *literary constructions.* The signifier becomes the signified, form becomes matter. Poor insignificant Mr. Marblehall, unnoticed by his fellow citizens, comes to nothing, or rather to that illusion which the story represents. That Welty changed old Mr. Grenada into old Mr. Marblehall and the town of Brewster into Natchez corroborates her wish to satirize at the same time the artificiality and anachronism of any literature about the Old South and its myth *and* the traditional way of creating character. She inaugurates here a new kind of character without past existence, which heralds the heroes of the *nouveau roman.*

Duly provided with a stylized mansion, ancestors, and a wife, Mr. Marblehall still lacks what would make him exist: a life. This is the narrative problem which is presented when we read that Mr. Marblehall, in his desire to catch up with time, or the others, is a bigamist. To insert oneself into the flow of time by claiming a past, a present, and a future, and to force the town's attention, is to accede to existence. But this existence is kept doubtful throughout the story:

> Nobody cares. Not an inhabitant of Natchez, Mississippi, cares if he is deceived by old Mr. Marblehall. Neither does anyone care that Mr. Marblehall has finally caught on, he thinks, to what people are supposed to do. This is it: they endure something inwardly—for a time secretly; they establish a past, a memory; thus they store up life. He has done this; most remarkably, he has even multiplied his life by deception; and plunging deeper and deeper he speculates upon some glorious finish, a great explosion of revelations . . . the future. (pp. 96–97)

It all amounts to a matter of vision, and vision is what founds the dialectics used in "Old Mr. Marblehall": *to see and to show on the narrative level, to show oneself and [not] be seen on the narrated level.* The injunction to "watch" is the key word of the text; added in the revised version, it centers the whole story on the creative act which takes place between the puppeteer and his audience. This injunction is obviously addressed by the narrator to the reader, but it is also addressed by Mr. Marblehall to the other characters in the narrative. The positive exchange in the first case becomes negative or null in the second. If we look at the last scene, when old Mr. Marblehall imagines he is discovered by his second son, we are warned that it *cannot happen,* for the *whole* passage is based on the sum of all the different signs attached to his different lives. This scene is purely fictitious in the narrative with no other reality than the writing to give it existence. The text, then, can be read as a kind of staging of Welty's *ars poetica:* writing is a matter for illusion; it begets it while it feeds on it. "Old Mr. Marblehall" fictionalizes the process of writing; it is the imposture of narration.

"Kin" also deals with imposture: what a fraud a family portrait is. Here the structure is based upon the principle of the play within a play. André Gide noted this device in his *Journal,* in reference to the famous Van Eyck painting "The Wedding of the Arnolfi." In it, the guests, that is to say, the witnesses, those who testify to the truth of the event, are not shown directly but as reflections in a mirror. In "Kin," Welty also uses the device of a mirror to represent opposition, but the shift is no longer in space as with the Arnolfi (the witnesses standing where we stand, so to speak) but in time. The mirror does not reflect directly a part of the scene which is presented to the spectator or reader, but the fragment of another scene, of which it constitutes the only material proof, thus putting the first picture into perspective. The beauty of the story comes from the perfect adequacy of the medium for the subject: one must look at the portrait of the great-grandmother in order to understand the meaning of a story about people coming to have their picture taken. "Kin" treats the myth of the Old South after the manner of Monet or Vuillard: only fragments on the shimmering surface. Certainly, Eudora Welty satirizes the nostalgia, but at the same time she celebrates the South, whose essence remains immortal because it is steeped in vivid sensations.

"Kin" is a comedy whose obvious target is Sister Anne, vulgar, money-grabbing, without scruples or delicacy, who relinquishes her duties to the dying Uncle Felix and desecrates the house by letting an itinerant photographer use it. Her gain will be her own picture taken for free.

Two objects form the critical distance, the portrait of Great-grandmother Jerrold and the stereoscope. By a narrative perversity the point of view is Dicey's, who, like Laurel McKelva, is the Southerner gone North who comes back home to visit. The aptness of her remarks is such that we believe her—we are, in fact, in great danger of being taken in by Dicey's lively, charming speech. The extreme impressionistic—and postmodern—fragmentation of the narration, the intermingling of the present and the past, hides the counterpoint, which we see only at the end of the story. In "Old Mr. Marblehall," the Southern way of life was doubled; here it is tripled as it would be in a series of mirrors endlessly reflecting the same picture, producing an effect of closure. Thus three versions of Southern life are presented almost identically (Welty uses the same words). They consist of a present positive image (Dicey revisiting the South), a negative one (Sister Anne), and a much earlier one (the heroic past of the family). The function of the first scene is to establish, *en transparence,* that conventional code by which we can appreciate the structure. For all its beauty and polished appearance this society is essentially racist, materialistic, frivolous and irresponsible. But these flaws, so deeply engrained in the Southern way of life, appear unpleasant only after they are *repeated* in the text:

> It was two-thirty in the afternoon, after an enormous dinner at which we had had company—six girls, chattering almost like ready-made bridesmaids—ending with wonderful black, bitter, moist chocolate pie under mountains of meringue, and black, bitter coffee. (p. 539)
>
> "What do I see? Cake!" (*CS,* p. 548) (Sister Anne's first words of greeting.)
>
> . . . Uncle Harlan, who could be persuaded, if he did not eat too much, to take down the banjo later. (p. 557)

Welty deepens this critique of the family by holding the portrait of Great-grandmother Jerrold in tense relation with the photograph of Sister Anne. Their differences are only superficial, for Anne's photograph is the comical version of the portrait of the great-grandmother—the same vanity, the same desire to appear to advantage in both instances, above all, the same artificiality in the setting. The photographer uses a backdrop—a "blur of . . . yanked-down moonlight"—just as the itinerant painter did, to produce "the same old thing, a scene that never was" (p. 560).

The evocation of the heroic life of the great-grandmother, the founder of the family, is tinted with the same nostalgia and exotic overtones as the views shown in the stereoscope by Uncle Felix: wonderful cities to which the optical machine added the fascination of haziness. In effect, the heroic has become a postcard, rather, a yellowed photograph, something that can be discarded like the old Confederate musket which is kept behind the door like a broom. What the short story "Kin" presents is a series of old-fashioned portraits on the art of living in the South, but it also shows how they were *made up.* Did this legend ever exist? Or was it born out of a series of conventional embellishments? Welty requires that we remove all that is artificial, all that depersonalizes, just as we know that the veil behind the photograph or the canvas is not true. Dicey realizes this when she looks at her great-grandmother's eyes, which are her own, strangely authentic in this artificial portrait. As she leaves Mingo, she takes away with her one last "photograph," another faded and yellowed one too, the blurred, indistinct vision of the country neighbors waiting under the porch. Their faces are identical, yet each carries its impenetrable secret, its identity.

The counterpoint upon which the story is built functions like a stereopticon or a stereoscope, both of which juxtapose images that are seen in relief. Whatever the specific mechanism, the principle is one of duality with the result either of increased distinctness or blurring. This provides the key to "Kin." The superimposition of diverse attitudes, nearly identical throughout the ages, gives a unique picture which both permits one to see what is called "the Old South," and at the same time suggests something evanescent. On this apparent contradiction rest the dialectics of "Kin": to seize the myth one must start from the present, not the other way around. "Kin" is a fraud. The fraud of a family picture, the fraud of a loving family. By choosing appearances, artificiality, and the absurdly false, the living perpetuate an *illusion.* Yet, true values are seen, true courage exists. By rejecting false romanticism, Welty says, people can live authentically: the beauty and idealism of the South are all there. In this respect, "Kin" is a plea for the South, this South, which in a purely postmodern reading may amount to traces only. Memories are, paradoxically, as evanescent and immortal as smells, the exquisite smells of the pinks and four-o'clocks that Aunt Beck would give to her visitors as she walked them to the gate—as if, what is left of people, and life, amounted to no more than mere traces.

In an essay entitled "Literary History and Literary Modernity," Paul de Man arrives at the insight that "one is soon forced to resort to paradoxical formulations such as defining the modernity of a literary period as the manner in which it discovers the impossibility of being modern."[21] Paradoxical formulations are what would best define Euroda Welty's fiction. The first, as suggested by Paul de Man, is the urge repeatedly to try new techniques to express deeper truths about man, and at the same time, the awareness that this is illusory. There is also the effort to imprison the spirit of the moment and to know that it is past already—which is but one aspect of man's old quarrel with time since he is bound to meet defeat in his very accomplishment. The second paradox is to be very much a Southerner and at the same time to transcend, even disavow, the South, to stand outside in order to see better inside and to know the very desperation and impossibility of the enterprise. And, more important perhaps, it is to be alert and critical and distant and yet to use that very distance to encompass with greater love, with more comprehending love, all that is human. At the heart of Welty's modernity there is a lucidity that is never cold or ruthless even when scalding, a despair that can still love, and is above all a saving comic spirit.

Notes

1. Eudora Welty, *The Golden Apples,* in *The Collected Stories of Eudora Welty* (New York: Harcourt Brace Jovanovich, 1980), pp. 459–460. Subsequent references to the stories of *A Curtain of Green, The Wide Net, The Golden Apples,* and *The Bride of the Innisfallen* follow the text of *The Collected Stories.* Pagination is noted parenthetically.

2. Eudora Welty, "The House of Willa Cather" (1974), in *The Eye of the Story: Selected Essays and Reviews* (New York: Random House, 1978), pp. 51–52.

3. Eudora Welty, *The Optimist's Daughter* (New York: Random House, 1972), p. 136.

4. The word *modernité* was coined in 1849 by Chateaubriand and used, disparagingly, to oppose a romantic landscape with storm and gothic architecture to modern bureaucracy. A few years later Baudelaire took up the word to praise Constantin Guys, "the painter of modern life," for his desire to record moments and scenes from contemporary life. He valued this painter's efforts to extract poetry from fashion, eternal beauty from transience. *Curiosités Esthétiques,* "Le peintre de la vie moderne" (1863).

5. See Ruth M. Vande Kieft, *Eudora Welty* (New York: Twayne, 1962).

6. See "The Love and the Separateness in Miss Welty," *Kenyon Review,* 6 (1944), 257.

7. Quoted by Ihab Hassan in "Wars of Desire, Politics of the Word," *Salmagundi* (1982); rpt. in *Representation and Performance in Postmodern Fiction,* ed. Maurice Couturier (Delta 1983), pp. 47–55, 50.

8. For detailed discussion of postmodernist fiction, see *Representation and Performance,* especially the first part entitled "Theory," and Regis Durand's brilliant essay, "The Disposition of the Familiar." This essay is centered on James and Walter Abish, and started my own reflections on the unfamiliar in Welty.

9. See Sartre, *L'Imaginaire; Psychologie phénoménologique de l'imagination* (Paris: Gallimard, 1940), p. 232, and *L'Imagination* (Paris: PUF, 1981), p. 162.

10. See Tony Tanner, "Frames and Sentences," in *Representation and Performance,* pp. 21–32, 25.

11. See Regis Durand, "The Disposition of the Familiar," pp. 73–84, in *Representation and Performance.* Durand quotes from a typed version of Walter

Abish's paper that was circulated at the Nice conference on Postmodern fiction, April 1982.

12. *Ibid.*

13. This is Chester Eisinger's perceptive reading of the scene, although I think the scene too "framed" in the threatening sense of the word to be truly pastoral. See "Traditionalism and Modernism in Eudora Welty," in *Eudora Welty: Critical Essays,* ed. Peggy W. Prenshaw (Jackson: University Press of Mississippi, 1979), p. 10.

14. I am quoting here from Couturier's "Presentation of the Topic," pp. 3–8, in *Representation and Performance.*

15. Derrida, "Living ON: Border Lines," quoted by Tanner in *Representation and Performance,* p. 22.

16. Eudora Welty, "Words into Fiction" (1965), in *The Eye of the Story,* p. 144.

17. Freud, "The Uncanny" (1919), in *On Creativity and the Unconscious* (New York: Harper, 1958), pp. 122–161.

18. Quoted by Robert Scholes in *The Fabulators* (New York: Oxford University Press, 1967), pp. 68–69.

19. Scholes, *The Fabulators,* p. 12.

20. Welty, "Words into Fiction," p. 144.

21. Paul de Man, *Blindness and Insight: Essays in the Rhetoric of Contemporary Criticism* (New York: Oxford University Press, 1971), p. 144.

Patricia S. Yaeger

Woman's language has recently become the subject of a set of elaborate and contradictory mystifications. While a number of American feminist critics have begun to join French theorists in asserting that language is a patriarchal institution, French feminists like Hélène Cixous, Marguerite Duras, and Luce Irigaray additionally insist that this institution can be transcended, that woman's writing is an ecstatic possibility, a labor of mystery that can take place in some fruitful void beyond man's experience. "We the precocious, we the repressed of culture," says Cixous in "The Laugh of the Medusa." "Our lovely mouths gagged with pollen, our wind knocked out of us, we the labyrinths, the ladders, the trampled spaces, the bevies—."[1] If past repressions have become the source of woman's strength, the discovery of her secret and self-perpetuating language will give woman "access to her native strength; it will give her back her goods, her pleasures, her organs, her immense bodily territories," delivering paradise and more (p. 250). In a 1975 interview in *Signs* Marguerite Duras echoes and extends parts of Cixous' theory, arguing not only that woman can discover her own private and libidinal realm of connotation through writing but that men and women live in different linguistic cultures; they write from radically different perspectives. "Men . . . begin from a theoretical platform that is already in place, already elaborated," she says. "The writing of women is really translated from the unknown, like a new way of communicating rather than an already formed language. But to achieve that, we have to turn away from plagiarism."[2] Plagiarism, as Duras defines it, is any complicity with masculine ideology, theatricality, or rhetorical style. "Feminine

Reprinted by permission of the Modern Language Association of America from *PMLA,* 99 (October 1984), 955–73. This is a revised version of an essay which first appeared in *PMLA,* 99 (October 1984), 955–973, and is reprinted by permission of the Modern Language Association of America.

literature is a violent, direct literature," she insists. "To judge it, we must not—and this is the main point I want to make—start all over again, take off from a theoretical platform" (p. 425). "Translated" from subterranean depths, women's writing must resist cooperation with the tradition, must avoid the temptation to be patrilineal. In this essay I wish to argue, however, that women's writing employs a *useful* form of "plagiarism." Women who write are not only capable of appropriating myths, genres, ideas, and images that are "populated" with patriarchal meaning; they are continually endowing a male mythos with their own intentions and meanings. According to this argument women write about their own lives by appropriating masculine traditions and transforming them, adapting what has been called "phallocentric" diction to fit the needs of "feminocentric" expression. While this view is necessarily controversial it will lead, I hope, to an interesting thesis: although the plots that women construct for their heroines continue to focus on, and therefore in a sense to privilege, the dominant sex/gender system, the language that women writers have begun to develop to subvert or deconstruct this system is at once traditional and feminocentric. Language is not a reductively patriarchal system but a somewhat flexible institution that not only reflects but may also address existing power structures, including those conditioned by gender.

"Language," as Mikhail Bakhtin argues in his essay "Discourse in the Novel," "is never unitary. It is unitary only as an abstract grammatical system of normative forms, taken in isolation from . . . the uninterrupted process of historical becoming that is characteristic of all living language."[3] Disruptive, emotional, nonhegemonic, language, according to Bakhtin, is open to intention and change. Moreover, both spoken and written language are dynamic and plural, and, as such, language resists all attempts to foster a unitary or absolute system of expression within its boundaries. This does not mean, however, that language itself is either nonpossessive or free from obsession. As Bakhtin explains, "language is not a neutral medium that passes freely and easily into the private property of the speaker's intentions; it is populated—overpopulated—with the intentions of others" (p. 294). The process of its transformation is dialogic; that is, this process involves a dialectical interaction between words, between styles, between points of view. According to Bakhtin, this interaction is highly visible in the novel:

> The prose art presumes a deliberate feeling for the historical and social concreteness of living discourse, as well as its relativity, a feeling for its

> participation in historical becoming and in social struggle; it deals with discourse that is still warm from that struggle and hostility, as yet unresolved and still fraught with hostile intentions and accents; prose art finds discourse in this state and subjects it to the dynamic-unity of its own style. (p. 331)

Bakhtin argues that we are accustomed to think of the novel in terms of thematic unities or structural polarities but that the novel is neither univocal nor dialectical in structure. "The style of a novel is to be found in the combination of its styles; the language of a novel is the system of its 'languages' " (p. 262). The novel, then, is polyphonic it is composed of various styles, speech patterns, and ideologies that interact dynamically as a "heteroglossia," or many-languaged discourse. In the novel various stratifying forces come together and diverge, styles speak or argue with one another, barely constrained by the shifting framework of the author's intentionality. The novel, Bakhtin explains, is not a closed system in which style is controlled by authorial monologue. Instead, it represents, or results from, a dynamic conversation, a dialogue between those heterogeneous styles that, even as they are woven into a new plot and reinterpreted by an author, still speak with the intentions of their previous contexts.

Bakhtin's theories of linguistic evolution, of dialogism, and of heteroglossia will give us a useful vocabulary and a new perspective from which to examine the central tensions between men's and women's writing. Using his framework of ideas I will discuss Eudora Welty's *The Golden Apples,* a beautifully crafted and gender-preoccupied novel whose emphasis on sexuality and intertextuality has not been fully comprehended.[4] By focusing on Welty's dialogue with the "already formed" language of the masculine canon, specifically on her appropriation of themes and images from the poetry of William Butler Yeats, we will see that Welty's appropriation of Yeats's poetic imagery is neither a destructive form of "plagiarism" nor a source of disempowerment but a potent rhetorical and ideological strategy.

In the final moments of "June Recital," the second story in *The Golden Apples,* Cassie Morrison is possessed—erotically—by a poem:

> Into her head flowed the whole of the poem she had found in that book. It ran perfectly through her head, vanishing as it went, one line yielding to the next, like a torch race. All of it passed through her head, through her body. (p. 330)[5]

The poem is William Butler Yeats's "Song of Wandering Aengus" [*sic*], which tells the story of a man driven by the "fire" in his mind to seek an object equal to his desire. He finds this object in "a glimmering girl / With apple blossom in her hair / Who called me by my name and ran / And faded through the brightening air." After calling his name she disappears, but in her echoing image the wanderer discovers his vocation:

> Though I am old with wandering
> Through hollow lands and hilly lands,
> I will find out where she has gone,
> And kiss her lips and take her hands;
>
> And walk among long dappled grass,
> And pluck till time and times are done
> The silver apples of the moon
> The golden apples of the sun.[6]

Yeats's poem focuses on the simultaneous impotence and persistence of the male poet's will to define himself through a feminine muse. And yet the final tone of the poem is one of self-assurance: "I will find out where she has gone," the speaker says, equating his discovery of the "glimmering girl" with a capacity to conjure presence out of absence, closure out of uncertainty, eroticism out of ennui. The feminine persona who enables the poet to create this sense of presence has the quality of a projection: she is the shadow or penumbra of the speaker's mind, the figment of *his* imagination. Although she enters the poem as an Ovidian enigma, returning briefly to human form after an immersion in nature, by the end of Yeats's poem she has been reabsorbed not only by nature but by the poem itself, her body becoming metaphor for the sexual plenitude of the landscape where the poet gathers his images. In Yeats's poem, in other words, the "glimmering girl" is assimilated into a masculine story. Even though she has been the first to call him by his name, she is also echoing the sound he wants to hear—"the name of the father"—enabling him to speak as she gives birth to his poem.

Although it has become a commonplace of feminist analysis to argue that patriarchal culture and writing undermine women's creativity, throughout *The Golden Apples* Eudora Welty makes extensive use of the "Song of Wandering Aengus" as well as of "Leda and the Swan." Paradoxically, she finds these texts useful because of their masculine bias; they provide tropes of the imagination that must be redefined to include women as well as men. On the most primary level Welty borrows images from the "Song of Wandering Aengus" to describe those women characters who find themselves in a situation like that of the glimmering girl. At the end of "June Recital" Cassie Morrison is dispossessed by Yeats's poem; she utters only a few words from Aengus' song before falling back "unresisting" into her dreams. Maideen Sumrall, whose very name, with its sense of warmth and seasonality, its alliterative syllables, resembles that of Yeats's muse, is another avatar of the glimmering girl and commits suicide soon after sleeping with Ran MacLain and preventing his suicide. Maideen's lover and the narrator of her story, Ran is the son of Miss Snowdie and King MacLain, a couple who are avatars not only of the glimmering girl and the Wandering Aengus but of the folk heroine Snow White and her wandering prince. As true to her name as Maideen is to hers, Snowdie is an albino who must stay out of the light; her house becomes both coffin and palace where she is always at home, always on view for her prince's pleasure. Snowdie is not simply kept out of the light; she is deprived of the vision and will to wander. "We shut the West out of Snowdie's eyes of course," her neighbor and friend Katie Rainey explains, referring to more than Snowdie's feeble vision (p. 270). Snowdie's husband, King, by contrast, is a roustabout who wanders through the forest, wild-eyed and white-suited, in search of maidens to distress. King is not only the legendary maker of community babies but the designated wanderer, the procreator of the more erotic and exuberant aspects of the communal plot.

Strangely, it is this most stereotypical of male roles that Welty reverses first in *The Golden Apples.* King becomes both "muse" and narrative subject in the fables that the women of Morgana tell themselves as they go about their work. "With men like King, your thoughts are bottomless" (p. 274), says Katie Rainey at the end of "Shower of Gold." King, like the glimmering girl, has the capacity to disappear and reappear, not just in fact, but in women's fancies.

Why is this role reversal important in our estimation of Welty's stories? In order to understand Welty's expropriation of Yeats's poetry, we need to examine Bakhtin's theory of the novel at closer range. For Bakhtin, novels are "multiform in style and variform in speech and voice" (p. 261); they are created by mingling many styles and genres. This "mingling" is progressive and dialectical. The novel, Bakhtin argues, both enacts and represents "a radical revolution in the destinies of human discourse" (p. 367). The novelist joins disparate languages and inserts disruptive points of view into dominant discourses and ideologies. As a result, the novel records a situation and becomes the site of struggle. At the same time, although the novel's openness to historical change can provide an increasingly flexible medium for deconstructing dominant mythologies, in numerous situations countermythologies remain difficult to voice. Since language is "overpopulated with the intentions of others," the novelist has at his or her disposal only those words that are already qualified or inscribed by others; writing occurs within a hostile linguistic environment. "Not all words for just anyone submit equally easily to this . . . seizure and transformation into private property: many words stubbornly resist, others remain alien, sound foreign in the mouth of the one who appropriated them and who now speaks them" (p. 294). This struggle against constraining ideologies is complicated by the fact that words may not submit easily to the writer's will. The limiting "intentions and accents" of a language system can be inscribed to such a depth that words become difficult to reappropriate even in new dialogic contexts. As linguistic and social patterns reinforce one another over time, language may change only to remain the same.

What feminist critics have come to call "patriarchal" discourse is clearly a variant of this general linguistic tendency. But women writers have begun to find voices: they continue to free language from the constraints of a mother or "father" tongue; and they have discovered within the multi-vocal structure of the novel fertile ground for their own reappraisals of history. Welty, for example, incorporates Yeats's poetry into *The Golden Apples* in order to reveal the limitations of his mythology of gender while extending the imaginative power that this mythology brings to male speakers to women as well. Welty uses the energy generated by Yeats's traditional images to question the source of these images and to challenge the masculine nature of his themes.

In order to reveal the hidden zone of women's desires, Welty employs several rhetorical strategies. First, to describe those women characters who wish to become wanderers or storytellers and to protest their positions in a hierarchical and gynophobic society, Welty needs a discourse that is adequate to her characters' complexities—a discourse that is articulate, resonant, and capable of expressing women's aspirations. Instead of abandoning the tradition and creating the new dispensary of images that feminists like Duras have envisioned, Welty expropriates and redefines images from the masculine tradition; she places her own prose or prose intentions in dialogue with what has already been said. "The prose writer," Bakhtin explains, "makes use of words that are already populated with the social intentions of others and compels them to serve . . . new intentions, to serve a second master" (pp. 299–300). But in order to create this dialogic tension Welty must simultaneously call on and interrupt the singularity of Yeats's fictions; she must rupture his language with an intensity of her own. Welty's strategy, then, is to preserve, to intensify, and yet to anatomize Yeats's poems. She inserts fragments from Yeats's "Song of Wandering Aengus" and "Leda and the Swan" into her own prose contexts, simultaneously challenging and calling upon a well-known male plot.

For example, in "Sir Rabbit," the third story in *The Golden Apples*, Mattie Will, a young woman bored with her sedentary marriage, imagines making love to King in the forest. As she sits on her front porch, churning and dreaming, she stages his gargantuan approach: "When she laid eyes on Mr. MacLain close, she staggered, he had such grandeur, and then she was caught by the hair and brought down as suddenly to earth as if whacked by an unseen shillelagh." While Mattie Will's fantasy begins as a clever parody of "Leda and the Swan," it develops into a serious commentary on the poem itself: "But he put on her, with the affront of his body, the affront of his sense too. No pleasure in that!" Quarreling with Yeats's mythology of gender, Welty recontextualizes his diction; she bestows several of his most memorable phrases on her own female speaker.

> She had to put on what he knew with what he did—maybe because he was so grand it was a thorn to him. Like submitting to another way to talk, she could answer to his burden now, his whole blithe, smiling, superior, frantic existence. (p. 338)

While Mattie Will's precursor Leda had no power to control her own fate, Mattie Will has a measure of control over her own story. Welty's references to "Leda" enable us to measure the relative autonomy of Mattie Will's fantasy even as they remind us that women's desire for pleasure is still inscribed by a male economy: "And no matter what happened to her, she had to remember, disappointments are not to be borne by Mr. MacLain, or he'll go away again" (p. 338). King's "burden," or song, replicates the masculine impositions of Wandering Aengus, and yet Welty herself could be said to answer to Yeats's "burden" in this story; she submits his language to her own system of accents, her own "way to talk."

Some readers have taken Mattie's fantasy of lovemaking for a real encounter with King in the forest.[7] Why does "Sir Rabbit" have this effect on its readers? Certainly, there is no first-person narrator, as in "A Shower of Gold," to cast doubt upon the narrator's reliability. In addition, Welty invites us to identify—here, and in other stories—with the structures of idealization and fable that add a patina of glamor to the everyday tedium of women's lives. But Mattie Will is day-dreaming; her dreams are inspired by the very taboos that deny them: "Junior Holifield would have given her a licking . . . just for making such a story up, supposing, after she married Junior, she had put anything in words. . . . Poor Junior!" (p. 333).

Readers may mistake Mattie Will's imaginary adventure for reality because they confuse the shared ideology of Welty's Morgana with the painful and contradictory reality this ideology works to hide. An ideology is a set of beliefs that allows individuals to experience themselves as unified or coherent in a society that is neither. In "A Shower of Gold," King MacLain and Snowdie are asked, within the communal mythos, to represent the ideological extremes of male and female identity. By representing these extremes, they play delicious roles in the fantasy lives of Morgana women, but insofar as these women talk about the extremes of King's and Snowdie's identities as if they were inevitable, the "naturalness" of these extremes is bolstered or reinforced. If it is natural for men to be boisterous, libidinal, and free-spirited like King, and for women to be pale, patient homebodies like Snowdie; if it follows that men are afraid of home and family since children are both silly and burdensome, then the women of Morgana must be content with yarning and churning; they must put up with their lot. What Welty emphasizes, however, as she moves from "A Shower of Gold" to "Sir Rabbit" is something far more liberating: the restrictive myths that the neighborhood women need to fantasize about King lead them paradoxically to identify with his power. "He was going like the wind, Plez swore to Miss Lizzie Stark. . . . But I bet my little Jersey calf King tarried long enough to get him a child somewhere. What makes me say a thing like that? I wouldn't say it to my husband, you mind you forget it" (p. 274).

In "Sir Rabbit" Mattie Will also imagines that her husband is conveniently missing from the story. Junior Holifield has been knocked cold, made oblivious not just to King's desire but to Mattie's as well. The dialectical structure of *The Golden Apples* prepares us for this subterfuge. After discovering the controlling gender myths of the Morgana community in the first story, we learn their results in "June Recital." Since the community only idealizes wandering men and sedentary women, there is no space in Morgana for women wanderers. Women who want to be visionaries like Wandering Aengus, or roustabouts like King MacLain, must either become self-destructive or deviant (that is, commit suicide like Mrs. Morrison, go crazy like Miss Eckhart, or become unhappily promiscuous like Virgie Rainey), or—they may let this impulse go underground by imagining wild, compensatory stories about themselves and King, the designated wanderer.[8]

Thus mythos and ethos work together. But while this imaginative wandering is limited in scope, it also provides a motive for liberation. Throughout the novel, Welty uses Yeats's poems "to write what cannot be written," to extend the scope of Mattie Will's story. Though Mattie Will can only draw on the limited myths of her community, she tries, in a rush of sexual energy conveyed through the images Welty has borrowed from "Leda and the Swan," to reinscribe these limits, to become the author of her own sexuality. And while the images that Welty selects to describe Mattie Will's revisionary reading of her world are comic, they hint at something beyond community:

> Then when he let her fall and walked off, when he was out of hearing in the woods, and the birds and woods-sounds and the wood-chopping throbbed clearly, she lay there on one elbow, wide awake. A dove feather came turning down through the light that was like golden smoke. She caught it with a dart of the hand, and brushed her chin; she was never displeased to catch anything. Nothing more fell. (pp. 338–339)

In imagining what happens to Mattie Will after the rape, Welty revises both of Yeats's poems; she is in dialogue not only with his sense of an ending but with his reading of women's creativity as well. In "Sir Rabbit" it is not King but Mattie Will who ventures imaginatively through the forest, alone with whatever her imagination can conjure. "In the woods she heard sounds, the dry creek beginning to run or a strange man calling, one or the other, she thought, but she walked right up on Mr. MacLain again, asleep—snoring" (p. 339). Like Wandering Aengus, Mattie Will hears the call of a stranger whom Welty has deliberately associated with the glimmering girl. " 'You boys been sighting any birds this way?' the white glimmer asked courteously, and then it passed behind another tree. 'Seen my dog, then?' " (p. 334).

> His coat hung loosely out from him, and a letter suddenly dropped a little way out from a pocket—whiter than white.

> Mattie Will subsided forward onto her arms. Her rear stayed up in the sky, which seemed to brush it with little feathers. She lay there and listened to the world go round. (p. 340)

Like a cherubic version of Zeus, Mattie Will could almost be said to resemble a baby swan as King's letters (his quills, his white and authorial feathers) fall from him and begin to describe Mattie Will's fledgling, if less than philosophic imagination. But these feathers are also signs of Zeus/King's sexual triumph, and Mattie Will's sense of vocation is short-lived:

> . . . presently Mr. MacLain leaped to his feet, bolt awake, with a flourish of legs. He looked horrified. . . .
>
> "What you doing here, girl?" Mr. MacLain beat his snowy arms up and down. "Go on! Go on off! Go to Guinea!"
>
> She got up and skedaddled. (p. 340)

Yeats's mythology is both temporalized and satirized in Welty's prose, and a modicum of creative power is translated to woman from man. But while King becomes the "other" that Mattie Will's fantasy transforms, he also blocks her deeper hearing; she misses the "dry creek beginning to run or a strange man calling" and stumbles instead upon an old man who is swearing and snoring. Seeking a romance within herself, Mattie Will rediscovers the limits of domesticity: "Junior Holifield would have given her a licking . . . just for making such a story up, supposing, after she married Junior, she had put anything in words" (p. 333). Although Mattie Will's fantasy becomes a lyric of sexual subordination in which only King's sons can inherit his freedom and power, her exuberant metaphors in this fantasy within a fantasy give evidence of a playful—if not yet powerful—imagination, unfairly constrained.

> But as she ran down through the woods and vines, this side and that, on the way to get Junior home, it stole back into her mind about those two gawky boys, the MacLain twins. They were soft and jumpy! That day, with their brown, bright eyes popping and blinking, and their little aching Adam's apples—they were like young deer, or even remoter creatures . . . kangaroos. . . . For the first time Mattie Will thought they were mysterious and sweet—gamboling now she knew not where (pp. 340–341)

The bitter memory of Mattie Will's earliest sexual experience has been transformed by this forbidden seizure of linguistic and imaginative power, and it is in this capacity of imagination that Mattie Will Holifield née Sojourner most resembles Eudora Welty herself. We must distinguish, however, between Mattie Will's persona and Welty's own authorial voice. "The activity of a character in a novel is always ideologically demarcated," Bakhtin suggests. "He lives and acts in an ideological world of his own[;] . . . he has his own perception of the world that is incarnated in his action and in his discourse" (p. 335). Mattie Will makes her own mistakes, and yet her "ideological world" is useful to Welty as an arena in which Yeats's authoritative language and Welty's own intended themes begin to clash. If Mattie Will is a figure of the artist as a young woman, she is also a symbolic site where the dialogic interactions of text and intertext become visible. Since she is unable to imagine terms for herself beyond those provided by the erotic plot, Mattie Will's fantasy represents the limited scope of creativity that Morgana society confers—even on women of strong imagination.

In *The Golden Apples* Welty has invented a complement of characters who replicate even as they relativize the patterns of Yeats's poetry. She achieves this primarily by giving the figure of Yeats's glimmering girl a literary if not a social status equal to that of Yeats's wanderer. Women like Mattie Will, Snowdie MacLain, Maideen Sumrall, and Cassie Morrison do not remain peripheral to Welty's plot; they become instead the central "actors" on the stage of her story. Welty not only redefines female desire in her revisions of "Leda"; she also breaks the "Song of Wandering Aengus" into a series of quotations spoken by Cassie and a set of fragmentary images defining both male and female characters. She alters the poem's context and its meaning by insisting that Yeats's poem has two protagonists and that each protagonist incarnates a different aspect of woman's story. If at times Welty's female characters resemble the passive, mysterious figure of the glimmering girl whom Yeats portrays as the object of man's desire, in other moments they resemble the ostensible subject of Yeats's poem, Aengus, in their imagination and their desires.

In "The Wanderers," for example, the last story of Welty's novel, King MacLain reminisces that he once nicknamed Katie Rainey "Katie Blazes" because of her tendency as a child to set her cotton stockings on fire at a dare. " 'Whsst! Up went the blazes, up to her knee! Sometimes both legs. Cotton stockings the girls used to wear—fuzzy, God knows they were. Nobody else among the girls would set fire to their legs. She had the neighborhood scared she'd go up in flames at an early age' " (p. 438). Throughout *The Golden Apples* this imaginative fire is associated with woman rather than with man. And yet, in describing Katie's charred stockings Welty has overliteralized the opening images of Yeats's poem to emphasize that Katie's desires and the social limits of those desires are in conflict. The stockings become an image of impotence, of Katie's inability to go "out to the hazel wood" because a fire was in her legs. But it is in the character of Miss Eckhart, one of Snowdie MacLain's boarders, that Welty has invented the most direct and disturbing counterpart to Yeats's male wanderer. Miss Eckhart, a piano teacher fiercely devoted to her pupils and her art, sets a literal "fire in her head" the day she escapes from the county asylum and returns to Morgana. Having given the daughters of Morgana's community a forbidden vision of the passion, the genderless ecstasy available to the woman artist, Miss Eckhart is ostracized and incarcerated—punished more severely for her iconoclasm than are the men of Morgana. But Miss Eckhart tries, in her own peculiar way, to remain close to both the male economy of power and the female economy of nurturance. She passes the gift of her insight and her disobedience to Virgie Rainey, her protégée and Katie Rainey's daughter: "Miss Eckhart had had among the pictures from Europe on her walls a certain threatening one. It hung over the dictionary, dark as that book. It showed Perseus with the head of the Medusa" (p. 459). The threat of the picture comes from its frightening invitation to female passion and creativity:

> Miss Eckhart, whom Virgie had not, after all, hated. . . . had hung the picture on the wall for herself. She had absorbed the hero and the victim and then, stoutly, could sit down to the piano with all Beethoven ahead of her. With her hate, with her love, and with the small gnawing feelings that ate them, she offered Virgie her Beethoven. She offered, offered, offered—and when Virgie was young, in the strange wisdom of youth that is accepting of more than is given, she had accepted *the* Beethoven, as with the dragon's blood. That was the gift she had touched with her fingers that had drifted and left her. (p. 460)

After Katie Rainey's funeral Virgie Rainey not only contemplates the community that has constrained both her and her mother; she also accepts Miss Eckhart's "gift," her absorption of "the hero and the victim" embodied in the frightening picture of the Medusa and Perseus. In "Women's Time" Julia Kristeva outlines a similar pattern of feminist inquiry: "the habitual and increasingly explicit attempt to fabricate a scapegoat victim as foundress of a society or a countersociety may be replaced by the analysis of the potentialities of *victim/executioner* which characterize each identity, each subject, each sex."[9] Virgie begins to propound for herself a pattern of meditation and self-engagement in which she achieves a freedom she has always sought—not by enacting the violent stories that have been thrust on heroic men like Perseus but by achieving a dialectical vision of the rhythms of victim and victimizer that are the pulse of every heroic and gender-specific plot. "In Virgie's reach of memory a melody softly lifted, lifted of itself. Every time Perseus struck off the Medusa's head, there was the beat of time, and the melody. Endless the Medusa, and Perseus endless" (p. 460).

This dissociation of the story of Perseus from its mythic origins is characteristic of Welty's writing. Her prose is an absorbing exercise in freeing language from previous meanings. As Bakhtin explains in "Discourse in the Novel," the seizure and redefinition of any story whose traditional meaning has seemed synonymous with "truth" has far-reaching consequences:

> By "dissociation" we have in mind here a destruction of any absolute bonding of ideological meaning to language, which is *the* defining factor of mythological and magical thought. An absolute fusion of word with concrete ideological meaning is, without a doubt, one of the most fundamental constitutive features of myth, on the one hand determining the development of mythological images, and on the other determining a special feeling for the forms, meanings and stylistic combinations of language. (p. 369)

If it is mythological thinking that makes language seem absolute in its affirmation and expression of a "patriarchal" authority, then by subverting the seemingly inviolable fusion of word and ideology, by converting "authoritative discourse" into a new form of metaphor, Welty also challenges the view of reality this language represents. Perseus, as Virgie understands, is finally as culpable and as benign as the Medusa herself. Their terrible and seemingly archetypal hatred and love are only elements in an endlessly painful linguistic melody through which our gender differences are maintained. But finally it is more than the gender-specific structures of Yeats's poems or the gynophobic nature of Greek myth that Welty protests in *The Golden Apples.* She protests, as well, that "dark" dictionary which sits beneath Miss Eckhart's picture, a dictionary as blinding as the picture's frame. "Around the picture—which sometimes blindly reflected the window by its darkness—was a frame enameled with flowers, which was always self-evident—Miss Eckhart's pride. In that moment Virgie had shorn it of its frame" (pp. 459–460). Welty begins to "free" language systems that have encouraged us to associate gynophobia and heroism. Like Virgie she has altered their reflections, released them from their frames, allowing language to express something more powerful: the "fire" in women's minds that it has sought to contain.

While it could be argued that Welty's transformations of the canon's "alien" mythologies should come under the auspices of Harold Bloom's theory of "the anxiety of influence" or Gilbert and Gubar's theory of "the anxiety of authorship," clearly Welty's intertextual dynamics are of a different order. Welty, for example, does not deny, repress, or disguise her obligation to Yeats; she emphasizes her own comic resourcefulness by expropriating Yeats's poems in unexpected ways. Welty has, moreover, taken the title of *The Golden Apples* from the "Song of Wandering Aengus," as if to signal Yeats's complicity in her story. But her title is also ambiguous; it evokes Atalanta's golden apples and the fruit of the Hesperides. Yeats's poem resonates from the beginning, then, in a number of different contexts. Neither a strong misreading nor a simple repetition, Welty's use of the "Song of Wandering Aengus" is dialogic.

We can define dialogic discourse, or what Bakhtin calls "dialogic heteroglossia," as the reciprocal action or play that occurs among a novel's collective and heterogeneous systems of language. "In it the investigator is confronted with several heterogeneous stylistic unities, often located on different linguistic levels and subject to different stylistic controls" (p. 261). The novel's incorporation of poetry, however, presents a different set of opportunities and problems. Unlike the novel, the poem tries, Bakhtin argues, to be monovocal:

> Poetry also comes upon language as stratified, language in the process of uninterrupted ideological evolution, already fragmented into "languages." . . . But poetry, striving for maximal purity, works in its own language *as if* that language were unitary, the only language, as if there were no heteroglossia outside it. Poetry behaves as if it lived in the heartland of its own language territory. . . . (p. 399)

When the poem is incorporated into a prose text, however, the poetic voice ceases to possess the illusion that it is "alone with its own discourse": it can be altered—even violated—by a new prose context.

> As soon as another's voice, another's accent, the possibility of another's point of view breaks through the play of the [poetic] symbol, the poetic plane is destroyed and the symbol is translated onto the plane of prose. . . . In this process the poetic symbol—while remaining, of course, a symbol—is at one and the same time translated onto the plane of prose and becomes a double-voiced word: in the space between the word and its object another's word, another's accent intrudes, a mantle of materiality is cast over the symbol. (pp. 328–329)

The prose writer who quotes another's poem in her or his text changes that poem's meaning and orientation by representing the poem's symbols in a different light. This operation occurs in Welty's prose when Yeats's figural fire becomes the fire literally blazing up Katie Rainey's legs or the "fire in the head" of Miss Eckhart. And yet, even within these simple examples, Welty's transformation of Yeats's images acquires new complexity. Welty may impose a new accent or point of view onto Yeats's poem (women, like men, have imaginations or fires in their minds), but she also allows Yeats's poem to work on her own images and characters (women who have "fires" in their minds are still unable to escape the role of victim, of literally "glimmering girl"). Although Welty reaccents Yeats's poem with her own powerful intentions, at the same time this process is limited by the recalcitrance of Yeats's language and plot.

The woman in *The Golden Apples* who is compared most frequently to Yeats's glimmering girl is Cassie's mother, Catherine Morrison. Like many of the women Welty portrays in *The Golden Apples,* Mrs. Morrison sees herself as a failed artist: " 'Could you have played the piano, Mama?' 'Child, I could have *sung,*' " she tells her daughter with bitter pride (p. 293). To inscribe Mrs. Morrison's now-frivolous life, Welty transposes the imagery associated with Yeats's muse into a modern key. While the wanderer sees "a glimmering girl, with apple-blossom in her hair," who fades into "the brightening air," Cassie Morrison experiences her mother as a vanishing or evanescent fragrance. "Her bedroom door had been closed all afternoon. But first her mother had opened it and come in, only to exclaim and not let herself be touched, and to go out leaving the smell of rose geranium behind for the fan to keep bringing at her" (p. 287). Cassie's younger brother, Loch, Mrs. Morrison's favorite child, is also disturbed by his mother's disappearances.

> By leaning far out he could see a lackadaisical, fluttery kind of parade, the ladies of Morgana under their parasols, all trying to keep cool while they walked down to Miss Nell's. His mother was absorbed into their floating, transparent colors. Miss Perdita Mayo was talking, and they were clicking their summery heels and drowning out—drowning out something. . . . (p. 280)

If Welty's prose suggests a transposition of the call Wandering Aengus hears as he begins his quest, these women hear nothing as they chatter mindlessly on the way to a summer party, "drowning out—drowning out something. . . ." At this moment Mrs. Morrison, like the glimmering girl, disappears from view, "absorbed" by the other women's transparency. Later in the novel she fades altogether, for we learn in "The Wanderers" that she, like Maideen Sumrall, has committed suicide. Just as Yeats's glimmering girl becomes an object, a mirror for Aengus's desires, so Mrs. Morrison has become an "object" to herself, a mirror to the desires of her community, and only through suicide can she speak her despair. Ironically, it is not until after her death that someone calls Mrs. Morrison by her name. To commemorate her mother's death, Cassie first marks the grave with a stone angel and then plants her own front yard with a bed of narcissi that spell out "Catherine." By writing her mother's name in floral letters, Cassie is attempting to bring her mother back into the communal garden: she does not allow Catherine Morrison to have a plot of her own even in death. Moreover, Catherine Morrison's death is reincorporated into the myth of Narcissus, making her once again the "echo" of a masculine story.

But beneath the lackadaisical surface of Mrs. Morrison's life as it is described in "June Recital," Welty invites us to see something unvoiced and ominous—the glimmer of an untold story. From the beginning of "June Recital" Cassie's mother is more absent than present, reluctant to fulfill the chores of mothering, guilty about the fates of other women. Even Loch notices her vacant presence. "It was not really to him that his mother would be talking," Loch observes, "but it was he who tenderly let her, as they watched and listened to the swallows just at dark. It was always at this hour that she spoke in this voice—not to him or to Cassie or Louella or to his father, or to the evening, but to the wall, more nearly" (p. 328). In this moment we are allowed to see beyond the plot that has been scripted for her by her community and to look into the margins of Catherine Morrison's own story. As her voice moves back and forth in the fading light, she tells Loch her story about the garden party. Heard in this darkening context the garden "plot" becomes liminal, and we begin to read between the lines, to realize that Mrs. Morrison's speech is more nearly a parable about the permissible range of feminine creativity in this small Southern town than it is an anecdote about a ladies' social:

> "Listen and I'll tell you what Miss Nell served at the party," Loch's mother said softly, with little waits in her voice. She was just a glimmer at the foot of his bed.
>
> "Ma'am."
>
> "An orange scooped out and filled with orange juice, with the top put back on and decorated with icing leaves, a straw stuck in. A slice of pineapple with a heap of candied sweet potatoes on it, and a little handle of pastry. A cup made out of toast, filled with creamed chicken, fairly warm. A sweet peach pickle with flower petals around it of different-colored cream cheese. A swan made of a cream puff. He had whipped cream feathers, a pastry neck, green icing eyes. A pastry biscuit the size of a marble with a little date filling." She sighed abruptly.
>
> "Were you hungry, Mama?" he said. (p. 328)

If a number of characters in *The Golden Apples* are "just a glimmer at the foot" of someone's bed, if they replicate, even as they comment on, the limited powers of Yeats's muse, others, like Cassie's piano teacher, Miss Eckhart, initially appear as figures of capable imagination. Although by the end of "June Recital" Miss Eckhart has been ostracized and packed off to the County Farm, she maintains throughout the story a strange nobility and a will to wander. Even after she has taken leave of her senses, she is still able to resurrect a private teleology; she returns to the house where she taught piano lessons, as determined as Aengus to finish her story.

Miss Eckhart's attempted recreation and destruction of past events become the central dramatic action in "June Recital." As Cassie Morrison looks forward to an evening's hayride and creates a "tie-dye scarf" according to communal formula, her brother, Loch, watches the world outside his window and composes stories about the vacant house next door. Already the separation between genders has begun. Cassie's attention is focused on an object of feminine adornment that is safely unpredictable. Loch allows his mind to wander freely; his stories are fantastic, his metaphors inventive. As he watches Virgie Rainey and a "friendly" sailor making love on the second floor of the vacant house, Loch is established as a naive and unbiased observer who is already attempting to construct a metaphoric language to account for a world he does not understand. At first he is the only one to see an old woman enter the house and begin to putter about downstairs. Her behavior is strangely festive:

> The old woman was decorating the piano until it rayed out like a Christmas tree or a Maypole. Maypole ribbons of newspaper and tissue paper streamed and crossed each other from the piano to the chandelier and festooned again to the four corners of the room, looped to the backs of chairs here and there. When would things begin? (p. 283)

This is the room where Miss Eckhart used to give her June recitals, the room where every year she would come to life for one handsome, perfectible evening:

> Then she would look down ceremoniously at the sleepiest and smallest child, who had only played "Playful Kittens" that night. All her pupils on that evening partook of the grace of Virgie Rainey. Miss Eckhart would catch them running out the door, speaking German to them and holding them to her. In the still night air her dress felt damp and spotted, as though she had run a long way. (p. 315)

In her sweaty garment she resembles a benign goddess, in love with the world she has made, for like Yeats's wanderer she is a creator who has struggled, who seems to have "run a long way." Thwarted in love and in art she sustains herself by giving June recitals and imagining an artistic life for Virgie Rainey, who, at thirteen, is still passionately absorbed in her music:

> She played the *Fantasia on Beethoven's Ruins of Athens,* and when she finished and got up and made her bow, the red of the sash was all over the front of her waist, she was wet and stained as if she had been stabbed in the heart, and a delirious and enviable sweat ran down from her forehead and cheeks and she licked it in with her tongue. (p. 313)

Images of sweating, of licking, of violence, of delirium bind child and woman together and reveal the price both must pay for their art. Too eccentric, too foreign and impassioned for Morgana, Miss Eckhart loses her pupils and Virgie her inspiration. "Perhaps nobody wanted Virgie Rainey to be anything in Morgana any more than they had wanted Miss Eckhart to be," Cassie reminisces, "and they were the two of them still linked together by people's saying that" (p. 306). Miss Eckhart's return from her banishment to the County Farm is poignantly ceremonial: she comes back to the place where she organized recitals and cultivated a talent in Virgie Rainey as beautiful and as violent as her own.

In decorating the room for the final recital Miss Eckhart refurbishes it with numerous mementos. The piano is crowned with magnolia blossom—Virgie's perpetual and too fragrant gift to her teacher. Earlier in the story the magnolia has been an emblem of exuberant and rebellious female energy, but at this final recital it becomes—like the nest Miss Eckhart weaves in the piano—a symbol of woman's defeat. Miss Eckhart is preparing her beloved objects—piano, magnolia, metronome, empty house—for a small and funereal conflagration:

> She wanted things to suit herself, nobody else would have been able to please her; and she was taking her own sweet time. She was building a bonfire of her own in the piano and would set off the dynamite when she was ready and not before.
>
> Loch knew from her actions that the contrivance down in the wires—the piano front had been taken away—was a kind of nest. She was building it like a thieving bird, weaving in every little scrap that she could find around her. He saw in two places the mustached face of Mr. Drewsie Carmichael, his father's candidate for mayor—she found the circulars in the door. (p. 316)

Just as this collage contains patriarchs who will be burned in effigy, so the house contains Virgie Rainey, whose participation in the erotic play overhead (an eroticism that, we are led to believe, has helped disconnect Virgie from her art) may be permanently ended. But in spite of the fire Miss Eckhart envisions in her head, her plot is poorly conceived from the start. As Loch explains to himself, watching her clumsy activities through his bedroom window, "only a woman" would try to start a conflagration in a breezeless room where the windows are down, their cracks stuffed with paper. Unlike Yeats's wanderer Miss Eckhart lacks the freedom or knowledge to take her fire to that traditional source of inspiration—the hazel wood with its attendant rhetoricity.

> She bent over, painfully, he felt, and laid the candle in the paper nest she had built in the piano. He too drew his breath in, protecting the flame, and as she pulled her aching hand back he pulled his. The newspaper caught, it was ablaze, and the old woman threw in the candle. Hands to thighs, she raised up, her work done. (p. 317)

This Promethean and painful act is thwarted at once. Two husky wanderers who have spent the day fishing have been watching Miss Eckhart through the window as she painstakingly decorates her recital hall and builds her empty nest. As she holds her candle to the paper they jump into the house with a yell.

> Old Man Moody and Mr. Bowles together beat out the fire in the piano, fighting over it hard, banging and twanging the strings. Old Man Moody, no matter how his fun had been spoiled, enjoyed jumping up and down on the fierce-burning magnolia leaves. So they put the fire out. . . . When a little tongue of flame started up for the last time, they quenched it together. . . . (p. 320)

Woman's "fierce-burning magnolia leaves," her "little tongue of flame," and her fiery piano are amusing objects to these men. But even in the moment when they play, childlike, with woman's fire, their pleasure edges toward sadism.

> She rose up, agitated now, and went running about the room, holding the candle above her, evading the men each time they tried to head her off.
>
> This time, the fire caught her own hair. The little short white frill turned to flame.
>
> Old Man Moody was so quick that he caught her. He came up with a big old rag. . . . He brought the cloth down over her head from behind, grimacing, as if all people on earth had to do acts of shame, some time. He hit her covered-up head about with the flat of his hand. (p. 322)

Her hair aflame, Miss Eckhart becomes an archetype of woman's fury and desire. Like Yeats's wanderer she has a "fire in her head," and yet the image turns in on itself and becomes parodic as she strikes back, not at society, but at herself. Her fire becomes a masochistic flame: it scorches before it illuminates. Miss Eckhart's resemblance to Yeats's wanderer, then, at once expands and collapses. Her aspirations are mediated by her culturally inscribed role as victim, as literally "glimmering girl."

"Old Man Moody was so quick that he caught her. . . ." Her hair in flames, her victimizer still in pursuit, woman is caught in a periphrasis, but her desire to change roles is not so much thwarted by Yeats's poem as it is expressed *through* the poem:

> When heteroglossia enters the novel it becomes subject to an artistic reworking. The social and historical voices populating language, all its words and all its forms, which provide language with its particular concrete conceptualizations, are organized in the novel into a structured stylistic system that expresses the differentiated socio-ideological position of the author amid the heteroglossia of his epoch. . . . in the novel heteroglossia is by and large always personified, incarnated in individual human figures, with disagreements and oppositions individualized. But such oppositions of individual wills and mind are submerged in *social* heteroglossia[,]. . . surface manifestations of those elements that play *on* such individual oppositions, make them contradictory, saturate their consciousness and discourses with a more fundamental speech diversity, (Bakhtin, pp. 300, 326)

Within the context of Welty's novel Yeats's poem becomes one of the voices that both describe and explain women's predicament within a society that represses their desires. His poem provides a set of differential images describing gender roles that Welty refracts with an even more frightening "speech diversity." Old Man Moody prevents Miss Eckhart from acting out her chosen role, and although he saves her life, his act is mediated by violent images of suffocation ("he brought the cloth down over her head from behind") and of sadism ("he hit her covered-up head about with the flat of his hand").

Shadows of an older mythology, the men portrayed in "June Recital" have been demystified in Welty's prose, brought down to earth. But if they move through Welty's world clumsily, ineptly, their cruelty is not abated; Welty asks them to enact, as if by rote, their older roles of victor and victimizer. Miss Eckhart and her pupils are harassed, for example, by the second roomer at Miss Snowdie's boarding house, the encyclopedia saleman Mr. Voight, who "would walk over their heads and come down to the turn of the stairs, open his bathrobe, and flap the skirts like an old turkey gobbler. . . . he wore no clothes at all underneath" (p. 294). Welty's humor is a mediating device to keep these stories about human derangement dialogic. But neither the humor nor the dialogism obscures the fact that sexual, economic, and linguistic restraints are imposed on women at an early age. Cassie "herself had told all about Mr. Voight at breakfast, stood up at the table and waved her arms, only to have her father say he didn't believe it; that Mr. Voight represented a large concern and covered seven states. He added his own threat to Miss Eckhart's: no picture show money" (p. 295). Those women in Morgana who step outside traditional roles, who attempt to speak in the culture's excluded heteroglossia, either are denied scripts altogether or have scripts foisted on them. " 'Listen. You should marry now, Virgie,' " Jinny Love Stark shrieks at Katie Rainey's funeral. " 'Don't put it off any longer.' . . . She was grimacing out of the iron mask of the married lady. It appeared urgent with her to drive everybody, even Virgie for whom she cared nothing, into the state of marriage along with her" (pp. 444–445). But while the community tries to prevent another outbreak of pyromania, the reader who is attuned to Welty's revision of Yeats's poem sees another story altogether. The Morgana community acts together, man and woman alike, to prevent *feminine* acts of Prometheanism: woman is not allowed to steal man's holy fire.

In her essay "The Difference of View" Mary Jacobus asks for a feminist criticism that does more than reaffirm the concept of gender difference as opposition. Instead, Jacobus envisions an alliance of feminism and the avant-garde in which the traditional terms of linguistics, of psychoanalysis, and of literary criticism "are called in question—subverted from within." "Such a move has the advantage of freeing off the 'feminine' from the religion-bound, ultimately conservative and doom-ridden concept of difference-as-opposition which underlies Virginia Woolf's reading of the 'case' of George Eliot," Jacobus argues. "*Difference* is redefined, not as male *versus* female—not as biologically constituted—but as a multiplicity, joyousness and heterogeneity which is that of textuality itself."[10] In forging an alliance between avant-garde literary practice and feminist criticism, textuality "becomes the site both of challenge and Otherness; rather than (as in more traditional approaches) simply yielding the themes and representation of female oppression" (p. 12). This redefinition of difference should, according to Jacobus, encourage the transgression or "transversal" of gender boundaries and expose these boundaries "for what they are—the product of phallocentric discourse and of women's relation to patriarchal culture" (p. 12). A new feminist poetics should begin, then, to address the heterogeneous languages, the dialogism, the "pleasure edge" in women's writing, since this writing will be in conflict, in conversation, and, to some degree, in correspondence with the ideologies it is trying to dislodge.

In this essay I have begun to show how such an alliance of feminist criticism and "those pleasurable and rupturing aspects of language" that Jacobus identifies with the avant-garde may work together in the analysis of a literary text. One of Welty's strengths as a writer is her recognition that she need not be coerced by those stories that coerce her female characters; she feels small compunction at her own Promethean acts.

In the last sentence of *The Golden Apples* words and images that have been appropriated from the poetic contexts of the "Song of Wandering Aengus" and "Leda and the Swan" begin to reappear as part of the irresolution and diversity of Virgie's final vision:

> She smiled once, seeing before her, screenlike, the hideous and delectable face Mr. King MacLain had made at the funeral, and when they all knew he was next—even he. Then she and the old beggar woman, the old black thief, were there alone and together in the shelter of the big public tree, listening to the magical percussion, the world beating in their ears. They heard through falling rain the running of the horse and bear, the stroke of the leopard, the dragon's crusty slither, and the glimmer and the trumpet of the swan. (p. 461)

Is Welty hinting at her text's demythologization not only of Yeats's poetry but of that "sixty-year-old smiling public man" who dreams so poignantly "of a Ledaean body" in "Among School Children" and celebrates organic beauty in the "chestnut-tree, great-rooted blossomer"? Welty has transformed Yeats's wished-for organicism into a series of dissolving images; she links the death of the mythological "King" with Virgie's own multiple vision. And finally, in subjecting Yeats's poetic discourse to the heteroglossia of her own story, Welty has displaced the ending of his story with a beginning of her own: the unresolved yet resolute image of "the big public tree" sheltering two marginal and intemperate women who are, nonetheless, afoot with their visions.

Notes

1. Hélène Cixous, "The Laugh of the Medusa," in *New French Feminisms*, ed. Elaine Marks and Isabelle de Courtivron (Amherst: University of Massachusetts Press, 1980), p. 248. Further references to this work will be cited in the text.

2. Marguerite Duras, "An Interview with Marguerite Duras," by Susan Husserl-Kapit, *SIGNS*, 1 (1975), 425. Further references to this work will be cited in the text.

3. Mikhail Bakhtin, "Discourse in the Novel," in *The Dialogic Imagination*, trans. Caryl Emerson and Michael Holquist, ed. Michael Holquist (Austin: University of Texas Press, 1981), p. 288. Further references to this work will be cited in the text.

4. Only a few of Welty's critics have begun to discuss her prose in terms of feminist analysis or theory. For fine examples of such analysis see Mary Anne Ferguson's "*Losing Battles* as a Comic Epic in Prose," in *Eudora Welty: Critical Essays,* ed. Peggy Whitman Prenshaw (Jackson: University Press of Mississippi, 1979), Carol Manning's *With Ears Opening Like Morning Glories: Eudora Welty and the Love of Storytelling* (Westport, CT: Greenwood Press, 1985), and Louise Westling's *Sacred Groves and Ravaged Gardens: The Fiction of Eudora Welty, Carson McCullers, and Flannery O'Connor* (Athens: University of Georgia Press, 1985).

5. References to *The Golden Apples* (1949) follow the text of *The Collected Stories of Eudora Welty* (New York: Harcourt Brace Jovanovich, 1980). Page numbers are cited parenthetically in the text.

6. William Butler Yeats, *The Collected Poems of William Butler Yeats* (New York: Macmillan, 1968), p. 57.

7. See, for example, Carol Manning's reading of "Sir Rabbit" in *With Ears Opening Like Morning Glories: Eudora Welty and the Love of Storytelling,* pp. 100–103. Manning's analysis is representative of recent readings of "Sir Rabbit" in which the critic assumes the actuality of the episode; otherwise her analysis is very perceptive, especially her descriptions of King's mock heroism and Welty's comic flair.

8. Although a complete analysis of Welty's reading of gender in *The Golden Apples* is beyond the scope of this essay, the rest of the novel focuses on gender issues with a thorough dialectical force. After exploring the constrictions that an asymmetrical sex/gender system imposes on women, Welty begins in "Moon Lake," and then in "The Whole World Knows" and "Music from Spain," to address the pain this asymmetry creates for men as well. For a reading of this dialectic in "Moon Lake," see my "The Case of the Dangling Signifier: Phallic Imagery in Welty's 'Moon Lake,' " in *Twentieth Century Literature,* 28 (Winter 1982).

9. Julia Kristeva, "Women's Time," trans. Alice Jardine and Harry Blake, *SIGNS,* 7 (1981), 34.

10. Mary Jacobus, "The Difference of View," in *Women Writing and Writing about Women,* ed. Jacobus (New York: Barnes and Noble, 1979), p. 12. Further references to this work will be cited in the text.

Nancy K. Butterworth

Since such seminal studies as Robert Penn Warren's "The Love and Separateness in Miss Welty" and Harry Morris's "Eudora Welty's Use of Mythology," it has become traditional to interpret Welty's characters in terms of mythological and cultural archetypes. Welty's black characters frequently have evoked such parallels. In addition to the obvious reference to the Egyptian resurrection myth implied by her name,[1] Phoenix Jackson in "A Worn Path" has been compared to the pagan fertility figures Kore, Demeter, and Persephone, Osiris, Attis, and Adonis, as well as Theseus and Aeneas (Ardolino, 1–6); knight questers such as the Red Cross Knight and Don Quixote; Bunyan's Christian, a Magi, and Christ.[2] Little Lee Roy in "Keela, The Outcast Indian Maiden" has been likened to the archetypal scapegoat Le Roi Mehaigné, the maimed Fisher King (May), the albatross in *The Rime of the Ancient Mariner* (Warren), and American Negro folk tricksters such as Brer Rabbit (Appel, *Season,* 146). Powerhouse, more simplistically, has been described as "a virtual Negro Paul Bunyan" (Appel, "Powerhouse's," 222).

Although such "superimpositions" of external ideas, as Morris terms them (40), always risk distorting the text, a majority of these mythological and symbolic readings are valid because they add resonances that enrich our understanding of the characters' roles. Welty's own comments on her use of name symbolism and the influence of remembered fairy tales and myths further support such interpretations.[3] Commentaries on her black characters, however, sometimes obfuscate more than they reveal. One obvious reason is our sensitivity to the race issue, which has made it tempting to oversimplify the narrative events to fit our own conceptions of history and how the races ought to have behaved.

Recent revisionist criticism, in particular, frequently falsifies Welty's portrayals of black-white relations in earlier eras. For example, John

From *Eudora Welty: Eye of the Storyteller,* Dawn Trouard, ed. Kent, Ohio (1989). Reprinted with permission of the Kent State University Press.

Hardy's "Eudora Welty's Negroes," in *The Image of the Negro in American Literature*, is, paradoxically, both sentimental and satirical. Although his attitude is somewhat inconsistent,[4] Hardy views Phoenix as "a saint":

> One of those who walks always in the eye of God, on whom He has set His sign, whether ordinary men are prepared to see it or not. For we realize finally that she has done nothing for herself, for her own advantage, either psychological or material. Just because sanctity is never self-regarding, she must see herself as a sinner. But in the ultimate perspective she is, by virtue of her sanctity, exempt from the usual requirements of economic and social morality. (229)

Conversely, he argues that those who fail to see her as such are the whites, and particularly the white women. He concludes that "There is nowhere in modern literature a more scathing indictment of the fool's pride of the white man in the superiority of his civilization, of his fool's confidence in the virtue of the 'soothing medicine' he offers to heal the hurts of that 'stubborn case,' black mankind" (229). John R. Cooley, in "Blacks as Primitives in Eudora Welty's Fiction," accuses Welty of failing to "develop her racial portraits with sufficient sensitivity or depth" (27) and criticizes her for creating a primitive idyll in "A Worn Path," making it "difficult to cut through the reverence and romance which cloud the story, in order to see the babe as a pathetic image of life caught in the stranglehold of white civilization." He cynically questions whether Welty intended the story as a myth of the phoenix perishing in its own ashes (24–25).

Such polemical demythologizings conflict with Welty's persistent refusal to use fiction as a platform, particularly for political or sociological issues, as well as her downplaying and even disavowal of racial implications in her stories.[5] Even in "Keela, The Outcast Indian Maiden," "Where Is the Voice Coming From?" and "The Demonstrators," which treat racial interactions directly, she eschews authorial statement or facile solutions or dichotomies. Thus, although we condemn his act, we are brought to understand the mundane motives for a lower-class white's murder of a black civil rights worker in "Where Is the Voice Coming From?"; the guilt-ridden Steve and cynical civil rights worker in "Keela" and "The Demonstrators," respectively, are portrayed as ethically equivocal; and even such white characters as Max and Dr. Strickland, who attempt to mediate between the races and ameliorate oppression and illness, remain largely ineffectual. The blacks, too, range from virtuous victims to perpetrators of wanton violence, but most of them are merely traditional family members coping with tragedy as best they can. One of Welty's greatest achievements as a writer is that she refuses to rewrite history but rather presents individualized conflicts and tensions, in all of their disturbing ambiguity.

Although there have been some balanced commentaries on the race relations in "A Worn Path"—in particular, Elmo Howell's "Eudora Welty's Negroes: A Note on 'A Worn Path' "[6]—one aspect of the story that has not been adequately explored is the portrayal of Phoenix Jackson as an almost allegorical representation of black people's traits and behaviors from slave times to the story's present. Alfred Appel, Jr., has suggested such a reading when he describes the story as "an effort at telescoping the history of the Negro woman" (*Season*, 166), but he doesn't develop it.

The most compelling reason for seeing Phoenix as an avatar of her race is her almost mythic age. When Phoenix asks the nurse to forgive her momentary senility, she explains, "I never did go to school, I was too old at the Surrender" (*CS*, 148). If we assume that Phoenix was eighteen or more at Emancipation and posit the present action of the story to be around 1940, when it was written, she would be approximately 100 years old. Further corroboration for her age is afforded by her boast when dancing with the scarecrow, "I the oldest people I ever know"; the hunter also marvels that she "must be a hundred years old" (*CS*, 144, 146). This extreme age serves a symbolic function of allowing her personally to have spanned the entire history of the black people from antebellum days to those just prior to the civil rights movement.

Such an interpretation requires considerable caution so as not to reduce the story to mere allegory. It is essential to emphasize—as Stella Brookes does concerning Joel Chandler Harris's Uncle Remus (47–48)—that Phoenix is not a stereotypical or stock black character but a real human portrait with a distinctive personality. In interviews and essays, Welty has explained the key image that suggested the story to her imagination:

> One day I saw a solitary old woman like Phoenix. She was walking; I saw her in the middle distance, in a winter country landscape, and watched her slowly make her way across my line of vision. That sight of her made me write the story. I invented an errand for her, but that only seemed a living part of the figure she was herself: what errand other than for someone else could be making her go? (*Eye*, 161)

She conflated this experience with another on the Old Canton Road when an elderly black woman stopped to talk with her; the woman's remark, "I was too old at the Surrender," Welty tells us, "was indelible in my mind" (*Conversations*, 168). The nexus of Phoenix's character for Welty seems to have been her sense of urgency, her "desperate need" to reach her goal. She notes that Phoenix's "going was the first thing, her persisting in the landscape was the real thing. . . . The real dramatic force of a story depends on the strength of the emotion that has set it going. . . . What gives any such content to 'A Worn Path' is not its circumstances but its *subject:* the deep-grained habit of love" (161).

Phoenix particularizes these attributes of persistence and enduring love through her own distinct set of decorums and devotions, such as wearing tied shoes into town and her somewhat dubious adherence to the eighth commandment (although in her own estimation she "stoops" when she retrieves a dropped coin, she does not in conning a few more pennies and accepting the "charity" medicine for her grandson). Phoenix's personality also comprises a complicated mixture of shrewdness—"Five pennies is a nickel" (*CS,* 149)—and childlike unself-consciousness—shown when she talks aloud to herself and warns all of the "foxes, owls, beetles, jack rabbits, coons, and wild animals" to keep out of her way (*CS,* 141). Her composite of character traits is somewhat like conflating Ida M'Toy with the bird women in "A Pageant of Birds." This complexity, along with her distinctive voice and humor (" 'Old woman,' she said to herself, 'that black dog come up out of the weeds to stall you off, and now there he sitting on his fine tail, smiling at you' " [*CS,* 145]), keep Phoenix from falling into mere quaintness or caricature.[7]

Phoenix's individuality, though, does not preclude another, simultaneous, view of her as a symbolic representative of her race. Such an interpretation helps to elucidate otherwise confusing statements or situations in the surface narrative. For example, one of the more cryptic passages in Welty's fiction occurs when Phoenix walks "past cabins silver with weather, with the doors and windows boarded shut, all like old women under a spell sitting there," and she says, " 'I walking in their sleep,' . . . nodding her head vigorously" (*CS,* 144). Her strong identification with these "women" (the white woman in town who ties her shoes is termed a "lady" [*CS,* 147]) suggests that they are the matriarchs of her race whose dreams she views herself as proudly carrying on. Indeed, in her own almost trancelike state, she seems to gain strength from their vicarious vision of her persisting in the landscape while they doze.

The content of Phoenix's dream becomes clearer at the conclusion of the story when she sees the gold-framed document (presumably a diploma) nailed up on the clinic wall, and the narrator asserts that it "matched the dream that hung up in her head" (*CS*, 147). On the surface level, the document verifies that she has reached her specific dream or goal of obtaining the medicine (" 'Here I be,' she said" [*CS*, 147]), though she ironically has a memory lapse about her mission immediately afterward. On a deeper level, the diploma also seems to represent her respect for education, which is reiterated later in the scene. Wonderful pathos is evoked by the formally unschooled Phoenix wishing education for herself, her grandson, and, by implication, her people. This dream also may inform part of her faith that her grandson, though frail in body, will prevail and prosper.

Viewing Phoenix as an emblem of her people also helps to explain the title, "A Worn Path," which seems to imply that others have trod and retrod the same arduous path before her. Echoes of slave times can be heard in her chant as she heads up the hill, "Seem like there is chains about my feet, time I get this far" (*CS*, 143), as well as in the images of confinement and persecution, such as the barbed-wire fence, one-armed black men, and the threatening black dog. These symbolic references could refer specifically to the difficulties encountered by the blacks, as well as more generally to any enslaved or downtrodden people from the times of the early Egyptians and Greeks (from whom her name derives) on through the twentieth century.

Finally, this reading explains a number of Phoenix's encounters with whites, both real and imaginary. On the surface level, the story consists of a simple journey composed of about twelve obstacles—external or internal—which Phoenix must overcome to obtain her goal (*Season*, 167). These encounters take on deeper meaning when seen as symbolic trials or tests of her faith. Robert Welker suggests this interpretation when he refers to the "visions" which sometimes tempted wayfaring knights so as to divert them from their final purpose (203–04). Likewise, Phoenix is tempted at numerous points to forestall her journey, as exemplified by the scene in which she marches across the hollow log, "like a festival figure in some parade," and then hallucinates a little boy bringing her a slice of marble cake which she finds "acceptable" (*CS*, 143).

If taken literally, this vision makes little sense; however, it makes a great deal of sense if we see it as a symbolic role reversal in which Phoenix is tempted to accept the dream—the marble cake—rather than the reality of economic equality. This scene bears much resemblance to the parallel one in town when Phoenix requests the nice-smelling white lady to tie her shoes for her, which Hardy so incorrectly interprets as an "outrageous request," one of "the ways in which southern Negroes have learned to take subtle revenge on the 'superior' race, to exploit, for their own material or psychological advantage, the weakness of white pride" (228–29). On the simplest level, both scenes involve wish-fulfillment fantasies—one imaginary and the other realized—in which Phoenix probably does gain psychological pleasure from being waited upon by those whom she previously served. However, in neither does she seem vindictive toward the whites; she merely accepts with dignity what she considers her "due" (Howell, 30–31; Robinson, 26; and Dazey, 92–93). Further, both situations carry a covert danger; for if Phoenix were to remain eating imaginary marble cake or allowing others to care for her, she would not complete her necessary journey.

Phoenix's vulnerability is also made explicit in the scene just prior to the hunter's entrance. Evoking her earlier hallucinations or misperceptions of reality, the setting is imbued with a fairy tale aura: a road which cuts "deep, deep . . . down between high green-colored banks" of the swamp, with live oaks meeting overhead, making it "as dark as a cave." The sleeping alligators and Cerberus-like black dog which suddenly rears up out of the weeds suggest covert dangers and unprovoked violence which catch her unawares: "She was meditating, and not ready, and when he came at her she only hit him a little with her cane. Over she went in the ditch, like a little puff of milkweed" (*CS*, 145). Her inability to help herself is shown by her drifting into a dream of rescue.

Perhaps the most troubling incident in the whole story concerns her encounter with the young white hunter. At first he appears to be sympathetic as he helps her out of the ditch. Yet almost immediately the situation takes on uncomfortable undertones in the reversal of usual youth-age decorums when the hunter cheerily condescends to her as "Granny" and swings her through the air like a child. His apparent charity of dropping the nickel is also belied by his later assertion that he would give her a dime, if he had "*any money*" with him (*CS*, 146, emphasis added).[8] Finally, the tone darkens with the implications of his hunting bobwhites—both Phoenix and the grandson are linked with frail birds[9]—and his seemingly sadistic act of turning his gun on her.

It is difficult not to condemn the hunter's behavior (Welty herself refers to him as a "really nasty white man" [*Conversations*, 335]).[10] One way of gaining more perspective on his behavior is to interpret this scene broadly as an allegory of the racial stances of the early twentieth century. All of the hunter's actions can be explained in terms of accepted social behavior of the rural South in the 1930s and 1940s, which would have allowed a young white man—a simple "red neck" hunter—some degree of domineering byplay with the curious old black woman. Welty does not distort the man's realistic responses to Phoenix, much as, two decades later, she similarly refuses to pretty up the depiction of the equivalent lower-class white city dweller who murders a black civil rights worker (Medgar Evers) in "Where Is the Voice Coming From?".

More specifically, each of the characters' actions in this scene symbolically represents a particular stage in the pre–civil rights era treatment of blacks. For example, for an indeterminate time before the hunter's arrival, Phoenix waits patiently, merely dreaming of salvation. At one point she reaches up her hand expectantly, "but nothing reached down and gave her a pull" (*CS*, 145). After the zeal of Reconstruction, which Phoenix missed out on because she was too old to be educated, a period of indifference to blacks' welfare persisted well into the early decades of the twentieth century. When the hunter finally arrives, Phoenix uses her vulnerability, lying flat on her back "like a June-bug waiting to be turned over" (*CS*, 145), to obtain her simple need of being helped out of the ditch. Likewise, when the blacks so desperately required help out of the social, educational, and economic ditch, whites finally reached out a hand to aid them, though only perhaps because they appeared so helpless. The next stage is symbolized by Phoenix's having to grovel on her knees for the nickel, which the hunter avers he does not have. The hunter's threatening act of pointing his gun at her and his false advice—"stay home, and nothing will happen to you" (*CS*, 146)—seem prophetic of southern whites' stance during the mid-fifties when blacks began to demand equal opportunities and dignity. Had Phoenix given in to this temptation to remain passive, she would not have obtained the much-needed medicine. Finally, the hunter fails to comprehend the dire necessity of her mission, mistakenly believing she is merely going to see Santa Claus. He is not, in a last analysis, so much malicious as insensitive (Robinson 24).

The final scene at the clinic has also drawn considerable commentary on the failure of charity—in the sense of the Latin *caritas* or Christian love.[11] Yet to see the white attendant and nurse merely as representing the callous welfare state is simplistic. The attendant, who does not know Phoenix's case, displays a clinical sort of charity, dispensed without care or personalization: "A charity case, I suppose" (*CS*, 147). Yet it is noteworthy that at the end of the story she offers Phoenix a small personal gratuity for Christmas. The nurse does act impatiently when Phoenix lapses into senility, but only after five patient attempts to elicit the needed information regarding the grandson.

This scene focuses two of the most significant motifs of the story: Phoenix's unreserved love for her grandson and her hope for his future. The slightly humorous suspense afforded by her momentary lapse of memory functions to undercut the tendency to sentimentalize a tragic situation. When she finally remembers, Phoenix expresses one of the most powerful definitions of Christian love imaginable: "I not going to forget him again, no, the whole enduring time. I could tell him from all the others in creation" (*CS*, 148). She is also adamant in her faith that, despite his seeming frailty, he is going to survive. The flame, bird, and windmill (Isaacs 81; Ardolino 7) imagery in the final scene reinforces the virtuous cycle by which she keeps her grandson alive through her persistent care; his need likewise gives her a reason to live. To overlook the real suffering in both their lives is to distort. Yet to interpret this scene cynically, as Cooley does, as the blacks swallowing the lye (lie) of racist condescension and occasional charity (24)—or to view Phoenix as some sort of misguided Don Quixote flapping at imaginary windmills (Daly 138)—misses the point that Phoenix, in her slow, plodding, and often interrupted course, has overcome every temptation and obtained her goal.

Thus, the truth of the racial interactions in "A Worn Path" lies somewhere between Hardy's, Cooley's, and Appel's encomiums of the blacks and excoriations of the whites and Howell's almost complete exoneration of both:

> There is no conflict between Phoenix and the white world, and there is no hate. . . . The whites who confront Phoenix reflect the usual attitudes of their generation toward the Negro. . . . [T]he charity of the whites, meager as it is, is proffered in kindliness and received as such. (Howell 31; see also Vande Kieft, *Eudora Welty* 140)

Whereas the former interpretations are too polemical, the latter is perhaps overly sanguine. The story does portray interracial tension and misunderstanding, if not overt conflict. To obtain her meager needs, Phoenix has to remain in her subservient role as requester. Although she avoids the more obvious near-parodic ploys, such as Uncle-Tom obsequiousness or Sambo antics, she does rely—consciously or unconsciously—on her shrewdness, senility, and even minor thievery. The whites also evince at least degrees of insensitivity toward Phoenix, but seemingly more out of callous incomprehension than deliberate cruelty. Finally, however, the mythic aura of the story mitigates the impact of these political issues, allowing the reader to apprehend Phoenix whole, as no single character within the story does.

Notes

1. The earliest critical reference to the mythological phoenix is William Jones. Two interesting studies parallel Phoenix's physical description with other birds. See Donlan, who also interprets Phoenix's encounters with the small boy and the hunter as manifestations of the sun god Ra; and Nostrandt, who traces Phoenix as an inversion of an old Norse folktale in which a selfish woman is transformed into a woodpecker.

2. Almost all of these interpretations are implicit in Isaac's seminal (though too loosely argued) study of the story. Welker and Gower (203–06) make suggestive parallels to religious questers. The most detailed study of the Christian imagery, including specific analogues to the Passion Week, is Keys (354–56). Daly offers an existentialist interpretation which views Phoenix as less like Christ and Bunyan's Christian than Don Quixote. See also Trefman.

3. Welty, "And They Lived Happily Ever After" 3; *OWB*, esp. 8, 99. See also her *Conversations* interviews with Van Gelder, Buckley, Freeman, Gretlund, Maclay, Haller, and Jones (4, 107–08, 174, 224–25, 275, 313, and 324, respectively).

4. Hardy's treatment of blacks is difficult to understand because it is internally contradictory. Clearly he intends his treatment of Phoenix to be sympathetic (see also his comments on Welty's characters in the introduction and conclusion [221, 232]). Yet he confusingly refers to Phoenix's "outrageous request" that the white woman tie her shoes as an example of "the ways in which southern Negroes have learned to take subtle revenge on the 'superior race,' to exploit, for their own material or psychological advantage, the weaknesses of white pride" (228–29).

5. Welty's "Must the Writer Crusade?" (*Eye* 146–58) is her most thorough discussion of what she considers the author's appropriate role in regard to morality and reforming society. For specific comments on race, see her *Conversations* interviews with Clemons, Bunting, Kuehl, Buckley, Walker, Ferris, Freeman, Gretlund, Royals and Little, Brans, and Jones (31, 48, 83–84, 99–103, 136–37, 166, 182–84, 225, 259, 299–300, and 337, respectively), as well as the preface to *The Collected Stories of Eudora Welty* (x–xi). In the Brans interview, she remarks that making Phoenix black was not a deliberate decision, such as "I am now

going to write about the black race. I write about all people." She continues somewhat facetiously, "I think all my characters are about half and half black and white." Later in the same interview, however, she admits that only a black person "would be in such desperate need and live so remotely away from help and . . . have so far to go" (*Conversations* 300). She also notes that Phoenix is a common black name (*Conversations* 51); see also Freeman's interview (*Conversations* 188). Davis (5) interestingly notes the irony in the practice of slaveholders who named slaves and other chattel for classical personages. Within a larger cultural context, he sees this practice in Welty's fiction as "both a constant reminder of the past and a testament to the capacity to turn derision into dignity."

6. See also Vande Kieft, *Eudora Welty* (rev. ed., 140); and Moss (147–49) which asks some very difficult questions about the race issues in the story, especially regarding those readers who have been searching to find illiberal racial attitudes.

7. See Bartel; Feld 64–65; and Robinson 24. For dissenting views, see Cooley (23) and Hardy (226).

8. This scene is analyzed in great detail by Robinson (25–26).

9. Ardolino (8) relates the dove symbolism with Song of Solomon 2:10–13; Welker and Gower (204–05) also notes New Testament birds to which Welty may have been alluding. Throughout Welty's fiction birds seem to be signs of beneficence. See, for example, the scene in "Keela, The Outcast Indian Maiden" in which at the moment when Little Lee Roy recognizes Steve, "a sparrow alighted on his child's shoe" (*CS* 43), and the conclusion of "The Demonstrators" in which Dr. Strickland watches the hen and the cock and peacefully recalls how his estranged wife's "eyes would follow the birds when they flew across the garden" (*CS* 621), as well as "A Pageant of Birds."

10. Casty (6) captures the dualism of the hunter well, seeing him as exemplifying "the imperfect mixture that is mankind." See also Moss 149–50 and Robinson 24–27. Cooley lamentably claims that the "white reader may identify himself with the hunter" (24). Recent studies of race relations in Welty's fiction, particularly Vande Kieft on "The Demonstrators" and "Where Is the Voice Coming From?" and Coulthard's study of "Keela, The Outcast Indian Maiden," represent perceptive and balanced treatments of the complex and tragic issue of racism.

11. Hardy (227–29) presents the most scathing interpretation of their actions. See also Appel, *A Season of Dreams* 16; and Cooley 24. Welker and Gower (205) offer a necessary corrective that "all Christians, through Grace, are 'charity cases' "; the "obstinate case," they further argue, suggests Original Sin, "the nature of the human condition."

Chronology

1909 April 13, Eudora Alice Welty born, the first of three children, to Mary Chestina and Christian Webb Welty in Jackson, Mississippi.

1925 Graduates from Central High School, Jackson.

1927 Attends Mississippi State College for Women.

1927–1929 Earns B.A., University of Wisconsin, Madison.

1930–1931 Attends Columbia University School of Business, New York City; studies advertising.

1931 Returns to Jackson to live after the death of her father.

1931–1933 Works on newspapers and for Jackson radio station.

1933–1936 Works as publicity agent for the WPA in Mississippi; takes photographs as she travels throughout the state.

1936 Has a show of photographs in New York City. Publishes first short stories: "Death of a Traveling Salesman" and "Magic."

1940 Diarmuid Russell becomes Welty's agent.

1941 Wins second prize, O. Henry Memorial Contest Award for "A Worn Path." Summer at Yaddo. Publishes *A Curtain of Green,* with an introduction by Katherine Anne Porter.

1942 Publishes *The Robber Bridegroom.* Wins first prize, O. Henry Memorial Contest Award, for "The Wide Net."

1942–1943 Awarded Guggenheim Fellowship.

1943 *The Wide Net and Other Stories* published. Wins first prize, O. Henry Memorial Contest Award, for "Livvie is Back."

1944 Receives award from the Academy of Arts and Letters. Works on staff of *New York Times Book Review* for six months.

1946 *Delta Wedding* published.

1949 *The Golden Apples* published.

1949–1950 Guggenheim Fellowship renewed; travels to England, France, and Italy.

1951 "The Burning" published; wins second prize, O. Henry Memorial Contest Award.

1952 Elected to National Institute of Arts and Letters. Travels to England and Ireland.

1954 *The Ponder Heart* and *Selected Stories* published.

1955 Publishes *The Bride of the Innisfallen.* Receives the William Dean Howells Medal from the Academy of Arts and Letters for *The Ponder Heart.* Travels to Europe; participates in Cambridge University conference on American literature; delivers lecture, "Place in Fiction."

1956 *The Ponder Heart,* adapted as a play, opens on Broadway.

1958 Made Honorary Consultant in American Letters, Library of Congress.

1958–1959 Receives Lucy Donnelly Fellowship Award from Bryn Mawr College.

1960 Receives Ingram Memorial Foundation Award in Literature.

1962 "Three Papers on Fiction" published.

1970 Publishes *Losing Battles.* Receives Edward McDowell Medal.

1971 Publishes *The Optimist's Daughter.* Receives the National Institute of Arts and Letters Gold Medal, and a National Book Award nomination for *Losing Battles.*

1972 Receives Christopher Book Award for *One Time, One Place.*

1973 Wins the Pulitzer prize for *The Optimist's Daughter.*

1978 *The Eye of the Story: Selected Essays and Reviews* published.

1980 Publishes *The Collected Stories of Eudora Welty.* Receives the National Medal of Literature and the Medal of Freedom Award.

1983 Delivers first annual Massey Lectures in the History of Civilization at Harvard University. These lectures become her short autobiography, *One Writer's Beginnings.*

1984 *One Writer's Beginnings* published. Wins American Book Award and National Book Critics Circle Award, and the Common Wealth Award for Distinguished Service in Literature from Modern Language Association of America.

1987 Receives National Medal of Arts.

Selected Bibliography

Works by Eudora Welty

A Curtain of Green. New York: Doubleday, 1941.
The Robber Bridegroom. New York: Doubleday, 1942.
The Wide Net, and Other Stories. New York: Harcourt Brace Jovanovich, 1943.
Delta Wedding. New York: Harcourt Brace Jovanovich, 1945.
The Golden Apples. New York: Harcourt Brace Jovanovich, 1949.
The Ponder Heart. New York: Harcourt Brace Jovanovich, 1954.
The Bride of the Innisfallen, and Other Stories. New York: Harcourt Brace Jovanovich, 1955.
The Shoe Bird. Harcourt Brace Jovanovich, 1964.
Losing Battles. New York: Harcourt Brace Jovanovich, 1970.
The Optimist's Daughter. New York: Harcourt Brace Jovanovich, 1970.
One Time, One Place: Mississippi in the Depression; A Snapshot Album. New York: Random House, 1978.
The Eye of the Story: Selected Essays and Reviews. New York: Random House, 1979.
The Collected Stories of Eudora Welty. New York: Harcourt Brace Jovanovich, 1980.
One Writer's Beginnings. Cambridge: Harvard University Press, 1984.
Photographs. Jackson: University Press of Mississippi, 1989.
A Writer's Eye: Collected Book Reviews, ed. Pearl Amelia McHaney. Jackson: University Press of Mississippi, 1994.

Books and Collections

Appel, Alfred Jr. *A Season of Dreams: The Fiction of Eudora Welty.* Baton Rouge: Louisiana State University Press, 1965.
Bryant, J. A. Jr. *Eudora Welty.* Minneapolis: University of Minnesota Press, 1968. (Minnesota Pamphlet No. 66)
Issacs, Niel D. *Eudora Welty.* Steck-Vaughn Southern Writers Series, no. 8. Austin, Texas: Steck-Vaughn, 1969.
Manz-Kunz, Marie-Antoinette. *Eudora Welty: Aspects of Reality in Her Short Fiction.* Bern: Francke, 1971.
Howard, Zelma Turner. *The Rhetoric of Eudora Welty's Short Stories.* Jackson: University and College Press of Mississippi, 1973.

Desmond, John F., ed. *A Still Moment: Essays on the Art of Eudora Welty.* Metuchen, New Jersey, and London: The Scarecrow Press, 1978.

Dollarhide, Louis, and Ann J. Abadie, eds. *Eudora Welty: A Form of Thanks.* Jackson: University Press of Mississippi, 1979. Proceedings of the 1977 University of Mississippi Welty Conference. [Contents: "Eudora Welty and the Southern Idiom" / Cleanth Brooks; "Clement and the Indians: Pastoral History in *The Robber Bridegroom*" / Michael Kreyling; "Woman's World, Man's Place: The Fiction of Eudora Welty" / Peggy W. Prenshaw; "Precision and Reticence: Eudora Welty's Poetic Vision" / William Jay Smith; "Water, Wanderers, and Weddings: Love in Eudora Welty" / Noel Polk; "A Form of Thanks" / Reynolds Price; "Eudora Welty: A Friend's View" / Charlotte Capers.]

Prenshaw, Peggy Whitman, ed. *Eudora Welty: Critical Essays.* Jackson: University Press of Mississippi, 1979. [Contents: "Traditionalism and Modernism in Eudora Welty" / Chester E. Eisinger; "The Other Way to Live: Demigods in Eudora Welty's Fiction" / John Alexander Allen; "A Structural Approach to Myth in the Fiction of Eudora Welty" / Robert L. Phillips, Jr.; "The Recovery of the Confident Narrator" / J. A. Bryant Jr.; "Henny Penny, Eudora Welty, and the Aggregation of Friends" / Albert J. Griffith; "Marrying Down in Eudora Welty's Novels" / John Edward Hardy; "The Role of Family in *Delta Wedding, Losing Battles* and *The Optimist's Daughter*" / Jane L. Hinton; "The World of Eudora Welty's Women" / Elizabeth M. Kerr; "Woman's Vision; The Worlds of Women in *Delta Wedding, Losing Battles,* and *The Optimist's Daughter*" / Margaret Jones Bolsterli; "Eudora Welty's Mississippi" / Albert J. Devlin; " 'All Things Are Double': Eudora Welty as a Civilized Writer" / Warren French; "Renewal and Historical Consciousness in *The Wide Net*" / F. Garvin Davenport Jr.; "Fairchild as Compromise Protagonist in *Delta Wedding*" / M. E. Bradford; "Ambiguous Necessity: A Study of *The Ponder Heart*" / Brenda G. Cornell; "Morgana'a Apples and Pears" / Merril Maguire Skaggs; "Golden Apples and Silver Apples" / Julia L. Demmin and Daniel Curley; "Techniques as Myth: the Structure of *The Golden Apples*" / Danièle Pitavy-Souques; "*Losing Battles* and Winning the War" / Robert B. Heilman; "*Losing Battles* as a Comic Epic in Prose" / Mary Anne Ferguson; "A Long Day's Living: The Angelic Ingenuities of *Losing Battles*" / Seymour L. Gross; " 'A Battle with Both Sides Using the Same Tactics': The Language of Time in *Losing Battles*" / Douglas Messerli; "Social Form and Social Order: An Examination of *The Optimist's Daughter*" / Thomas Daniel Young; "The Eye of Time: The Photographs of Eudora Welty" / Barabara McKenzie; "Constructing Time and Place: Eudora Welty in the Thirties" / Elizabeth A. Meese; "Words into Criticism: Eudora Welty's Essays and Reviews" / Michael Kreyling; "Looking with Eudora Welty" / Ruth M. Vande Kieft.

Kreyling, Michael. *Eudora Welty's Achievement of Order.* Baton Rogue: Louisiana State University Press, 1980.

Evans, Elizabeth. *Eudora Welty.* New York: Frederick Ungar, 1981.

Randisi, Jennifer Lynn. *A Tissue of Lies: Eudora Welty and the Southern Romance.* Washington, D.C.: University Press of America, 1982.

Devlin, Albert J. *Eudora Welty's Chronicle: A Story of Mississippi Life.* Jackson: University Press of Mississippi, 1983.

McDonald, W. U. Jr. *The Short Stories of Eudora Welty: The Evolution of Printed Texts.* Toledo: William S. Carlson Library, 1983. Catalog of an exhibit at The Ward M. Canaday Center of Carlson Library, The University of Toledo, March–April, 1983.

Manning, Carol S. *With Ears Opening Like Morning Glories: Eudora Welty and the Love of Storytelling.* Westport, Connecticut, and London: Greenwood Press, 1985.

Westling, Louise Hutchings. *Sacred Groves and Ravaged Gardens: The Fiction of Eudora Welty, Carson McCullers, and Flannery O'Connor.* Athens: The University of Georgia Press, 1985.

Bloom, Harold, ed. *Eudora Welty: Critical Views.* New York: Chelsea, 1986. [Contents: "*A Curtain of Green*" / Katharine Anne Porter; "Love and Separateness in Eudora Welty" / Robert Penn Warren; "*Delta Wedding* as Region and Symbol" / John Edward Hardy; "The Mysteries of Eudora Welty" / Ruth M. Vande Kieft; "The Art of Eudora Welty" / Joyce Carol Oates; "The Onlooker, Smiling: An Early Reading of *The Optimist's Daughter*" / Reynolds Price; "Three Tributes" / Malcolm Cowley, Walker Percy, Robert Penn Warren; "Eudora Welty and the Southern Idiom" / Cleanth Brooks; "Technique as Myth: The Structure of *The Golden Apples*" / Danièle Pitavy-Souques; "A Long Day's Living: The Angelic Ingenuities of *Losing Battles*" / Seymour Gross; "*The Robber Bridegroom* and the Pastoral Dream" / Michael Kreyling; "Eudora Welty's South Disdains Air Conditioning: An Interview" / Raad Cawthorn; "Gossip and Continuity in Eudora Welty" / Patricia Meyer Spacks.]

Devlin, Albert J., ed. *A Life in Literature.* Jackson: The University Press of Mississippi, 1987. [Contents: "A Conversation with Eudora Welty" / Albert J. Devlin and Peggy Whitman Prenshaw; "Eudora Welty: Visited and Revisited" / Ruth M. Vande Kieft; "Words Between Strangers: On Welty, Her Style, and Her Audience" / Harriet Pollack; "More Notes on River Country" / Mary Hughes Brookhart and Suzanne Marrs; "The House as Container: Architecture and Myth in *Delta Wedding*" / Dorothy G. Griffin; " 'Because a Fire Was in My Head': Eudora Welty and the Dialogic Imagination" / Patricia S. Yaeger; "The Loving Observer of *One Time, One Place*" / Louise Westling; "Mothers, Daughters, and One Writer's Revisions" / Helen Hurt Tiegreen; "Subject and Object in *One Writer's Beginnings*" / Michael Kreyling; "The Antiphonies of Eudora Welty's *One Writer's Beginnings* and Elizabeth Bowen's *Pictures and Conversations*" / Peggy Whitman Prenshaw.]

Vande Kieft, Ruth M. *Eudora Welty.* New York: Twayne, 1962; rev. New York: Twayne, 1987.

Trouard, Dawn, ed. *Eudora Welty: Eye of the Storyteller.* Kent: Kent State University Press, 1989. [Contents: "American Folk Art, Fine Art, and Eudora Welty: Aesthetic Precedents for 'Lily Daw and the Three Ladies' " / Ruth D. Weston; "June Recital: Virgie Rainey Saved" / Carey Wall; " 'Contradictors, Interferers, and Prevaricators': Opposing Modes of Discourse in Eudora Welty's *Losing Battles*" / Susan V. Donaldson; " 'The Assault of Hope': Style's Substance in Welty's 'The Demonstrators' " / Suzanne Ferguson; "Eudora Welty and the Dutiful Daughter" / Elizabeth Evans; "The Strategy of Edna Earle Ponder" / Marilyn Arnold; "Sibyls in Eudora Welty's Stories" / Peter Schmidt; "How Not to Tell a Story: Eudora Welty's First-Person Tales" / Ann Romines; "The Terrible and the Marvelous: Eudora Welty's Chekhov" / Jan Nordby Gretlund; "Realities in 'Sir Rabbit': A Frame Analysis" / Daun Kendig; "From Metaphor to Manifestation: The Artist in Eudora Welty's *A Curtain of Green*" / Cheryll Burgess; "Of Suffering and Joy: Aspects of Storytelling in Welty's Short Fiction" / Danièle Pitavy-Souques; "Going to Naples and Other Places in Eudora Welty's Fiction" / Noel Polk; "From Civil War to Civil Rights: Race Relations in Welty's 'A Worn Path' " / Nancy K. Butterworth; "Falling into Cycles: *The Golden Apples*" / Thomas L. McHaney; " 'Where Is the Voice Coming From?': Teaching Eudora Welty" / Ruth M. Vande Kieft.]

Turner, Craig W., and Lee Emling Harding. *Critical Essays on Eudora Welty.* Boston: G. K. Hall and Co., 1989.

Gygax, Franziska. *Serious Daring from Within: Female Narrative Strategies in Eudora Welty's Novels.* Westport: Greenwood, 1990.

Carson, Barbara Harrell. *Eudora Welty: Two Pictures at Once in Her Frame.* Troy, NY: Whitson Publishing Co., 1992.

Mark, Rebecca. *The Dragon's Blood: Feminist Intertextuality in Eudora Welty's* The Golden Apples. Jackson: University Press of Mississippi, 1994.

Mortimer, Gail L. *Daughter of the Swan: Love and Knowledge in Eudora Welty's Fiction.* Athens and London: University of Georgia Press, 1994.

Bibliographies

Smythe, Katherine Hinds. "Eudora Welty: A Checklist," *Bulletins of Bibliography* 21 (January–April 1956): 207–8.

Gross, Seymour L. "Eudora Welty: A Bibliography of Criticism and Comment." *Secretary's News Sheet,* Bibliographical Society, University of Virginia, no. 45, (April 1960).

Jordan, Leona. "Eudora Welty: Selected Criticism." *Bulletin of Bibliography* 23 (January–April 1960): 14–15.

McDonald, W. U. Jr. "Eudora Welty Manuscripts: An Annotated Finding List." *Bulletin of Bibliography* 24 (September–December 1963): 44–46.

———. "Eudora Welty Manuscripts: A Supplementary Annotated Finding List." *Bulletin of Bibliography* 31 (July–September 1974): 95–98, 126, 132. "Eudora Welty Manuscripts: A Second Supplement." *Eudora Welty Newsletter* 2 (Winter 1978): 4–5.

Thompson, Victor H. *Eudora Welty: A Reference Guide.* Boston: G. K. Hall, 1976.

Blayac, Alain. "The Eudora Welty Collection at the Humanities Research Center, the University of Texas at Austin." *Delta* 5 (November 1977): 83–88. [In French.]

Givner, Joan. "The Eudora Welty Collection, Jackson, Mississippi." *Descant: The Texas Christian University Literary Journal* 23 (Fall 1978): 38–48.

Van Noppen, Martha. "Eudora Welty Scholarship, 1959–1976: A Supplementary Checklist." *Eudora Welty Newsletter* 2 (Summer 1978): 10–12. [Supplements Thompson, *Eudora Welty: A Reference Guide.*]

Tomlin, Ronald E. "The Eudora Welty Collections at the Mississippi Department of Archives and History." *Eudora Welty Newsletter* 3 (April 1979): 10–12.

Brookhart, Mary Hughes. "Welty's Current Reception in Britain: A Checklist of Reviews." *Eudora Welty Newsletter* 7 (Summer 1983): 1–5.

Emerson, O. B. "Reviews of *Collected Stories:* A Preliminary Checklist." *Eudora Welty Newsletter* 7 (Winter 1983): 4–6.

Prenshaw, Peggy Whitman. "Eudora Welty." In *American Women Writers: Bibliographical Essays.,* ed. Maurie Duke, Jackson R. Bryer, and M. Thomas Inge. Westport: Greenwood Press, pp. 233–67.

Swearingen, Bethany C. *Eudora Welty: A Critical Bibliography, 1936–1958.* Jackson: University Press of Mississippi, 1984.

McDonald, W. U. Jr., and Robert Alan Shaddy. *A Guide to the Eudora Welty Collection at the Ward M. Canaday Center for the Special Collections.* Toledo: University of Toledo Libraries, 1993.

Polk, Noel. *Eudora Welty: A Bibliography of Her Work.* Jackson: University Press of Mississippi, 1994.

Special Welty Issues

Shenandoah 20 (Spring 1969)
Mississippi Quarterly 39 (Fall 1986)
Mississippi Quarterly 46 (Spring 1993)
Southern Quarterly 32 (Fall 1993)

General Studies

Warren, Robert Penn. "The Love and Separateness in Miss Welty." *Kenyon Review* 6 (Spring 1944): 246–59.

Hicks, Granville. "Eudora Welty." *English Journal* 41 (November 1952): 461–68. Also in *College English* 14 (November 1952): 69–76.

Morris, Harry C. "Eudora Welty's Use of Mythology." *Shenandoah* 6 (Spring 1955): 34–40.

Jones, William M. "Name and Symbol in the Prose of Eudora Welty." *Southern Folklore Quarterly* 22 (December 1958): 173–85.

Daniel, Robert. "Eudora Welty: The Sense of Place." In *South: Modern Southern Literature in Its Cultural Setting*, ed. Louis D. Rubin Jr. and Robert B. Jacobs. New York: Doubleday Dolphon, 1961, pp. 276–86.

Buswell, Mary Catherine. "The Love Relationships of Women in the Fiction of Eudora Welty." *West Virginia University Bulletin Philological Papers* 13 (December 1961): 94–106.

Gossett, Louise Y. "Violence as Revelation: Eudora Welty." In *Violence in Recent Southern Fiction*, ed. Louise Y. Gossett. Durham: Duke University Press, 1965, pp. 98–117.

Inge, M. Thomas "Eudora Welty as Poet." *Southern Humanities Review* 2 (Summer 1968): 310–311. Reprints Welty's poem "There."

Gross, Seymour L. "Eudora Welty's Comic Imagination." In *The Comic Imagination in American Literature*, ed. Louis D. Rubin, Jr. New Brunswick, New Jersey: Rutgers University Press, 1973, pp. 319–28.

Robinson, Clayton. "Faulkner and Welty and the Mississippi Baptists." *Interpretations: Studies in Language and Literature* 5 (1973): 51–54.

Meyers, Susan L. "Dialogues in Eudora Welty's Short Stories." *Notes on Mississippi Writers* 8 (Fall 1975): 51–57.

Gingrich, Arnold. "Goosing a Gander." *Esquire* 84 (December 1975): 14, 161. [Concerning *Esquire*'s rejection of an unidentified Welty story.]

Cole, Hunter M. "Welty on Faulkner." *Notes on Mississippi Writers* 9 (Spring 1976): 28–49.

Chaffee, Patricia. "Houses in the Short Fiction of Eudora Welty." *Studies in Short Fiction* 15 (Winter 1978): 112–14.

Chronaki, Bessie. "Eudora Welty's Theory of Place and Human Relationships." *South Atlantic Bulletin* 43 (May 1978): 36–44.

Simpson, Lewis P. "The Southern Aesthetic of Memory." *Tulane Studies in English* 23 (1978): 207–27.

Binding, Paul. "Mississippi and Eudora Welty." In *Separate Country: A Literary Journey Through the American South*, Paul Binding. New York: Paddington Press, Ltd., 1979, pp. 131–48.

Rubin, Louis D. Jr. "Growing Up in the Deep South: A Conversation with Eudora Welty, Shelby Foote, and Louis D. Rubin, Jr." In *The American*

South: Portrait of a Culture, ed. Louis D. Rubin Jr. Baton Rouge: Louisiana State University Press, 1980, pp. 59–85.

Evans, Elizabeth. "Eudora Welty: The Metaphor of Music." *Southern Quarterly* 20 (Summer 1982): 92–100.

McAlpin, Sara. "Family in Eudora Welty's Fiction." *Southern Review* n.s. 18 (Summer 1982): 480–93.

Vande Kieft, Ruth M. "Eudora Welty: The Question of Meaning." *Southern Quarterly* 20 (Summer 1982): 24–39.

Moreland, Richard C. "Community and Vision in Eudora Welty." *Southern Review,* n.s. 18 (Winter 1982): 84–99.

Flower, Dean. "Eudora Welty Come from Away." *Hudson Review* 38 (Autumn 1985): 473–80.

Watkins, Floyd C. "Eudora Welty's Natchez Trace in the New World." *The Southern Review* 22 (Autumn 1986): 708–26.

Mortimer, Gail L. " 'The Way to Get There': Journeys and Destinations in the Stories of Eudora Welty." *Southern Literary Journal* 19 (Spring 1987): 61–69.

Kreyling, Michael. "The Natchez Trace in Eudora Welty's Fiction." *The Southern Quarterly* 30 (Fall 1991): 24–34.

Studies of Individual Works: A Curtain of Green

General

Porter, Katharine Anne. "Introduction" to *A Curtain of Green.* Garden City, New York: Doubleday, Doran, 1941, pp. ix–xix.

Boyle, Kay. "Full-Length Portrait." *New Republic* 24 (November 1941): 707.

Bogan, Louise. "The Gothic South." *Nation* 153 (6 December 1941): 572.

Carson, Gary. "Versions of the Artist in *A Curtain of Green:* The Unifying Imagination in Eudora Welty's Early Fiction." *Studies in Short Fiction* 15 (Fall 1978): 421–28.

Butters, Ronald R. "Dialect at Work: Eudora Welty's Artistic Purposes." *Mississippi Folklore Register* 16 (Fall 1982): 33–39.

Kreyling, Michael. "Modernism in Welty's *A Curtain of Green and Other Stories.*" *Southern Quarterly* 20 (Summer 1982): 40–53.

Peterman, Gina D. "*A Curtain of Green:* Eudora Welty's Auspicious Beginning." *Mississippi Quarterly* 46.1 (Winter 1992–93): 91–114.

"A Piece of News"

Brooks, Cleanth, and Robert Penn Warren. "Interpretation." In *Understanding Fiction,* ed. Cleanth Brooks and Robert Penn Warren. New York: Appleton-

Century-Crofts, 1943, pp. 143–146. [Revised in the second edition of *Understanding Fiction* (New York, 1959), pp. 128–133; revision also reprinted in Brooks and Warren, eds., *The Scope of Fiction.* New York: Appleton-Century-Crofts, 1960, pp. 108–33.]

Hollenbaugh, Carol. "Ruby Fisher and Her Demon-Lover." *Notes on Mississippi Writers* 7 (Fall 1974): 63–68.

"The Key"

Opitz, Kurt. "Eudora Welty: The Order of a Captive Soul." *Critique* 7 (Winter 1964–65): 79–91.

"Petrified Man"

Helterman, Jeffery. "Gorgons in Mississippi: Eudora Welty's 'Petrified Man.' " *Notes on Mississippi Writers* 7 (Spring 1974): 12–20.

Walker, Robert G. "Another Medusa Allusion in Welty's 'Petrified Man.' " *Notes on Contemporary Literature* 9 (March 1979): 10.

Jones, Libby F. "The Stories of Welty's 'Petrified Man.' " *Notes on Mississippi Writers* 18 (1986): 65–72.

Berlant, Lauren. "Writing the Medusa: Welty's 'Petrified Man.' " *Studies in Short Fiction* 26 (Winter 1989): 59–70.

"Keela, the Outcast Indian Maiden"

Hardy, John Edward. "Eudora Welty's Negroes." In *Images of the Negro in American Literature,* ed. Seymour L. Gross and John Edward Hardy. Chicago: University of Chicago Press, 1966, pp. 221–32.

McFarland, Ronald E. "Vision and Perception in the Works of Eudora Welty." *Markham Review* 2 (February 1971): 94–99.

Fischer, John Irwin. " 'Keela, the Outcast Indian Maiden': Studying It Out." *Studies in Short Fiction* 15 (Spring 1978): 165–71.

Coulthard, A. R. " 'Keela the Outcast Indian Maiden': A Dissenting View." *Studies in Short Fiction* 23 (Winter 1986): 35–41.

"The Whistle"

McDonald, W. U. Jr. "Welty's 'Social Consciousness': Revisions of 'The Whistle.' " *Modern Fiction Studies* 16 (Summer 1970): 193–98.

"Why I Live at the P.O."

May, Charles E. "Why Sister Lives at the P.O." *Southern Humanities Review* 12 (Summer 1978): 243–49.

Du Priest, Travis. " 'Why I Live at the P.O.': Eudora Welty's Epic Question." *Christianity and Literature* 31, no. 4 (1982): 45–54.

"A Memory"

Lief, Ruth Ann. "A Progression of Answers." *Studies in Short Fiction* 2 (Summer 1965): 343–50.

Ginsberg, Elaine. "The Female Initiation Theme in American Fiction." *Studies in American Fiction* 3 (Spring 1975): 27–37.

Gray, Richard J. "Eudora Welty: A Dance to the Music of Order." *Canadian Review of American Studies* 7 (Spring 1976): 57–65; rpt. in *Literature of Memory,* ed. Richard J. Gray. Baltimore: Johns Hopkins University Press, 1977, pp. 150–52, 174–85, 261.

"Clytie"

Jones, William. "Growth of a Symbol: The Sun in Lawrence and Eudora Welty." *University of Kansas City Review* 26 (1959): 68–73.

Griffith, Albert J. "The Numinous Vision: Eudora Welty's 'Clytie.' " *Studies in Short Fiction* 4 (Fall 1966): 80–82.

"Old Mr. Marblehall"

Brooks, Cleanth, and Robert Penn Warren, "Interpretation." In *Understanding Fiction,* ed. Cleanth Brooks and Robert Penn Warren. New York: Appleton-Century-Crofts, 1943, pp. 479–80.

"A Visit of Charity"

Bradham, Jo Allen. " 'A Visit of Charity': Menippean Satire." *Studies in Short Fiction* 1 (Summer 1964): 258–63.

"Flowers for Marjorie"

Gretlund, Jan Nordby. "Welty's Photos of New York in the Depression and 'Flowers for Marjorie,' " *Eudora Welty Newsletter* 5 (Summer 1981): 4–5.

"A Curtain of Green"

Arnold, St. George Tucker. "The Raincloud and the Garden: Psychic Regression as Tragedy in Welty's 'A Curtain of Green.' " *South Atlantic Bulletin* 44 (January 1979): 53–60.

"Death of a Traveling Salesman"

Sederberg, Nancy. "Welty's 'Death of a Traveling Salesman.' " *Explicator* 42 (Fall 1983): 52–54.

Dessner, Lawrence Jay. "Vision and Revision in Eudora Welty's 'Death of a Traveling Salesman.' " *Studies in American Fiction* 15 (Autumn 1987): 145–59.

Hoberman, Michael. "Demythologizing Myth Criticism: Folklife and Modernity in Eudora Welty's 'Death of a Traveling Salesman.' " *Southern Quarterly* 30 (Fall 1991): 23–24.

"Powerhouse"

Kirkpatrick, Smith. "The Anoited Powerhouse." *Sewanee Review* 77 (January–March 1969): 94–108.

Balliett, Whitney. "Jazz: Fats." *New Yorker* 54 (10 April 1978): 110–12, 114–17.

Lampkin, Loretta M. "Musical Movement and Harmony in Eudora Welty's 'Powerhouse.' " *CEA Critic* 45 (November 1982): 24–28.

Getz, Thomas H. "Eudora Welty: Listening to 'Powerhouse.' " *The Kentucky Review* 4 (Winter 1983): 40–48.

Albert, Richard N. "Eudora Welty's Fats Waller: 'Powerhouse.' " *Notes on Mississippi Writers* 19 (1987): 63–71.

"A Worn Path"

Issacs, Neil D. "Life for Phoenix." *Sewanee Review* 71 (January–March 1962): 75–81.

Daly, Saralyn R. " 'A Worn Path' Retrod." *Studies in Short Fiction* 1 (Winter 1964): 133–69.

Moss, Grant Jr. " 'A Worn Path' Retrod." *College Language Association Journal* (Morgan State College) 15 (December 1971): 144–52.

Ardolino, Frank R. "Life Out of Death: Ancient Myth and Ritual in Welty's 'A Worn Path.' " *Notes on Mississippi Writers* 9 (Spring 1976): 1–9.

Keys, Marilynn. " 'A Worn Path': The Way of Dispossession." *Studies in Short Fiction* 16 (Fall 1979): 354–56.

Walter, James. "Love's Habit of Vision in Welty's Phoenix Jackson." *Journal of the Short Story in English* 7 (Autumn 1986): 77–85.

Saunders, James Robert. " 'A Worn Path': The Eternal Quest of Welty's Phoenix Jackson." *Southern Literary Journal* 25.1 (Fall 1992): 62–73.

The Wide Net

General

Trilling, Diana. "Fiction in Review." *Nation* 157 (2 October 1943): 386–87.

Rosenfeld, Issac. "Consolations of Poetry." *New Republic* 109 (18 October 1943): 525–26.

"First Love"

McFarland, Ronald E. "Vision and Perception in the Works of Eudora Welty." *Markham Review* 2 (February 1971): 94–99.

Devlin, Albert J. "Eudora Welty's Historicism: Method and Vision." *Mississippi Quarterly* 30 (Spring 1977): 213–34.

Holder, Alan. " 'It Happened in Extraordinary Times': Eudora Welty's Historical Fiction." In his *The Imagined Past: Portrayals of Our History in Modern American Literature.* Lewisburg, Pennsylvania: Bucknell University Press, 1980, pp. 125–46.

Marrs, Suzanne. "The Conclusion of Eudora Welty's 'First Love': Historical Backgrounds." *Notes on Mississippi Writers* 13 (1981): 73–78.

"The Wide Net"

Cluck, Nancy Anne. "*The Aneneid* of the Natchez Trace: Epic Structures in Eudora Welty's 'The Wide Net.' " *Southern Review,* n.s. 19 (Summer 1983): 510–18.

Donaldson, Susan V. "Meditations on Nonpresence: Re-visioning the Short Story in Eudora Welty's 'The Wide Net.' " *Journal of the Short Story in English* 11 (Autumn 1988): 75–91.

Carson, Barbara Harrell. "Eudora Welty's Tangled Bank." *South Atlantic Review* 48 (November 1983): 1–18.

Pollack, Harriet. "On Welty's Use of Allusion: Expectations and Their Revision in *The Wide Net, The Robber Bridegroom* and *At the Landing.*" *The Southern Quarterly* 29 (Fall 1990): 5–31.

"A Still Moment"

Pollack, Harriet. "Eudora Welty's Snowy Heron." *American Literature* 53 (January 1982): 723–25.

Cluck, Nancy Ann. "Audubon: Images of the Artist in Eudora Welty and Robert Penn Warren." *Southern Literary Journal* 17 (Spring 1985): 41–53.

"The Winds"

Manning, Carol S. "Little Girls and Sidewalks: Glasgow and Welty on Childhood's Promise." *Southern Quarterly* 21 (Spring 1983): 67–76.

"Livvie"

Smith, Julian. " 'Livvie'—Eudora Welty's Song of Solomon." *Studies in Short Fiction* 5 (Fall 1967): 73–74.

Prenshaw, Peggy Whitman. "Persphone in Eudora Welty's 'Livvie.' " *Studies in Short Fiction* 17 (Spring 1980): 149–55.

The Golden Apples

Morris, H. C. "Zeus and the Golden Apples: Eudora Welty." *Perspective* 5 (Autumn 1952): 190–99.

Bowen, Elizabeth. "The Golden Apples." In *Seven Winters: Memories of a Dublin Childhood & Afterthought: Pieces on Writing,* ed. Elizabeth Bowen. New York: Alfred A. Knopf, 1962, pp. 215–18.

Harris, Wendell V. "The Thematic Unity of Welty's *The Golden Apples.*" *Texas Studies in Literature and Language* 6 (Spring 1964): 92–95.

Blackwell, Louise. "Eudora Welty: Proverbs and Proverbial Phrases in *The Golden Apples.*" *Southern Folklore Quality* 30 (December 1960): 332–41.

Pawloski, Robert. "The Process of Observation: *Wineburg, Ohio* and *The Golden Apples.*" *University Review* 37 (June 1971): 292–98.

Carson, Franklin D. " 'The Song of Wandering Aengus': Allusions in Eudora Welty's *The Golden Apples.*" *Notes on Mississippi Writers* 6 (Spring 1973): 14–17.

Bryant, J. A. Jr. "Seeing Double in *The Golden Apples.*" *Sewanee Review* 82 (Spring 1974): 300–15.

———. "Recurring Metaphors: An Aspect of Unity in *The Golden Apples.*" *Notes on Contemporary Literature* 5 (September 1975): 4–7.

Pei, Lowry. "Dreaming the Other in *The Golden Apples.*" *Modern Fiction Studies* 28 (Autumn 1982): 415–33.

Pugh, Elaine Upton. "The Duality of Morgana: The Making of Virgie's Vision, the Vision of *The Golden Apples.*" *Modern Fiction Studies* 28 (Autumn 1982): 435–51.

Harrison, Suzan. "The Other Way to Live: Gender and Selfhood in *Delta Wedding* and *The Golden Apples.*" *Mississippi Quarterly* 44 (Winter 1990–1991): 49–67.

Donaldson, Susan V. "Recovering Otherness in *The Golden Apples.*" *American Literature* 63 (September 1991): 489–506.

Hankins, Leslie Kathleen. "Alas, Alack! or A Lass, A Lack? Quarrels of Gender and Genre in the Revisionist *Künstlerroman:* Eudora Welty's *The Golden Apples.*" *Mississippi Quarterly* 44 (Fall 1991): 391–409.

Pingree, Allison. "The Circles of Ran and Eugene MacLain: Welty's Twin Plots in *The Golden Apples.*" In *The Significance of Sibling Relationships in Literature,* ed. JoAnna Stephens Mink and Janet Doubler Ward. Bowling Green, Ohio: Bowling Green State University Popular Press, 1993, pp. 83–97.

"Music From Spain"

Opitz, Kurt. "Eudora Welty: The Order of a Captive Soul." *Critique* 7 (Winter 1964–65): 779–91.

Marilyn, Arnold. "Somnabulism in San Francisco: Eudora Welty's Western Story." *The Southern Quarterly* 27 (Summer 1989): 16–24.

"June Recital"

Pitavy-Souques, Danièle. "Watchers and Watching: Point of View in Eudora Welty's 'June Recital.' " Trans. Margaret Tomatchio. *Southern Review,* n.s. 19 (Summer 1983), 483–509.

"Sir Rabbit"

Carson, Franklin D. "The Passage of Time in Eudora Welty's 'Sir Rabbit.' " *Studies in Short Fiction* 12 (Summer 1975): 284–86.

"Moon Lake"

Manning, Carol S. "Male Initiation, Welty Style." *Regionalism and the Female Imagination* 4, no. 2 (1978): 53–60.

Yaeger, Patricia S. "The Case of the Dangling Signifier: Phallic Imagery in Eudora Welty's 'Moon Lake.' " *Twentieth Century Literature* 28 (Winter 1982): 431–52.

Caldwell, Price. "Sexual Politics in Welty's "Moon Lake" and "Petrified Man." *Studies in American Fiction* 18 (Autumn 1990): 171–81.

Scott, Michael. "Easter as Sexual Pathfinder in Eudora Welty's "Moon Lake." Crossroads 1 (Fall 1992): 35–38.

The Bride of the Innisfallen

General

Peden, William. "The Incomparable Welty." *Saturday Review* 38 (9 April 1955): 18.

Carter, Thomas H. "Rhetoric and Southern Landscapes." *Accent* 15 (Autumn 1955): 293–97.

"The Bride of the Innisfallen"

Liscio, Lorraine. "The Female Voice of Poetry in 'The Bride of the Innisfallen.' " *Studies in Short Fiction* 21 (Fall 1984): 357–62.

"Ladies in Spring"

Bolsterli, Margaret. "Mythic Elements in 'Ladies in Spring.' " *Notes on Mississippi Writers* 6 (Winter 1974): 69–72.

"Circe"

Goudie, Andrea. "Eudora Welty's Circe: A Goddess Who Strove with Men." *Studies in Short Fiction* 13 (Fall 1976): 481–89.

"No Place for You, My Love"

Jones, Alun R. "A Frail Traveling Coincidence: Three Later Stories of Eudora Welty." *Shenandoah* 20 (Spring 1969): 40–53.

"The Burning"

McBurney, William H. "Welty's 'The Burning.' " *Explicator* 16 (November 1957): item 9.

The Collected Stories

General

Howard, Maureen. "A Collection of Discoveries." *New York Times Book Review* 2 (November 1980): 1, 31–32. [Review of *The Collected Stories.*]

Uglow, Jennifer. "Journeys out of Separateness." *Times Literary Supplement* 110 (8 January 1982): 26. [Review of *The Collected Stories.*]

"The Demonstrators"

Romines, Ann. "The Power of the Lamp: Domestic Ritual in Two Stories by Eudora Welty." *Notes on Mississippi Writers* 12 (Summer 1979): 1–16.

"Where Is This Voice Coming From?"

Clerc, James. "Anatomy of Welty's 'Where Is This Voice Coming From?' " *Studies in Short Fiction* 23 (Autumn 1986): 389–400.

Hargrove, Nancy D. "Portrait of an Assassin: Eudora Welty's 'Where Is this Voice Coming From?' " *Southern Literary Journal* 20 (Fall 1987): 74–88.

Index

The Author

Carol Ann Johnston, assistant professor of English at Dickinson College, grew up in Gladewater, Texas, and received her Ph.D. from Harvard University. In addition to her work on Southern women writers, her research focuses on literature of the English Renaissance, and she is a published poet.